TURN
AROUND

Dearest
Esther,

Lots of love!

Lots of Love!

Health & happiness

Love Out

TURN AROUND

180 Degrees in 180 Days

BY ORIT ESTHER RITER

author of A Daily Dose of Emuna

MOSAICA PRESS

Mosaica Press, Inc.

© 2015 by Mosaica Press

Typeset and design by Daniella Kirsch

All rights reserved

ISBN: 1-937887-44-8

Published and distributed by:

Mosaica Press, Inc.

www.mosaicapress.com

info@mosaicapress.com

Printed in Israel

Divrei Berachah and Haskamah

There is a consensus among the leading spiritual leaders of this generation that those souls that are alive today in these challenging times before Mashiach are all here on earth to correct and strengthen *emunah*. For that reason, the tests of faith that our people are experiencing around the world are so difficult. Rebbe Nachman of Breslov accordingly teaches that the lack of *emunah* is the main factor in the delay of the *Geulah*. As such, spreading *emunah* is the key to terminating the long and painful exile of the Jewish people.

In light of the above, Mrs. Riter's *Daily Dose of Emuna*, as well as her new book, *180 Degrees in 180 Days* — in addition to being healthy food for thought and practical spiritual guides — are endeavors that are so important for this generation. May she be blessed in her efforts and may she help hasten the day when all of living flesh calls Hashem's name.

With the blessings of Torah and *emunah*,
Eliezer Raphoel (Lazer) Brody

Orit Esther Riter shines with the joy and clarity of the *emunah* that she teaches. I had the privilege of participating in an "Amen party" for a sick neighbor led by Orit Esther. She transformed a room full of grieving and worried women into a room full of inspired, joyful, connected-to-Hashem-and-to-each other, exalted spirits. The highest compliment: Orit Esther is what she teaches. In that lies the secret of her power to transform her readers.

Sara Yocheved Rigler
Author of *Holy Woman*

Though Jewish history has consisted of countless Jews since its beginning, it has usually been individuals who have changed the course of Jewish history, or at least allowed it to continue on in spite of the many forces that would do it in, G-d forbid. Sometimes it is national calamity that causes them to surface and leave their mark, sometimes it is personal misfortune, or even both. Whatever the reason, one thing is certain: Hashem Yisbarach chooses such people because of their latent greatness and loyalty to Torah values.

After reading about Mrs. Riter's personal journey and seeing some of her work, it is clear that she is one of those special people of Jewish history. *Emunah* is the foundation of Torah, and essential for a close and ongoing relationship with Hashem. However, it is also essential for surviving the trials and tribulations of the "birth pangs of Mashiach" which we seem to be going through at this time.

May Hashem Yisbarach grant her a long and healthy life, and may her influence only grow as she inspires more and more Jews to perform the ultimate *Kiddush Hashem* — trust and faith in G-d.

B'birchas HaTorah,
Pinchas Winston

Klal Yisrael has always had a collective *emunah*. While mighty empires living in the safety of their borders have perished, the stubborn survival of a handful of people — uprooted from its land and ruthlessly persecuted for more than two thousand years through expulsion, inquisition, pogroms and holocaust — is a testimony to its faith in the protection of Hashem.

The *emunah* of an individual in everyday life is not as well-grounded. Stresses and sufferings are constant challenges to the conviction that Hashem is in control of everything that happens, and that His judgment is fair and His kindness infinite.

Orit Esther Riter provides us with valuable reinforcements of *emunah*. These readings can support us when we falter and save us from the confusion and even despair that adversity may cause. They are an enhancement of our daily declaration of *Shema Yisrael*, and should be read daily.

Rabbi Abraham J. Twerski, MD

Many thanks to our generous contributors:

Aviva Aberman

Freyda Abrams

Shari Alter

Elvin Arastehmanesh

Lori Ashe

Katie Devorah Avrukin

Faige Bader

Betty Bendavid

The Berenstein Family

Allen and Susan Black

Mandana Bolour

Tracy Carno

Leah Chaimov

Rachel Cohen

Miriam Deverett

Chaya Edelson

The Edi Family

Tzippy Erblich

The Farajun Family

Sarah Friedman

The Gerowitz Family

Abbie Miriam Goldberg

Amanda Goldman

Elisheva Goldwater

Eileen Grama

Beth/Bat Sheva Haber

The Horenstein Family

Nellya Iskhakova

Yehuda Kramer

Kayla Krauss

Marla Krinitz

Tziporah Kushkuley

Vicki Last

The Ledder Family

Jessica Light-Lefkowitz

Rivka Rachel Levron

Marcia Levy

The Margolis Family

Miriam Maslin

Tamar Menasseh

Yehudis Chana Meshchaninov

Michelle Tamar Miller

Zahava Molad

Marina Mordukhayev

Jaci Nadav

Shoshana Packouz

Yocheved Pamensky

Fayge Parker

Sepi Paykar

Gail Perez

Susan Polevoy

Chavi Rabinowitz

Shahrzhad Rashti

Donna Meyer Reich

Lenore Richter

Debbie Rosalimsky

Leah Rubabshi

Elissa Sce

Anna Kaufman Sce

Teddy Scher

Steven Schlamovitz

Frannie Schmerling

The Schamroth Family

Alison Sklar

Chaya Soller

Sara Stobezki

Sandy Trencher

Janet Waller

Rivki Weiner

Jeanette Weinschel

The Weiss Family

Yael Werth

Shira and David Wiseman
and Family

Laureen Zisa

Table of Contents

Preface

*D*ear reader,

As a trained chef by profession, I imagined that if I were to ever write a book, it would be a cookbook. I never dreamed I would publish a book on Torah wisdom and inspiration! Yet, as the Yiddish proverb teaches, "Man plans and G-d laughs."

So what is my personal story? My path from chef to personal mentor, speaker and author was adorned with blessings. Some of these miracles were clearly visible to me at the time, others were disguised as traumas. Without *emunah* training under my belt, the benefits of these challenging times were often only revealed in retrospection.

In 2006, I experienced symptoms typifying a chronic auto-immune illness called multiple sclerosis (MS). Since I was expecting at the time, I erroneously presumed these symptoms were pregnancy related. Though test results suggested MS as a probability, the symptoms miraculously disappeared after three weeks. *Baruch Hashem*, I was able to complete my pregnancy and give birth with no further complications.

However, three months after my daughter was born, the symptoms reappeared. I underwent further tests, one of which was a spinal tap that proved unequivocally that I had MS. In retrospect, I realized that in His infinite compassion Hashem had granted me a year to gradually adjust to and process my new reality.

Representing the first major *nisayon* (challenge) of many, contracting MS provided a feeding-ground for my *emunah*. It enabled me the opportunity to see Hashem from a place of confusion and difficulty.

Many other trials and tribulations followed in quick succession. For instance, the near-drowning of our youngest daughter two weeks before she turned one served as another major *emunah* test. *Baruch Hashem,* she was saved and made a complete recovery — miracle of miracles! The experience of almost losing our daughter caused my MS to flare up. While in the hospital undergoing a procedure to control the relapse, we received a phone call that there had been a fire in the building which housed our family catering business. Our family thus lost all our equipment and food inventory due to water damage. We were not insured.

Hindsight is an exact science. If I only knew then that these multiple personal trials would serve to lead us to make *aliyah* within two years, I would definitely have felt much stronger and less anxious. Our family arrived with just enough money to put down a deposit on a rental apartment, purchase basic major appliances and start our life anew. However, at this point, I felt our family was experiencing a personal tsunami.

Yet... what does not break you, makes you! Instead of wallowing in the bleakness of our situation, with Hashem's help we summoned up the will to identify the messages Hashem was sending us through these intense challenges.

Over the last five years since making *aliyah*, we experience daily challenges like any other family. Through it all, we try to repeat and internalize the words *"Ein Od Milvado"* — that there truly is no other existence and reality other than Hashem. We continually work to train ourselves and implant *emunah* into our hearts.

Emunah enables us to view our individual and collective lives from a wider perspective. With *emunah*, we gain clarity and vision. In addition to injecting us with tranquility and inner peace, seeing events in our lives with *emunah* genuinely changes a person's life. Rebbe Nachman of Breslov teaches, "A person's life is greatly strengthened by *emunah*. When a man has *emunah*, even if he suffers, G-d forbid, he can comfort himself and revitalize himself."[1] When we see darkness but continue to believe in the light, eventually we see only light. That is the essence of *emunah*.

However, though I have been training my *emunah* muscles for a few years now, I must admit I am still in "*emunah* boot camp," always striving and learning to see Hashem in all that happens and to trust His loving guidance. As with all training, building our *emunah* muscles takes consistent effort.

I invite you to join me for six months — 180 days — on this life-changing journey of *emunah* training. Traveling the *emunah* path provides a remarkable opportunity to discover our true essence and to connect with our inner G-dliness.

With Hashem's help, this guidebook can illuminate the beginning of our way. Together, we can then uncover our true souls and ultimately allow them to shine.

Looking forward to traveling with you.

Wishing you *shalom*, *emunah* and *berachah* always,

Love,

Orit

---

1   *Sichos HaRan* 32.

Acknowledgments

"Mi-kol melamdai hiskalti — From everyone I have learned."[2]

Thank You, Hashem for granting me life, guidance and the ability to see beyond the physical realm. Thank you for gifting me with wisdom and understanding which enables me to learn and teach Your holy Torah. Thank you for choosing me to be part of Am Yisrael; *"Mi k'amcha Yisrael* — Who is like Your nation, the Jewish people!"

Hashem has placed in my life a dedicated staff of people who brought me to this point, and brought this book to fruition. This book is truly a mosaic, the product of craftsmanship and assistance from so many righteous souls of the Jewish people, working together with unity.

Without your ongoing familial love and support, dear Avraham, Shani, Netanel Raphael, Binyomin Shauel, Dovid and Chaya Rivka, I would not be able to learn, teach or share *emunah* to women at all hours of the day. My dear husband, Avraham, if there were an equivalent description for husbands such as is used to describe virtuous wives I would call you my *ish chayil!* You are a true servant of Hashem. By applying your Torah learning to everyday living, you are the perfect example of what it means to learn and to perform Hashem's holy *mitzvos.* I acknowledge and appreciate your patience and understanding and for teaching me by example.

---

2   *Tehillim* 119:99.

I thank you my precious children just for being you. You are kind, considerate and loving souls. Your G-dliness shines through and through. You uplift me when you speak *divrei emunah*. You make me smile when you tell me your "*emunah* experiences." Thank you for sharing me with others.

Ma, you are one of these instrumental and cornerstone people. Your words of encouragement constantly envelop me wherever I go. Particularly over the last few years, I appreciate more and more your *mesirus nefesh* (self-sacrifice) to ensure I received a Jewish education. Your sacrifice was fundamental to my *teshuvah* path. My reawakening undoubtedly came as a result of retrieving that which I learned in Yeshiva but had been tucked away for so long.

Aba, thank you for teaching me how to be excited about Judaism. You have a way of spreading your love and appreciation of Hashem in a unique way. This certainly has contributed to my enthusiastic love of Judaism and pride in my Jewish *neshamah*.

As my beautiful father and mother-in-law, Shauel and Ruti, you both teach me the importance of family unity and the value of steering away from *machlokes* (strife). Unquestionably, this has enhanced my teaching of *emunah* and my valuing of inner and outer peace.

My one and only older sister, Talia, I am most grateful to you. Your name depicts your character. Unlike the grandiosity of rain, you are like the *tal* (dew) that gently but effectively nourishes the earth. Thus, you teach me the importance of humility. Undeniably, this beautiful character trait helped steer me toward living a life of Torah and *mitzvos* in a manner that I pray is *l'shem Shamayim* (for the sake of Hashem only).

Rebbetzin Shirley Efrata, I acknowledge that you are responsible for igniting and continually directing my spiritual path. My wonderful friend, Chava Sela, introduced me to your insightful *shiurim*; lessons that radiate with words of *emes* (Hashem's truth).

Chaiya Danielle Ledder (D. Fine The Lines, Writing and Editing) — I attribute so many of my written accomplishments to you. Thank you for polishing my words to extract their shine. I appreciate your unique ability to pinpoint my exact message and then help me craft my expression with clarity. I am grateful for your immeasurable contribution to this book.

I direct a big thank you to you, Devorah Ohayon, for initiating the *emunah shiurim*. These *shiurim* began in your home in Beit Shemesh and *baruch Hashem* have now grown via the internet and Torahanytime.com to a wider audience of women across the globe. With no doubt, Torah Anytime is the reason Hashem created internet!

Zahava Molad, I hope you realize that the *Daily Dose of Emuna* website and many of our *emunah* projects and events are due primarily to you! You truly are the living definition of your name — *zahav* (gold). Your drive to spread *emunah* and "get the word out" is infectious and motivating. You are the engine driving *Daily Dose of Emuna*.

Tzippy Erblich, your home is the perfect setting for the weekly *shiurim* in Ramat Beit Shemesh. Your hospitality and gracious composure makes us all feel so welcome, and your place is the ideal hothouse for our flowering *emunah*.

I feel your enthusiasm even from a distance, Ariel-Sara Gerowitz! Your wisdom, creativity and experience have "made things happen." Please accept my heartfelt appreciation for everything you do.

Allison Griggs, your insight and care in spreading *emunah* to other women has been so helpful. Leah Rubabshi, Fayge Parker and Rivka Sima Berenstein — I thank you for repeatedly lending me your helping hands and warm hearts. And Shaindy Lebowitz, I hope you realize how much I appreciate your assistance and dedication to my writing.

I am very grateful to you, Kayla Krauss (of Graphics and Multimedia), for beautifully designing the *Daily Dose of Emuna* website with such care, expertise and without a "sigh." Elisheva Goldwater (of Imagine Graphics), I am grateful for your tremendous talent and exceptional poise and patience you employed to design the *emunah* flyers, logo and magnets.

It has been a true privilege to work with you, Rabbi Yaacov Haber, *shlita*, of Mosaica Press. Rabbi Doron Kornbluth, your highly professional craftsmanship has without a doubt transformed this book. Thank you both, and to your most professional and helpful staff, for ensuring this book became a reality.

To you, the sponsors of this book — I believe you are Hashem's holy emissaries, emissaries who brought this book into actuality. Your vital support animates the *emunah* events and projects, allowing them to be shared with others. Thank you and *tizku l'mitzvos*.

And finally, to you, the reader — you may be one of the many readers of the *Daily Dose of Emuna*, one of the viewers of *emunah shiurim* on Torahanytime.com or the *Daily Dose of Emuna* YouTube channel, or one of those whose comments and emails have touched my heart. Or, this might be your first exposure to these *emunah* lessons. Whoever you are, you are joining the worldwide group of people who strive to elevate themselves in their *avodas Hashem*. We are all a work in progress, and your learning inspires me to keep teaching. I love waving the *emunah* flag together with you. Thank you for working with me to make this world shine more brightly with *emunah* and G-dliness.

With gratitude to Hashem for weaving my life with all of these wonderful *neshamos*, and for enabling me to be one of Your emissaries.

Lecha Hashem haGedulah!

Introduction

*T*his book provides a step-by-step daily *emunah* program for the soul. It is my prayer that by following this program, your vision of life will become infused with *emunah*. Immersing myself in *emunah* has worked for me, now I want to share it with you!

So what is *emunah*? Our physical eyes see the outer shell of life; *emunah* vision pierces through the surface and sees within. *Emunah* broadens our vision so that we see the "bigger picture" of life, the hidden picture, not merely a limited, surface view of the world. It is accepting what is best for us without rationally knowing why it is so.

Yet, we do not need to actively implant *emunah* within us, we merely need to uncover or reveal it. The Jewish people was gifted with this *emunah* when we stood at Har Sinai. We accepted the Torah and then sealed our covenant with the words *na'aseh v'nishma* — we will do and then we will listen/understand.[3] This proclamation to Hashem vowed that the Jewish people would live by Hashem's will, regardless of the logic or rationale. We would only strive for knowledge to make sense of what we were doing after we already carried out Hashem's instructions. Thus, we agreed to remain loyal and committed to Hashem, His mandates and His will, whether difficult or comfortable — with or without rhyme or reason. This promise recognizes that Hashem knows us best and knows what is best for us. In this way, *emunah* is encoded in our DNA.

---

3   *Shemos* 24:7.

"All Your commandments are *emunah*."[4] As Jewish people we strive to live by *emunah*, performing the *mitzvos* even if the intellectual meaning is hidden, since we know Hashem is our G-d and He is a G-d of truth. However, in contrast to blind faith, *emunah* is founded on a reliable transmission of Jewish tradition from grandfather to father to son, generation after generation until this day. A sample size of three million people witnessed the experience of receiving the Torah. This unwavering chain provides strong evidence of Hashem's existence and authenticity.

At *Matan Torah* (the Giving of the Torah) we felt the *emes* (truthfulness) of the Torah from our innermost source — our souls. Our instincts were so attuned to living a life of Torah that we had no need to understand on an intellectual level, because the higher level of our *neshamah* was satisfied.

It is truly a gift to live life with a cognitive awareness that enables one to see the unseen and experience what cannot be touched. Hashem repeatedly reassures us that He will not forsake His people (aka the Jewish nation);[5] "*Banim atem l'Hashem Elokeichem* — You are children to Hashem."[6]

Yet, these days many of us often struggle to act on *emunah*, to feel Hashem's enveloping love. Why? In addition to the physical exile that Klal Yisrael suffers, part of our conscious mind went into "exile" as well. This is called *galus ha-da'as* (exile of knowledge). Thus, it is a struggle to regain that awareness of Hashem's Presence. The further away each generation is from *Matan Torah*, the weaker this link in the *emunah* chain naturally becomes. Nowadays, religion in the Western world is for the most part out of fashion. This day and age is defined by science and empirical knowledge. The Western world (stemming from Greek culture) only accepts empirical and scientific data as truth. Our free will is represented by our struggle to maintain our *emunah* in a world devoid of it.

---

4   *Tehillim* 119:86.

5   To mention a few passages: "He shall call upon Me, and I will answer him: I will be with Him in trouble; I will deliver him, and honor him" (*Tehillim* 91:15), "For Hashem's kindness will not leave us…" (*Yeshayah* 54:11), "Hashem will not abandon His people nor forsake His heritage" (*Tehillim* 94:14).

6   *Parashas Re'eh* 6:7.

A core of *emunah* is the belief that Hashem is and will always be with us and working on our behalf. Thus, part of working our *emunah* muscles involves persistently internalizing this message of Hashem's Presence. We must work hard to ignore any contrary message the outer world might "scream." We need to work hard to ensure we ignite the faith in our soul that Hashem is the Master Planner of every event, including the minutest details that occur in our individual and collective lives.

Fundamentally, when we pray for *chochmah* (wisdom), *binah* (understanding) and *da'as* (knowledge) we are asking to see the world from a G-dly perspective. Through Torah study we accumulate knowledge that moves us to change and take our wisdom and transform it into action. Ideally, this knowledge will serve to motivate and drive us. This is *the* foundation of willpower.

In simple terms, *da'as* is knowledge — understanding as a result of intellectual pursuit. However, on a deeper level, *da'as* represents a deep and real connection with that knowledge to the point where it affects all of our decisions, our actions and our ways of living. *Da'as* is the bridge between intellect and emotion. Therefore, when we live with *da'as*, we transition between knowing with the mind and feeling with the heart.

If we undertake Torah learning with the intent of bonding to Hashem, Hashem will grant us further *emunah*. We live a life of Torah and *mitzvos* in order to cleave to Hashem — to bond with the truthful reality of Hashem. Each time we do a mitzvah, pray, or try to emulate Hashem's *middos*, we peel away at the layers that distance us from the truth of Hashem's intimate Presence. It is immensely rewarding and ultimately soothing to know that without a doubt, we are never alone. We are bonded to an eternal power source of goodness Who orchestrates everything for our ultimate best. An *emunah*-based life provides us with guidance when the road ahead is unclear.

After I was officially diagnosed with MS in 2006, I lifted my eyes upward. I needed strength and there was only one true place to turn — Hashem! After all, MS is pronounced identically to the Hebrew word *emes* (Hashem's name, Truth).

There are four *emunah* buttons that we should strive to "press" (remember) when things aren't going as we planned (they are listed on our latest *emunah* magnet which is distributed worldwide for free):

1. It's all from Hashem — There is purpose!

2. Hashem is my Father — He loves me!

3. It must be good. My ultimate best!

4. What is the message Hashem is sending me?

By virtue of pressing these buttons we are better equipped with the ability to rise above life's challenges. There is purpose — it is all from Hashem!

The most remarkable part of the entire process of discovering Hashem is that we become deeply aware of our own essence — that is, who we are and why we are here. Finding the "real you" infuses one's life with meaning. Every Jewish soul contains a ray of G-dliness, capable of shining incredible endless light onto oneself and others. In this way, living a life of *emunah* enables us to live with focus and direction and minimize aimless living.

I pray that following this *emunah* program will enable all of us to live calmer, more G-d-centered and purposeful lives. I trust it will help us accept that He Who is in charge is coordinating everything for our very best, whether we can see it immediately on the surface or not. May it also enable us to be in touch with our own unique G-dliness within.

Hashem, may it be Your will that all that we learn bring *nachas ruach* to You, invoke *rachamei Shamayim* for Klal Yisrael and bring *yeshuos* and *nechamos* to those in need, Amen.

Where You Are

I looked for You,
It was late at night
Staring up at the blackened sky
A sign perhaps,
A shooting star,
Telling me just where You are...

I looked for You
In the morning light
Past the clouds that were floating by
Beyond the blue,
From near to far
Telling me just where You are...

I looked for You
But I didn't see
The answer right in front of me.
I closed my eyes,
No cloud, no star,
And found You there
Just where You are.

Poems by Leah Rubabshi, copyright 2015.
Used with permission.

What Lies Deep Within Us? | DAY 1 ◄

Emunah lies hidden within each and every one of us. It is something unseen to the human eye. The world appears to be run without a Creator, *chas v'shalom*, because He is concealed within our world. Knowledge of Him — *emunah* — is something that is discovered from within, a private bond between me and my Creator. Underneath layers of mundane thoughts and selfish desires lies an inner desire for this bond. Subconsciously, we really do want to be close to Him.

Tefillah unleashes and frees that hidden part of us that yearns for a deep relationship with Hashem. In order to reveal our *emunah* through *tefillah* we should strive to speak the words softly, so that only we can hear them. We should ask for our needs to be fulfilled because we want to use them to serve Him better. We ask for wisdom to understand the Torah. Give us health, so we can perform the *mitzvos*. We are truly drawn to serve Hashem and do His will. Through *tefillah* we are able to unravel this desire to cleave to Hashem.

R. Abraham Twerski teaches in his book, *Growing Each Day*, that *tefillah* is the way in which we make Hashem a reality in our lives, rather than an abstract concept. Focusing on the nature of our relationship to Hashem is a great way to begin understanding that reality.

GETTING PRACTICAL

Focus on the words of your tefillos. For instance, the phrase in Adon Olam stating, "B'Yado afkid ruchi — into His hands I entrust my soul," implants the idea that Hashem holds us in the palm of His hands. Take these words and allow yourself to feel tremendous security. Go through your day knowing that whatever happens, our Father, our Creator is always there, lifting us up!

In memory of Tzvia bat Mordechai z'l (11 Kislev) Dedicated lovingly by Marla Krinitz

Hashem Did It!

DAY 2

We can all seek and find Hashem's hand in the mundane. Rather than considering it to be some mystical or antiquated practice, finding Hashem's *hashgachah* (Divine intervention) in the most everyday places is *the* way to increase our *emunah*.

Seeking Hashem in every life event is mental training. One method of improving our Hashem-perspective is to regularly repeat the words "*Ein Od Milvado* — There is no one else but Him." *Ein, ein, ein* — there is no one, no one, no one! At first it might be difficult, but eventually it will become second nature. When something happens we will come to recognize almost immediately, "This is from Hashem, thank you, I love you Hashem." There is no annoyance or insult or good idea or opportunity that comes along without Hashem's intervention. It is *all* Him.

In order to see the bigger picture, we have to develop *emunah* — which requires "small thinking." It is minute-by-minute, investigative work — seeking and finding the Borei Olam everywhere, all of the time and in everything.

The list is endless. Consider the way your computer worked today. Or consider your couch, your chair, the books on your shelf, the tomatoes in your vegetable basket, your child's terrible-two tantrum, the insult your spouse unknowingly gave you — Hashem is in, around and involved in them all.

Blaming others for our frustrations only enmeshes each of us deeper into our personal *galus* (exile). Instead, we need to remind ourselves that everything that touches us in our life is just Hashem — it is not our spouse, children, sibling, boss, co-worker,

Hatzlocha in all to Deborah Rosalimsky and her sons Avi, Josh and Shai

38   TURN AROUND

neighbor or friend. He is in front, behind, around and in everything — our choices, our thoughts, our strengths and weaknesses. He is teaching us, communicating with us, guiding and leading us to the best place... our complete soul rectification.

GETTING PRACTICAL

To foster emunah, we are required to see that Hashem is the source of all that occurs in life. Next time you are compelled to blame another for your distress, try to remember this important teaching. See how it affects your response.

DAY 3 | Feeling Emunah in Our Hearts

Living in an *"emunah* world" is living in a place entirely united with HaKadosh Baruch Hu. It is an elevated state where we are completely conscious of Hashem's existence and closeness within our earthly reality.

A person may reach different levels of *emunah* at different phases in his life. The basic level is an intellectual belief that Hashem exists and guides the destiny of the world. However, as the Chazon Ish teaches in his *sefer, Emunah v'Bitachon,* the highest level of *emunah, emunah shleimah* (simple and complete belief) needs to be felt deep in our hearts. Just as we experience emotions such as joy, sadness and excitement, we are capable of feeling complete trust in HaKadosh Baruch Hu as a natural response to everything that occurs in our lives.

Although an important way to strengthen *emunah,* simply uttering words of *emunah* does not suffice. Our thoughts, feelings and actions should also be governed by our *emunah.* For instance, fulfilling the *mitzvos* with loyalty and carrying out the Borei Olam's will instills *emunah* in our hearts.

When we daven to Hashem with a warm heart and shower praise on Him, we ingrain *emunah* in our heart. Reciting *Tehillim* arouses our heart to live *bi-d'veikus* (bonding) to Hashem. Absorbing and appreciating the wonders of nature can also arouse awe of Hashem.

Hatzlocha in all to Deborah Rosalimsky and her sons Avi, Josh and Shai

Living life mindfully (aware of what is happening around and within us) is certainly of important value to increasing our *emunah.* Yet, this is a stepping stone. The next level we strive to reach and which occurs quite naturally as a result of our newfound expanded awareness is that our minds become attuned to a new way of thinking that never was before. We begin seeing Hashem in places, people, objects and events — a new vision of life begins to emerge seemingly out of nowhere. In spite of the fact that emotional work may require strength and effort, be assured that the outcome is irreplaceable; a polished point of view on life.

GETTING PRACTICAL

Although intellectually believing and trusting in Hashem is a good start, work toward instilling this feeling of trust in your heart. Doing mitzvos, davening, reciting Tehillim and marveling at creation are some ways of internalizing this feeling.

Choosing His People with Love

Every day we recite in our morning prayers before *Shema* the words, "Blessed are You Hashem Who chooses His people Israel with love." Hashem's love for His people is beyond our ability to grasp. In *Yirmiyahu*, it states, "Thus said Hashem, '... I have loved you with an eternal love, therefore I have extended loving kindness to you.'"[7]

The Talmud teaches us that "there are three whom Hashem loves — the one who controls his anger, the one who doesn't become drunk and the one who foregoes his own honor."[8] Nevertheless, Hashem's love for Israel surpasses all these other loves.

Though "I am Hashem who loves justice,"[9] His love for His children is even greater than His love of justice. The Zohar HaKadosh writes that if Hashem had to choose between His love for justice and His love for Israel, His love for Israel would triumph every time, just as with any loving father.[10]

Every Jewish heart harbors a fiery eternal love for Hashem. Yet, this passion is often buried under layers of transgressions and impure thoughts. Sins, impure thoughts and negative emotions detach us from Hashem, making it difficult for us to feel His love. We don't need to reinvent the wheel or attempt to create a new love. Rather, we are instructed to cleanse our hearts of transgressions and thus uncover and reveal the love which already exists.

As the Zohar HaKadosh laments, if only those who transgress Hashem's word knew how deep His

---

7   32:1,2.
8   *Pesachim* 113b.
9   *Yeshaya* 61:8.
10   III, 99b.

love runs for them, and how closely connected He wishes to be, they would "pick up their hems" and run to Him with all their strength.[11]

GETTING PRACTICAL _____

Hashem has an intrinsic love for us, His people. Keeping the Torah and mitzvos expresses our deep love for Hashem. Chapter 18 in Tehillim expresses Dovid HaMelech's deep love for Hashem. Recite it with renewed intent as you focus on feeling unconditional love toward Hashem based on lifelong gratitude.

---

11   II, 5b.

It Is All a Gift

"And you shall love Hashem, your G-d, with all your heart and all your soul and all your resources."[12]

Ideally, our love for Hashem should be unconditional. Rather than being dependent on receiving something from Him, our love should be present no matter what we receive from Him. Yet, realistically, most of us may initially strive to relate to Hashem with conditional love. We recognize where all of life's gifts come from and how kind HaKadosh Baruch Hu is to us. As our awareness of Hashem's Presence increases, this leads to a greater understanding of His compassionate ways.

Think about it: Where does everything we have come from? Every idea, every thought, every feeling, every intricate part of our body, our soul, our children, our spouse, our family and our money are gifts bestowed on us by Hashem. All of these gifts are an expression of Hashem's love and kindness to us. We don't deserve them — rather, they are a reflection of Hashem's altruistic affection.

We are often falsely led to believe that everything we successfully complete is done "with the help of Hashem." This reasoning is faulty. Hashem is in complete control and is all-powerful. He is not just "helping us" — He runs the world! He does not even need our help! In order to internalize this fully we have to nullify our ego and admit our dependence on the Borei Olam. It's not just feeling humble — it's living with *emes*, truth. Everything in this world belongs to the *Melech HaOlam*. We are merely temporary guardians of

In memory of Charna bat R' Benzion HaLevi z'l (Jennie Jaye Tenzer, 6 Elul) Dedicated lovingly by Shira & David Wiseman and Family

---

12   *Devarim* 6:15.

our lives and possessions which are gifted to us in order to serve Hashem.

Ultimately, after internalizing all the blessings Hashem has bestowed on us and living with gratitude for them, we may begin to attempt to work toward forging an unconditional loving bond with Him. Instead of loving Him because of what He gives to us, we may finally learn to love Him no matter what, for His very existence — just as He loves us!

If we stop and take stock of all the gifts Hashem bestows upon us we should feel an intense, heartfelt love for Him.

GETTING PRACTICAL

Each day, repeatedly list every single minute detail and blessing in our lives in order to sharpen our senses and see how Hashem takes care of us. This is the beginning of what it means to love HaKadosh Baruch Hu conditionally.

The Gift of Shabbos

Every Shabbos we partake of the future world, of the peace and harmony of *yemos haMashiach* (the days of Mashiach). By observing Shabbos we are in essence preparing and readying ourselves for the day when it is all Shabbos.

Shabbos keeps us aware of our final goal in life. It is very easy to become excessively involved and indulged with the matters of this world, but Shabbos is our weekly reminder of a higher reality. We get to unplug from the world and enter into a zone of quiet and spiritual reflection. We receive life-giving power.

Everything we eat on Shabbos necessitates preparation beforehand. The same is true of eternity. When speaking of the future reward the Talmud teaches us, "Whoever prepares food before Shabbos, will have what to eat on Shabbos."[13] Every time we prepare for Shabbos, we are also reminding ourselves to prepare for the World to Come. We remind ourselves that our stay in this world is but a preparation for something much loftier.

Reishis Chochmah teaches us that Shabbos is a "sign of eternity,"[14] meaning that the door to eternity is left a crack open for us to see and experience. We have the opportunity to feel what the future world will be like and live in total harmony with HaKadosh Baruch Hu.

When *Bnei Yisrael* asked Hashem at Har Sinai how they would know what the World to Come would be like, they were told that they could sample it once

*In memory of R'
Elimelech ben R'
Tuvia z'l (Milton
Tenzer, 11 Shvat)
Dedicated
lovingly by
Shira & David
Wiseman and
Family*

---

13   *Avodah Zarah* 3a.

14   *Shemos* 31:17.

a week on Shabbos. Therefore, *Chazal* teach us that Shabbos is a taste of Heaven on Earth;[15] a taste of pure spirituality.

GETTING PRACTICAL ⎯⎯⎯⎯⎯⎯⎯⎯⎯

Twenty-five hours of achieving balance and harmony within; this is the gift of Shabbos. Shabbos offers a transcendent frame of mind after the culmination of a week's work. Let's see it as a dip into the World to Come where all is prepared and we are simply there to enjoy.

---

15   *Berachos* 57b. See also Maharal in *Netzach Yisrael*, 46.

Reawakening Our Awareness

The best possible feeling in this world is to attach ourselves to the Source of all good — HaKadosh Baruch Hu. Thinking about and speaking to Hashem constantly reawakens the awareness that He is with us right here and now. This brings Hashem to a place that is here on earth with us, removing the distance that the *yetzer hara* tries so desperately to create between us.

Even when the *Melech HaOlam* is hidden from our intellects, He is perceived by and revealed in our hearts. The Sfas Emes teaches that Hashem is present in all creation, though His existence is hidden from the human eye.[16] Therefore it is our calling to uncover His being through awakening our awareness when we go about our mundane, everyday activities.

The Rama quotes the *pasuk* in *Tehillim*, "*Shivisi Hashem l'negdi tamid*,"[17] and teaches that our *tzaddikim* lived constantly with the acute awareness of Hashem in their hearts. Though not easy, it is actually a very simple concept — to live with complete faith. It is all a matter of habit of the mind.

The Baal Shem Tov has taught that a person is wherever his thoughts are. If I think about Hashem, I am with Him. The way to attach oneself to Hashem is not through mental clarification and intellectual understanding, but through total faith. When talking to the Borei Olam we should make a direct connection by referring to Him as "You," for instance, "You, Hashem, are with me."

One way to bring Hashem into our lives is through the act of simple contemplation of the world around

In memory of Shraga Favish Ben Yosef Chaiyim HaCohen z'l Dedicated lovingly by the Ledder Family

---

16   *Parashas Shemini.*

17   16:8.

us. The *pasuk* in *Tehillim*, "*Mah rabu ma'asecha Hashem kulam b'chochmah asisa* — How wondrous are Your works, they are all made with wisdom,"[18] teaches us just this. Look around and be awestruck by Hashem's infinite wisdom and imprint on creation.

GETTING PRACTICAL

Hashem is right here waiting for us to allow Him entry. Speaking unpretentious words such as, "I know You are with me every step I take. You are standing by my side and I am never alone. Even when I am lost, You are still watching over me," will build an awareness that will stay with us always.

---

18   104:24.

A Rope of Hope

"You shall walk after the L-rd your G-d, and fear Him, and fear Him, and keep His commandments, and obey His voice, and you shall serve Him, and hold fast to Him."[19]

In *Hilchos Teshuvah*, the Rambam explains that there are both illnesses of the soul and the body. Each of these physical and spiritual illnesses can be divided into two categories — those that are harmful but not life-threatening, and those that are potentially fatal.

Despair is a grave illness of the soul that endangers our very existence. A despairing person loses hope, giving up on the possibility of salvation and suffering intense depression as a result. To avoid this, we should strengthen ourselves with *emunah* even in the most miserable and discouraging situations.

After being diagnosed with Multiple Sclerosis, a chronic auto-immune disease harming the body's neurological system in 2006, I abandoned thoughts of sadness and replanted my life on *emunah*-based ground. Living with *emunah* was a choice — and is one daily. It is not always easy, but is always the right choice — even at the hardest of times.

The Hebrew word *shachar* (dawn) is translated to mean black or darkness. Why? Because at the exact moment when the night's darkness becomes most intense, that is when *shachar* appears and the sun begins to rise. Thus, the concept of dawn is a source of great comfort, serving to eradicate despondency.

The power of hope in determining halachic questions is elucidated by the Gemara in its discussion about returning lost objects.[20] The issue of whether

---

19   *Devarim* 13:5.
20   *Bava Metziah* 21a–22b.

or not one must return a lost object depends, in part, on the owner's (objective) mental state. If the owner can be presumed to have become so anguished as to have given up hope, then the object is presumed to be ownerless and need not be returned. However, if the situation is such that the owner can be presumed to have retained hope of retrieving his object, then it is still considered to be his. Keeping up hope, not giving up, determines who you are, what you are associated with, and who you "belong to."

Nowhere is despair more imminent and prevalent than in these times, the generations before the Mashiach. HaRav Noam Elimelech beautifully summarizes this point as follows:

"In the generation before Mashiach comes, Hashem will extend a rope for Klal Yisrael to grasp. The difficulties that they will experience during this time will cause the rope to shake intensely. Those who are weak and foolish will let go. Those who are wise will continue to hold on through the power of their *emunah*."[21]

GETTING PRACTICAL

Deep inside, we all harbor a storehouse of inner strength. We have to rely on this strength to continue holding on to Hashem's rope of hope, despite the circumstances. The Izhbitzer Rebbe used to talk of how destructive it is to give up hope. Whatever the situation, as long as we keep our hope alive, there remains a potential cure, a potential redemption or a potential salvation to the crisis. What can you be more hopeful about?

---

21   *Sefer MiPeninei Noam Elimelech.*

Heartfelt Emunah

"And they shall make for Me a sanctuary, and I will dwell amongst them."[22]

Fundamental to Judasim is the concept that Hashem, the Torah and Israel are one. What does this mean? Hashem is as intrinsic to our bodies as all of our limbs and organs. If we do not "feel" Him inside us, it is as though we are disconnected from a part of our own body; we are numb to our inner essence. But in which part of our body should we feel Hashem?

The mind may be our intellectual center but our heart is our sanctuary, the emotional seat of our body. The heart has the ability to sense things both internally and externally. Hashem is present in each of our hearts. To truly feel *emunah* for Hashem in our hearts — as opposed to our minds — this organ needs to be receptive and accessible. In order to sense Hashem in everything around us, we are required to be conscious of our emotional core.

Intellectual *emunah* in Hashem refers to the mental knowledge that Hashem exists, and that He created, creates and controls everything occurring in this world every second. This level of *emunah* is important — very important — but alone it is not effective enough to enable us to transcend the vicissitudes of life. True tranquility flows only after we have worked hard to transform intellectual *emunah* into *emunah she'ba-lev* (heartfelt *emunah*).

Practically speaking, only with heart-based *emunah* we are able to internalize the truth of *gam zu l'tovah* — everything is good because it is all from

In memory of Sara Deena bat R' Elimelech z'l (S. Deena Voroba, 11 Iyar) Dedicated lovingly by Shira & David Wiseman and Family

---

22   *Shemos* 25:8. A sanctuary — a holy abode for Hashem to "reside" within us; in our hearts.

Hashem and Hashem is and does only good. Hashem runs the world with a specific purpose in mind. All that happens is in perfect harmony with this ultimate purpose. Internalizing this truth in our hearts enables us to transcend all challenges such as difficulties with livelihood, illness, marital turmoil or tragedy *chas v'shalom.*

The greatest distance in the world is the gap between our mind and heart. Our lifetime task is to minimize this distance, allowing *emunah* to resonate deep within and enabling us to weather the inevitable storms of life.

GETTING PRACTICAL

Can you feel Hashem in your heart? The measuring rod to size where you stand with your emunah is by means of judging how frustrated you are with the circumstances of your life: the greater the emunah, the less the heartache. Repeat the words gam zu l'tovah — I know this is good even though I don't understand. It will pierce the heart and eventually become second nature.

Sing and Dance to Hashem!

Hashem chose Dovid HaMelech to write *Sefer Tehillim*. Why was Dovid chosen? The answer is simple, yet it highlights an important message. Dovid HaMelech endured tremendous difficulties, hardships and suffering. He — *davka* (precisely) — was fitting to sing praises to G-d. The entire *Sefer Tehillim* reflects his desire and will to cleave to Him, despite his challenges.

What is so righteous about singing hymns of thanks to Hashem? The very act of singing reflects the acknowledgment that everything that happens in our life, including all the trials, is for the best. In *Tehillim*, Dovid HaMelech writes, *"L'Dovid mizmor chesed u'mishpat ashirah lecha Hashem azameirah* — Of Dovid, a song. I shall sing of kindness and judgment; to You, Hashem, I shall sing."[23] We learn from this verse that whether Dovid HaMelech experienced kindness or strict justice from Hashem in his life, he continued to sing to HaKadosh Baruch Hu in the same way; retaining the same level of *emunah*!

Singing uplifts one's spirits and strengthens one's heart. In the merit of us singing to the *Melech Olam* in times of trouble, Hashem "acts" as our shield and protects us. Our *emunah* is compared to a shield, as is written in *Tehillim*, *"V'Atah Hashem magen ba'adi* — But You, Hashem, are a shield about me."[24]

Dancing also affects our *emunah*, as is written elsewhere in *Tehillim*, *"Hafachta mispadi l'machol li* — You have turned my lament into dancing for me."[25] Dovid

In memory of Yosef Binyamin ben Moshe Aharon Alter z'l (Joseph Voroba, 5 Tishrei) Dedicated lovingly by Shira & David Wiseman and Family

---

23   101:1.
24   3:4.
25   30:12.

HaMelech declares before Hashem that in the merit of his dancing, Hashem sweetens decrees and changes his sadness into happiness. He danced for Hashem even in private and merited to feel the resulting joy. His entire life was redefined due to his strong *emunah* in Hashem's everlasting compassion and love.

GETTING PRACTICAL

Dovid HaMelech was chosen to write Tehillim because he sang songs and danced to Hashem even during challenging times. Sing and dance for G-d, even when it is difficult. Doing so will leave you uplifted, and with a higher level of closeness to Him, acknowledging that all is for the best.

No Complaints!

The smaller we are, the more we complain. The bigger we let ourselves grow, the less we will complain.

Everything that Hashem does is for the best. Complaining over one's life circumstances may be due to either lack of *emunah* or a lack of *hakaras hatov* (gratitude). Let's explore each possible cause.

Emunah is the foundation of Judaism. What is *emunah*? *Emunah* is defined as faithful belief — that whatever we have is exactly what we need, and whatever we do not have is precisely what we do not need. If our *emunah* is frail, our internal Jewish make-up can tumble down. Complaining about our difficulties is basically like saying, "Something here is just not good." This core belief reflects a lack of trust that Hashem knows what is truly in our best interests.

Admittedly, it is often difficult to acknowledge that suffering in the moment is truly in our best interests. Essentially we need to suspend logic and to have patience. We also have to exercise *dan l'kaf zechus* (giving the benefit of the doubt). To whom?

To G-d Himself.

A humbled spirit is needed to internalize the knowledge that our vision is limited and we often cannot see the long-term benefits of suffering or difficulties. Our lives span only a minute portion of the world's history. This can be compared to walking into the cinema in the middle of the movie and expecting to understand the entire plot! How can we possibly understand?

The other cause of complaining is a lack of gratitude. Failing to express gratitude for the endless gifts bestowed upon us, those that we notice and most of which go unnoticed, makes us essentially ingrates undeserving of additional benevolence. If we only take the time to stop, consider and focus on the outpouring of *rachamei Shamayim* we would be compelled to say Thank you rather than complain.

GETTING PRACTICAL

This is the generation of entitlement. It is so easy to feel that we deserve it all, yet this is a formula for internal destruction. Let's stop complaining. Hashem gives us exactly what we need — we lack nothing — and we have so much to be thankful for.

Talk to Hashem

Hisbodedus means personal secluded prayer with HaKadosh Baruch Hu. This is a positive way to foster inner peace. A daily conversation with Hashem will ultimately result in a surge of *koach* to deal with turmoil *r"l* when it arises. Practicing *hisbodedus* enables us to touch *emes*, the truth that lies in our heart.

Our hearts are often covered over by many layers of impurities. These impurities of the heart can be created by the following:

- being earthly-minded and becoming overly attached to the material toys of this world

- immoral thoughts, speech and actions that we have stocked up on, "thanks" to the cunning tactics of the *yetzer hara*

- our egotism — relying on our own might and thinking that we are in control of it all

- lack of Torah study and sluggish performance of *mitzvos*

- depleted stores of *emunah*

However, Rebbe Nachman teaches "*Ein yeush ba'olam klal* — There is no despair in this world." Everything can be repaired through *hisbodedus*. It is a simple practice. Sit down with your favorite drink and talk. Talk freely in your own language and words, empty out what is weighing heavily on your heart. "Hashem I need You, I miss You. I want to feel so much closer to You than I do, but I can't hold on anymore, I am losing it!"

Effective *hisbodedus* requires honesty. It is a priceless opportunity to get in touch with the real you and

In memory of Shmuel Yechezkel ben Shlomo z'l (21 Adar) Lovingly remembered and deeply missed by his daughter

lay the cards out on the table before the Borei Olam. He knows what is going on, more than we think He knows, and more than we want Him to know... but He knows. Now it is time for us to reveal it to ourselves.

Hisbodedus offers an outlet to pour out all of our disappointments, frustrations, anxieties and concerns. It is also an opportune time to confess all of our sins and do *teshuvah* for guilty thoughts, speech and actions. Effective *hisbodedus* also requires regular daily practice, even for ten minutes a day.

GETTING PRACTICAL

Hisbodedus is a private, daily, honest conversation with Hashem that enables us to invest in our own wellbeing and foster inner peace. It is a worthwhile investment for us. There is no cost, but the results are priceless!

The Power of Shabbos Kodesh

Shabbos is the center of creation and the heart and soul of reality. The power of Shabbos provides us with an additional soul, a pure light, as is written in *Tehillim*, "*Hotziah mi-masger nafshi* —Take my soul out of confinement."[26]

Shabbos frees us from the greed and enslavement of our physical being. Once released from our physicality, we can see our true purpose in life. Our earthliness is what imprisons us from being able to achieve a higher level of holiness. The spark of holiness that dwells deep inside each of us is exposed in the *zechus* (merit) of *Shabbos Kodesh*. On this holy day we can open our state of awareness and reach clarity of mind.

If we strive to attain holiness and attach ourselves to *emes* (Hashem's truth), we will become sensitive to the holiness of Shabbos and will become powerfully affected by this magnificent day. But how does one become a receptacle to receive this Shabbos holiness?

It is not merely observing the laws of Shabbos that makes us holy and draws us close to the Borei Olam. Rather, it is a continuous process of work and preparation done both throughout the week and also throughout our life that brings out the *Shabbos Kodesh* within us. Each of us has a personal *avodah* that enables us to reach this heightened state of holiness and awareness.

By simply paying attention to the names of the days of the week in the Hebrew language we can remind ourselves of Shabbos all week long. *Yom Rishon* (Sunday) reiterates that it is the first day after

In memory of Safta Nelly bat Aaron z'l (28 Sivan)

26   142:8.

Shabbos, *Yom Sheini* (Monday) the second day and so on. Shabbos is a precious gift from Hashem and its arrival should be awaited throughout the week.

GETTING PRACTICAL

Shabbos enables us to feel holy and spiritually transformed. However, achieving this level of kedushah is hard work, an individual challenge for each of us. Think of creative ways to prepare yourself during the week to create the proper vessel to receive this influx of holiness. For instance, you may hold off on purchasing and/or using something extra special during the week and do so only in the spirit of the upcoming Shabbos.

Power Prayer: Part I

When we talk to each other, our words usually don't reveal our innermost thoughts, opinions or feelings. In contrast, we should reveal all these deep innermost thoughts when we speak to Hashem.

Unfortunately, it is all too easy to daven without complete soul-baring or concentration. Davening with complete mindfulness and honesty is a challenge. It requires emotional honesty and effort. Ideally though, if we manage to daven mindfully, our words merely mimic our innermost thoughts. As we say at the end of *Shemoneh Esrei:* "Let the words of my mouth be accepted to You and the thoughts of my heart before You, Hashem."

Crying while davening is one physical indication that we have reached an ideal level of *kavanah* (intent). The tears demonstrate we have completely revealed our true inner self before HaKadosh Baruch Hu. When we cry, there is no discrepancy between our words and thoughts. A person does not cry and think about other things. This explains why *"sha'arei d'maos lo ninalim* — The gates of tears are never closed."[27]

How can we daven with complete openness and humbleness before Hashem? By internalizing the fact that Hashem is able to do anything and everything. For instance, when we recite the words in the *Shemoneh Esrei,* "*Teka b'shofar gadol* — Sound the great shofar" and "*Es tzemach Dovid avdecha* — The offspring of Your servant Dovid," we should remind ourselves that this really will happen — very possibly in the near future.

---

27   Baba Metzia 59a

When we pray "*Refaeinu Hashem* — Heal us, Hashem," we should truly believe that Hashem will heal us. We ought not to let our *yetzer hara* encourage us to doubt Hashem's powers to heal. We end the *tefillah* of *Shemoneh Esrei,* "*Hashem, Tzuri v'Goali* — My Rock and my Redeemer," and ask to be freed from these doubts and internalize our belief in Hashem's power to answer us.[28]

GETTING PRACTICAL

To achieve kavanah in davening, let us remember that Hashem is listening and all-powerful. We can practice deep intent with any activity. For instance before spicing up your next Shabbos meal say out loud, "Lichvod Shabbos Kodesh — In honor of the holy Shabbos." By doing so, we put purpose into our deeds and increase our emunah in Hashem.

---

28   Rabbi Tzadok HaKohen.

Power Prayer: Part II

Here are a few tips to enhance our davening and increase our *kavanah*. Ultimately, they will strengthen our *emunah* as well.

1. Reflect on **chasdei Hashem** (Hashem's kindness)

   Life itself is a gift. If we are here on this earth, we have already merited the greatest gift of all. Hashem's acts of kindness are far beyond our merits. Instead of davening with the attitude that we are entitled to be granted our wishes, our prayers should reflect humble gratitude and recognition for everything we have. We may not understand Heavenly calculations and why things happen the way they do. Yet, when we daven, it is useful to reflect with gratitude on everything Hashem represents. Hashem is eternally Kind, Generous and Good. Before we pray, it is useful to remind ourselves that He will give us anything we request at the right time — if it is for our ultimate good.

2. Request that a **chillul Hashem** (desecration of Hashem's name) be prevented

   Everything Hashem does can create a *kiddush Hashem* (honor to Hashem) in this world. One way to maximize the power of our requests during davening is to ask that our prayers be answered to deter doubters from arguing that Hashem does not listen or care. If Hashem would not answer our requests, it is possible that others with no *emunah* may erroneously presume that Hashem is either not listening or unable to fulfill

*In memory of
Chaya Pearl bas
Eliezer (Lazer) z'l
(17 Sivan)
Dedicated
lovingly by the
Gerowitz Family*

our requests. This may cause a *chillul Hashem*. Chana used this rationale when she davened to Hashem for a child. She feared that if He did not bless her with this miracle, others might create a *chillul Hashem* by proclaiming that "Hashem did not listen to the *tefillos* of a righteous woman."[29]

3. Understand that even if something is decreed to happen we must daven for it

Hashem wants us to realize what we need. The Western/Greek culture feeds us the false message that *"kochi v'otzem yadi* — my strength and the might of my hand made me all this."* In contrast, davening with the requisite *kavanah* requires the humble recognition that we can achieve nothing without the power and might of HaKadosh Baruch Hu. This humility causes a stir in *Shamayim* that enables the abundance to come down. We should recognize that everything we have, both life itself and the whole package deal, is all from Hashem. We are not able to do a thing — from breathing to eating to reading these words — without Hashem's "nod."

GETTING PRACTICAL

During davening, our attitude and words can enhance or detract from the power of our prayer. Our prayer session can be mediocre, or it can rise us up on eagle's wings. Let's try to work ourselves up into a passionate state and put fire and emotion into the words. If we do so, eventually the enthusiasm becomes real.

---

29   *I Shmuel* 2:1–10.

DAY 16 — Our Pain is Hashem's Pain

According to R. Asher Freund, our suffering in this world represents Hashem's wake-up call. Hashem is in pain both over the baseless hatred between Jews and the other evil acts which maintain our state of exile. R. Asher explains that we should share Hashem's distress. If we don't share His pain, then He shares a bit of "His pain" with us so that we may participate in His "anguish."

Why? One would think that suffering Hashem's pain would just lead us to despair — so what good can this do?

R. Asher explains that Hashem shares His pain with us so that we may cry to Him and arouse His *rachamim* (mercy) in order for Him to redeem us. Sharing His pain in this way is actually an act of compassion. As the central tenet of *Yiddishkeit* is simple, stubborn faith which prevents us from becoming broken, R. Asher instructs that during a *nisayon* we need to storm the Heavens with our cries. We should never remain silent over our pain and suffering, because the very purpose of our *nisayon* is to connect with Him. Remaining silent equates with giving up hope and leads to depression, a place of the evil inclination and the opposite of holiness.

If Hashem did not share His pain with us in the form of a *nisayon*, we may not be prompted to connect to Him in this way. I recently heard a talk by R. Shimshon Dovid Pincus who spoke on this issue. R. Pincus taught that we can achieve a heightened relationship with Hashem through the experience of pain. It serves as a reminder to "take hold of His hand" as it were and beg Him to help us through our challenges. When all around us everything is seemingly lost, what remains and always will remain is the reality of Hashem.

GETTING PRACTICAL _____

Our personal pain is part and parcel of Hashem's pain of our being in exile. The next time we feel personal discomfort we can associate it with the sorrow of the Shechinah and recognize its source.

We Are All Hashem's Children

We are all children of Hashem. Despite our human frailties and shortcomings, our bond with Him will never be severed. Hashem is our Father and we are His children. Parents do not divorce their children.

Because He is our Father, HaKadosh Baruch Hu showers us with special affection. Even those who willingly ignore Hashem's will still retain this special status. Rather than abusing our position, being aware of our status should motivate us to please our *Tatte* and bring Him *nachas* by thinking, speaking and acting according to His advice.

The more we try to follow Hashem's commandments, the more we will feel His love and closeness. Hashem sees our efforts to do His will and rewards us by revealing Himself. For this reason He gifted us with tools to feel His Presence — Torah and *mitzvos*.

If we hurt someone close to us (such as our spouse, children, friends or other family), the pain we feel lies in direct proportion to the extent of our love for them. An absence of emotional discomfort is an indication that we need to seriously examine our feelings and work on increasing our connection with that person.

Similarly, if we go astray and ignore Hashem's words, Hashem is "hurting" and we should feel similar emotional pain and remorse for causing Him pain. If we do not feel such remorse, it is time to work on our connection and love for Him. We do this by giving to Him in the way He asked — by following His Torah.

*In memory of
Shlomo ben Joya
z'l (3 Cheshvan)*

GETTING PRACTICAL

Hashem is our Father and He loves us as His children. By following His laws we connect to Him and experience a love which is pleasurable to us. If we ignore His Torah prescriptions, we hurt Him and ourselves in the process, just like we feel hurt when our actions cause pain to another loved one. Let's practice visualizing the pleasure we give to Hashem every time we fulfill His Torah.

The Faith and Trust

"In You, Hashem, I have taken refuge, let me never be ashamed; in Your righteousness let me escape. Incline Your ear to my prayer, quickly rescue me, be to me a rock of strength, a fortress of defense to deliver me. For You are my rock and my fortress, and for the sake of Your name — guide me and lead me."[30]

Dovid HaMelech composed this *pasuk* when he was fleeing from Shaul HaMelech, who was intent on killing him. Instinctively, when a person is in mortal danger he fearfully thinks only of his own survival. In contrast, Dovid HaMelech expressed his absolute trust in Hashem, even as he was running for his life.

The Radak provides a detailed commentary of this *pasuk* of *Tehillim*. He interprets the words, "In You, Hashem, I have taken refuge, let me never be ashamed," as reflecting Dovid HaMelech's confidence that in the merit of his trust in Hashem, he will never be put to shame. The dire straits that threatened him did not in any way compromise his belief that Hashem would never abandon him. Ironically, he believed that if he strengthened his *emunah* in the middle of this dangerous time, Hashem would in turn deliver him.

According to the Radak, even if his sins brought on the suffering, Dovid HaMelech knew Hashem would save him because of His merit and mercy — that is, "in Your righteousness let me escape." Although Shaul HaMelech was desperately pursuing him, Dovid HaMelech did not feel vulnerable. He said, "Incline Your ear to my prayer, quickly rescue me, be to me a rock of strength, a fortress of defense to deliver me."

---

30   *Tehillim* 31:2–4.

He was certain that Hashem would surround him with unshakable protection.

Dovid HaMelech concluded his prayer with the words, "For the sake of Your name, guide me and lead me." This prayer reflects a very pious level we should all strive for — to ask Hashem to rescue us so that Hashem (not we!) does not suffer over our predicament.

GETTING PRACTICAL

Let us strengthen our hearts with steadfast hope and unrelenting trust in Hashem. As a result Hashem will help us, safeguard us and rescue us in countless and amazing ways.

If You Want to Find Him - Look!

Hashem created the entire world and continues to take care and oversee every minute in constant detail. Of all creatures, man is the only one granted free choice. Our main choice is whether to live with the recognition that Hashem is our Creator, or whether we choose to ignore this vital connection.

The more we believe in HaKadosh Baruch Hu and search for His Presence, the more obvious His involvement in our lives. Though He is always here, we cannot see Him unless we put in the effort to find Him.

In contrast to the other nations, Hashem interacts with us, His beloved people, in a unique way. Part of *emunah* is recognizing this gift. Am Yisrael plays an integral role in this world — we are required to embrace this task with responsibility and purpose. It is vital to internalize the fact that we are irreplaceable as Hashem's treasured nation. The Borei Olam "yearns" for us to include Him in our lives and cherish His constant involvement.

If we only valued the treasure called heartfelt *emunah*, we would be motivated to work on building our trust in Hashem. It is the pillar we lean on when challenges arise; a support system intended to lift us up when it appears that everything around us is falling down.

It is our duty to actively look for Hashem in our lives and make use of this special gift. As the *sefer Orchos Chaim* teaches, "Trust Hashem with all your heart. Believe in His individual providence. With this, Hashem's Oneness will endure and be in your heart, when you believe that Hashem's eyes roam

In memory of Beryl Yisrael ben Rachel z'l (2 Adar Aleph) Dedicated lovingly by Leah Rubabshi

throughout the land, and sees all the ways of man, He examines their hearts... This is the special treasure of Yisrael over all other nations, and it is the foundation of the Torah."

GETTING PRACTICAL ⎯⎯⎯⎯⎯⎯⎯⎯

Do you see Hashem in every part of your life and welcome His Presence? Emunah is an innate gift that empowers us to do great things since emunah connects us to the source of all greatness.

| # Shabbos - Stop, Look and Listen

In order to emulate Hashem, we are commanded to cease creating for a period of time to ensure the cycle of creation continues. Generally speaking, there is little peace or sense of tranquility during the mundane week. Shabbos provides this missing ingredient that completes and perfects our week.

Shabbos is not about changing anything; it is about paying attention to what is already here. Essentially we "wake up" to our life on Shabbos; we taste the food placed in our mouths, we feel the presence of our family members. In effect, we are gifted with the opportunity to appreciate the simple blessings in life.

We go through life on automatic drive, many times not even noticing how we made it to where we are standing. Shabbos gifts us with the time to recognize what is important to us. When we stop, we notice. Paying attention to life is what we do on Shabbos. Consequently, we reveal our inner gratitude that was buried under our weekday acquisitions and successes. We have time to enjoy the taste of the World to Come; a world which in its entirety embodies the work which we have achieved throughout a lifetime.

By releasing ourselves from everyday life burdens, Shabbos enables us to hear the voice of our *neshamah*, even subconsciously. Rather than merely providing an opportunity to rest, Shabbos enables us to redirect our thoughts and our way of living. Our *mitzvos* are elevated and we appreciate more so their innate value.

In memory of Mazal ben Raphael z'l (16 Iyar) Dedicated lovingly by the Edi Family

GETTING PRACTICAL

Shabbos is an island of stillness — to cherish our lives. Let's pay attention to what and how much we have. Look out the window and relish the scenery of life. Sit and think how wonderful it is to stop, look and listen.

Have a Cup of Coffee... with Hashem

Sometimes, we fail to be comforted by the knowledge that all that Hashem does is for the best. Often, it is because the knowledge that Hashem loves us may be firmly in our minds — but has not yet trickled down to our hearts.

One successful path to achieving this mindset is through *hisbodedus*, regular, personal and secluded prayer with HaKadosh Baruch Hu. Why is it so important to do *hisbodedus*? Living in this rat race of a world, constantly scurrying around from place to place and from thought to thought, we often fail to stop and take the time to recollect our thoughts.

Hisbodedus helps us notice our racing thoughts, reset them, refocus and realign with Hashem. It also offers an opportunity to clean our slate from the burden of guilt that we carry around when we feel we have fallen short of our potential. It is a time to do *teshuvah* (repent), analyze ourselves and work on improving.

Having the courage to open up and have an honest discussion with the One Who knows us best is the perfect way to cleanse our heart. It helps us gain clarity for making the choices that stand before us. It strengthens us to handle difficulties with more ease. It enables us to live with more harmony, less criticism and increased joy. It is a must in today's world.

Secluded prayer is talking with Hashem without busying ourselves with other things. Sit with a cup of coffee and speak to the Borei Olam like you would to a friend. Telling Hashem everything from your

In memory of Osnat bat Bitiyo z'l (8 Sivan) Dedicated lovingly by the Mullodzhanov Family

innermost thoughts to your confused feelings is the greatest gift that awaits you when setting aside time for *hisbodedus*.

GETTING PRACTICAL ———————————

How do you empty your daily bag of burdens — disappointment, confusion, anxiety? Visit the awesome place to defuse these feelings. Hisbodedus is the place!

Simchah through Emunah

Dovid HaMelech writes, "For in Him will our hearts be glad, for in His Holy Name we trusted."[31]

Genuine *simchah* can only be achieved through complete trust in Hashem. There is no other way to attain inner peace and serenity than by relying on the One Who created us and continuously directs us on our journey of life. By internalizing the *emes* (true) fact that "I trust in the Borei Olam, He loves me and is doing the best for me now and always," we can reach endless happiness.

Knowing that Hashem is with us makes us feel strong — like a tiger walking on the street, not fearing anyone or anything. This feeling leads to contentment. We can rejoice in our good fortune that we are children of *Melech Malchei HaMelachim HaKadosh Baruch Hu!*

In the same *perek*, Dovid expounds, "May Your Kindness, O Eternal, be upon us, just as we long for You."[32]

We may stray from Hashem's ways and need to improve in our *avodas Hashem* (who doesn't?). Yet, it is crucial to remind ourselves that Hashem Yisbarach does not stop showering His everlasting kindness on us. To the degree that we are joyful we display our trust in His compassionate Fatherly love. We are His children and we will always be bound to Him.

One factor that often blocks us from receiving Hashem's blessings of kindness is our feeling that we are undeserving of His protection, *chas v'shalom. Emunah* in His love for us leads to *emunah* in ourselves

In memory of Leeor Devora z'l (20 Sivan) bat Shlomo Perl yblc"t
"...הוי שמאי אומר מקבל את כל האדם בסבר פנים יפות"
Dedicated lovingly by Allen and Susan Black

---

31   *Tehillim* 33:21.

32   33:22.

— that we are good and deserving of Hashem's infinite kindness to us. These thoughts can enable us to overcome the trap of the *yetzer hara* and instead hold steadfast onto our belief that Hashem loves us unconditionally and awaits our return to Him always. "Hashem has a plan and it is all for the best... for *my* ultimate best! I won't stop believing... I will keep yearning to improve my ways and grow closer in my relationship to Him." This is true joy — unconditional love and care by a loving Father.

GETTING PRACTICAL _____

Let's remind ourselves that in order to achieve lasting happiness, we need to have complete, internalized emunah in Hashem. And in order to have emunah in Hashem, we need to feel deserving of His love.

Hashem Loves Me

The Maharal teaches on his commentary in *parashas Lech Lecha*, "…Their actions, good or bad, contribute to the degree of closeness to Hashem or detract from it, but the selection itself [the fact that Am Yisrael was chosen to be His people] was nevertheless not a result of any action."[33] The *tefillah* of *Ahavah Rabah* (Hashem's abundant love) describes the endless love Hashem has for His beloved nation, no matter what. *Elokai* — My G-d; You are my G-d, who loves me with an eternal and unconditional love. *Ahavas Olam Ahavtanu* — an indescribable love, an indestructible love that lies deep within our hearts.

Hashem's love is not dependent on our actions, since we have been chosen through the merit of Avraham Avinu, the father of our nation. Though we are held responsible for our actions, and must give an accounting of our behavior, we nevertheless always remain part of the Jewish nation — for we are Hashem's children.

Love is the driving force of life. R. Noach Orloweck often teaches of the great importance of internalizing and reminding ourselves of Hashem's infinite love. He says it is vital to teach our children how much Hashem loves them, since this will inspire and empower them to fulfill their inherent potential.

We should be motivated to perform *mitzvos* and pray because of our loving relationship with Hashem. The word "*mitzvah*" stems from the root word *tzavta* (companionship), binding our soul to Hashem in companionship through the action of the mitzvah. In fact, the *mitzvos* were given to either help us feel

In amemory of Maya bat Osnat z'l (8 Cheshvan) Dedicated lovingly by the Mullodzhanov Family

---

33   *Netzach Yisrael*, ch. 11.

Hashem's love, to provide a way for us to express our love for Him and/or help us learn to love one another.

It is easier to love someone when we are happily receiving everything we want. However, our true love for Hashem is affirmed during the inevitable times of difficulty that our Creator creates for us. Thus, every morning and every night Hashem asks us to repeat the eternal message of *Shema*. The purpose of praying *Shema* twice daily serves to remind us that Hashem is One and His Name is One. Thus, all of our experiences — the happy, the easy, the moments of hardship — all stem from the love of the same HaKadosh Baruch Hu. The binding of the *tefillin* and the embrace of the *tallis* also serve as physical reminders of how Hashem wraps us, His people, in His love.

We must constantly pay attention to Hashem's never-ending love, which He shows for us in many different ways. Though our mortality and human frailty may mean we do not always understand His ways, filled with love for our Creator, our hearts will know everything He does is for our very best.

GETTING PRACTICAL ⸻

We can increase our love for Hashem by thinking of some of the ways that Hashem shows His endless love for us. Contemplating the gift of life is one poignant way or, we can wrap our arms around ourselves and remind ourselves that Hashem loves us, no matter what!

Tefillah Is Food for the Soul

The *avodah* in the Beis HaMikdash focused on bringing *korbanos* (sacrifices). The root word in the Hebrew language of *korbanos* is *karov* (close) — referring to coming close and cleaving to the Borei Olam. During this time, before the third and final Beis HaMikdash is built — may it come soon in our days — our *tefillah* humbly replaces the *korbanos,* partially filling the void.

Tefillah involves intimate talks with Hashem. *Tefillah* is an *avodah she'ba-lev* (a work of the heart). The word *avodah* implies effort. Struggling to connect to HaKadosh Baruch Hu takes regular practice and effort, particularly in an age where immediate and tangible results are expected.

The *yetzer hara* attempts to distance us from Hashem and leave us with a deep feeling of emptiness. The *yetzer hara* tries to push our worldly desires to the forefront of our lives. Successful *tefillah* practice weakens our *yetzer hara* by placing our spiritual desires ahead of these worldly desires. It is soul nourishment whose potency lies in overcoming the *yetzer hara*'s attempts to convince us that no one is listening to us.

How do we know our *tefillah* is on the right track? When we complete our prayer session feeling refreshed and energized, firmly attached to Hashem and refocused on our spiritual mission. Knowing that we have been listened to is a sure sign that our *tefillah* was meaningful. Walking away with a positive future outlook is a clear indication that we have dipped in our personal *mikveh.* *Tefillah* is food for the soul. It provides valuable

*In memory of
Avrech ben Zulai
z'l (4 Kislev)
Dedicated
lovingly by the
Arambayev and
Mirzakandov
Families*

ammunition to combat our *yetzer hara*. We need to increase our fighting chance against "the clever one" (aka *yetzer hara*). *Tefillah* is work — but the *avodah* is worth it!

GETTING PRACTICAL

Before we drift off mindlessly during tefillah, we should remind ourselves of the value of intimately connecting with Hashem and the power this has over our yetzer hara. Let's cherish the immense gift of closeness received when the battle is won.

Hashem, Show Me Your Way

"Horeini Hashem darkecha, ahalech ba'amisecha — Show me Hashem Your way, I will walk in Your truth."[34]

Ever since the sin of Adam, Hashem's Presence is hidden in this world. Our task is to reveal it. The *yetzer hara* ingeniously hides HaKadosh Baruch Hu from us, making it difficult for us to know which way to serve Hashem, what He wants from us and where He is in every situation.

We therefore need guidance to be led on the path of truth, the path of *emes*. The path of *emes* is reflected in the cool, calm recognition that every incident is truly the will of the Borei Olam. *Derech Hashem*, the path of Hashem, is a road of inner peace and focus. It is the ability to see obstacles in front of yourself as being an integral part of a Divine plan that will bring you closer to your eternal soul rectification.

Rather than being fooled into thinking that we are doing right because most people do so, when we are really wrong, we should be honest and make best use of our limited time in this world for the sake of our eternal good. Subsequently, we will realize that there is so much more we can and so much more we want to do... in order to bring *nachas ruach* (Divine pleasure) to HaKadosh Baruch Hu.

Most of our anguish is amplified when we stop learning Torah, thus causing us to forget our spiritual task. Torah is our pathway — and through its study we can better understand who we are and what we need to do. Otherwise, we will plan our lives based on our limited perspective, which may not be in line with our soul's mission.

---

34   *Tehillim* 86:11.

GETTING PRACTICAL

Honesty is an essential ingredient for character and spiritual development. Acknowledge deep in your core that "Your way, Hashem, is the best way." Try to envision giving your will over to Hashem for the mere reason that He knows what is best for you.

► DAY 26   # The Great Struggle

What is the essential difference between *emunah* and *bitachon*?

Emunah is in the realm of thought. *Bitachon* refers to the internalization of this knowledge through our daily decisions and actions.

Emunah represents the deep attachment to the Melech HaOlam in our hearts. *Bitachon* is putting into practice our desire to do His will. Our daily decisions and actions demonstrate the extent to which we have internalized this belief that everything that happens is only from Hashem, that it is all decreed from *Shamayim*.

We are required to do our *hishtadlus* — the minimal effort necessary in this natural, incomplete world as a result of the sin of Adam HaRishon and Chava. However, often when we act in this world, we see the results and erroneously conclude that our actions are responsible for the outcome. Therein lays the paradox between *bitachon* and *hishtadlus*. Although we carry out a physical act that seems to lead to a result, true *bitachon* reflects the realization that the result occurred only because Hashem willed it and wanted it that way. In other words, although it looks that way, our actions did not bring about the outcome. Hashem did.

As supremely rational beings, the illogic of this paradox can confuse us and cause us to struggle. Our eyes perceive the physical realm of this world. *Bitachon* lies beyond what is seen by the human eye. It is not logical. It is not rational. Our ability to struggle with this paradox and overcome the logical order of things testifies to our greatness.

GETTING PRACTICAL _____

Maintaining this daily balance between bitachon and hishtadlus is a lifetime nisayon (test). Let's remain alert and aware of this struggle. This is the first step in acquiring the proper armory to fight this lifetime battle.

We Are Invited

Shabbos is called an "inheritance beyond limit." Hashem loves us with such passion that He gives us the ultimate gift of Shabbos. Hashem "yearns" that we sense His affection on Shabbos — the day of intense Divine awareness.

Shabbos is a day filled with *da'as* that enables us to delve into the hidden secrets of the Torah and a deeper understanding of the teachings of *Chazal*. Our *neshamah yeseirah*, additional soul, lifts us up to embrace every word of learning and connect to the words of the *tefillos*. The lofty *zemiros* (songs) sharpen our spiritual consciousness to feel the *kedushah* of Shabbos.

On this holy day, we "marry" Hashem and proclaim at *Kiddush*, "Remember the Shabbos to sanctify it (*l'kadesh*)." *Kadesh* is the term used to bond husband and wife under the *chupah*. In order to achieve such closeness with Hashem, we should put aside any preoccupation that may distract us from bonding with Him.

The message of *Shabbos Kodesh* is to remove the barriers that were put up during the mundane workweek and unite in holiness. When we cease working and instead place our trust in the Borei Olam that only He controls our livelihood and our destiny, we earn the right to enter into such an exalted spiritual relationship.

What is the true meaning of *oneg* (delighting in) Shabbos? To cleave to Hashem in a manner that is impossible on any other day. We draw holiness from the physical delights and redirect them to heighten our keen awareness of Hashem's love for Klal Yisrael. For

In memory of Walter ben Sara z'l (1 Tishrei)

example, by glancing at the Shabbos table and the array of delicacies, we are filled with gratitude over the honor of being a *ben/bas melech*, the son/daughter of the King of Kings. The essence of the day lends itself to cuddle in the Borei Olam's arms and indulge in the physical and spiritual gifts He has bestowed on us.

GETTING PRACTICAL

Shabbos is Hashem's gift to us. Every week, Hashem cordially invites us to spend the day with Him and be His guest. We can prepare for this special "date" by dressing in fine clothes, straightening up our home and welcoming our special guest with smiles, song and glory.

Seeing G-d - in the Rice

The mundane workweek hides the holy essence of every material matter. The way to recognize the *kedushah* is to sharpen and increase our spiritual consciousness. How? By training our spiritual eye — looking and finding the Borei Olam in everything, including the less noticeable things — we increase our *emunah*. For example, we can train ourselves to see the Divine providence when a good idea pops into mind, or when our rice dish turns out just right.

Pirkei Avos teaches us, "*Lo alecha ha-melachah ligmor* — You are not expected to complete the task."[35] This teaches us that we are not held responsible for the outcome of our deeds, rather for the effort we extend to see the job through. In other words, when I prepare *challah* dough, gefilte fish — or rice — whether it turns out tasty and to everyone's liking is not in my hands. I will certainly invest time, effort and love into the preparation. However, if the *challah* burns, this was not because of my doing but was decreed to be so from Hashem.

This training of the mind is a type of work called *avodah she'ba-lev*, work of the heart. It honors Hashem by bringing Him into the everyday where nature seems to mask His constant Presence. After all, seeing Hashem in my cooking? That is one place many of us would not customarily attempt to seek Hashem! Yet it is a part of the *emunah* training program to see Hashem's blessing in the foods we cook. Food is essential for the body to remain healthy and strong; it is also an opportunity to recognize Hashem's

In memory of Elka Shprintza bas Moshe Chaim HaKohen z'l (8 Nissan) Dedicated lovingly by the Berenstein Family

---

35   2:21.

goodness and abundance He so lovingly bestows onto His world. Swirl your love and affection into the foods you prepare and ask Hashem to sprinkle in some Heavenly spice.

GETTING PRACTICAL

The Jewish people can stare into their rice dish and learn to appreciate Hashem from it. If we can see His kindness in the success and taste of our food, we are on the right track to finding His Presence and kindness in all areas of life.

No Existence Without Him

The Maharal explains that the amount to which we feel love and connection to the Borei Olam depends on the extent to which we understand that we cannot exist without His will; such an acknowledgment of our vulnerability aids us to connect with HaKadosh Baruch Hu.

The circumstances of our lives are ever-changing. We are in constant need of *rachamei Shamayim* (Divine mercy) for every single step and breath we take. This recognition of our lowliness and weakness encourages us to yield to Hashem's will and lowers our egotistic tendencies. When we empty out our *gaavah* (pride), we make room for Hashem's holiness to enter.

The letter *aleph* is the first letter of the Hebrew word *ani* (I). It represents the will, the ego. It is important that we see ourselves as being small compared to the magnitude of Hashem. Our prominence originates from being attached to infinite greatness. There is only one *aleph* in all of creation, only one King; that is Hashem.

How does this idea relate to *emunah*? Believing in *hashgachah pratis* (Divine providence) is the Jewish way of life. We are obligated to strengthen our trust in Hashem's providence. Recognizing *hashgachah pratis* helps us understand that everything happens regardless of whether we control it or desire a particular outcome. Success, failure or outcomes are not dependent on us.

The amount of effort we are required to invest in this level of *emunah* varies according to our level of

In memory of Chaim ben Esther z'l (4 Cheshvan) Dedicated lovingly by the Hayon Family

trust. Those with a great deal of trust in the Borei Olam only need to put in a small amount of effort in order to receive the necessary *emunah* for this recognition of *hashgachah pratis*. Yet, those of us with a smaller degree of trust in HaKadosh Baruch Hu need to toil more to reach that same level of tranquility and acceptance.

The Chazon Ish teaches us that when a person genuinely trusts in Hashem, Hashem will let him know that He is helping him and he will feel Divinely taken care of. This is a pretty good deal, no?

GETTING PRACTICAL

Let's ask ourselves the fundamental question, "How did I get here?" This is the first step to take when beseeching Hashem's intimate Presence in our lives. Hashem created the human race to be in a constant state of change and encased in layers of physicality. Calling out to Hashem and cutting through the layers of materialism enables us to see Him and recognize how dependent we are on Him.

A Marriage Made in Heaven!

In secular society, a marriage is defined as successful if it is a reciprocal give and take relationship. Society has trained us to think a certain way and has imbued us with commonly held beliefs and values. The media often plays a large part in this detrimental influence. It is time to reframe, folks! The Torah defines a successful relationship as one characterized by unconditional giving without any expectation of receiving back. This requires that we break away that "selfish" piece called the ego and allow the "giving" piece called the Divine soul to take charge. The emotion of kindness represents the soul's love for Hashem while the body desires immediate pleasure. This is part and parcel of the lifelong struggle we need to contend with in order to achieve character perfection and eternal rectification.

Our spouse is our *tikkun* (rectification) for things we need to improve. Our spouse often reflects the mirrored image of those traits that are hidden within us and is a tailor fit for the refinement of our soul. Often, our spouse seems to do things that do not seem fair or just. However, even if the relationship does not appear "fair game" in our eyes, we should remember that Hashem knows we need them. Through our spouse, we are being called to go beyond our natural tendencies in order to create harmony and peace in our home. Our task in our marriage is to give 100% unconditionally no matter what the result. In difficult times, we can gain the strength to do so by davening to Hashem and asking Him to help us to continue being a giver just as He is![36]

For Daniel Moshe ben Rachel Hatun v'Reuven Eliezer Avraham (28 Kislev). May our home always be filled with the Torah's light. With love, Alte Chaya bas Toba Shaindel v'Avraham Chaim

---

36   In some cases, one must consult a Rav for marital advice. This lesson does not refer to cases of abuse where the victim must receive help.

GETTING PRACTICAL

Unlike modern society, the Torah view of a marriage embraces unconditional love — a reflection of Hashem's love for us. Marital harmony is the perfect ground to practice emunah since it is an act of faith to trust that Hashem knows what He is doing by pairing us together with our spouse in order to help us improve. This is very important to remember and will contribute to marital peace.

Rendezvous

We were always close,
Rendezvous at night
Amidst quiet and solitude
Revealing secrets,
Telling all
With tears and yearning.

When the pain was too much to bear,
I couldn't speak.
I felt helpless,
And tried to escape my pain.
I was late for our meeting.

I was distracted.

The pain got worse,
You weren't there for me.
And I was more alone than ever.

Left to bear my grief,
I wondered what happened to our rendezvous
Amidst quiet and solitude.
And now the pain of being abandoned by You?

I came last night
To our meeting,
I wasn't late.
I looked for You,
And found You right away.
With tears and yearning,
I cried,
Knowing it was I who abandoned You,
While all this time
You were waiting for me...

Stand Strong!

Tension and worry are often caused by a breakdown of trust.

Society cannot exist without a solid foundation of trust. In order to function effectively, we are required to place our trust in others, including our doctors, co-workers, friends or family.

Emunah means trust in G-d.

It is the foundation on which every Jew should firmly stand. It builds internal and external focus and calm. It brings clarity when we are shrouded in doubt and uncertainty. To hold onto *emunah* is to hold onto our sanity. *Emunah* is effectively a fundamental therapeutic attitude to life, answering all questions and placing events in a positive perspective.

Throughout life, we all face inevitable *nisyonos* (difficulties), which can cause us tremendous instability. However, linking ourselves to HaKadosh Baruch Hu and remaining loyal to His will help us build a fortress to weather all storms. Even during the tough moments when there is no logical rationale as to why, trusting in Hashem helps us through to the inevitable peaceful oasis.

The world around us may often seem topsy-turvy in values, priorities and focus. Yet, a deep internal knowledge that Hashem's *derech* (Torah path) is the correct one and that He is holding onto us and guiding us to safety keeps us grounded.

Avraham Avinu was unshakeable in his *emunah* and he therefore merited that an entire nation be built from him. He went against the entire world and remained faithful to HaKadosh Baruch Hu in spite of the mockery that he had to endure. He trusted

*In memory of
R' Elazar Moshe
ben Miriam z'l
(18 Adar)
Dedicated
lovingly by your
talmid*

in Hashem and through his unwavering conviction, he became worthy to receive the needed Divine assistance that brought about the birth of the Jewish nation.

As his children, we have inherited his *emunah* DNA. Every one of us can and should follow in his path.

GETTING PRACTICAL

Enhancing the emunah that is already ingrained in every Jewish soul helps us stand strong and grounded throughout life. Life's circumstances can certainly cause uneasiness. However, remember that Hashem is in full control; this soothes the agitated soul.

Emunah is living in accordance with the *pasuk*, "*Hashlech al Hashem yehovecha v'Hu yechalkelecha* — Cast your burdens onto Hashem and He will provide you with your needs."[37] Having *emunah* means not feeling anxiety over our needs. We should throw our entire burden onto Hashem! Thus, in the face of trouble, it is vital to increase *emunah* and not become crushed in the face of adversity.

What is the difference between knowledge and belief? Knowledge is a product of the intellect, whereas belief begins where the intellect ends. By definition, intelligence is limited to what mankind can rationally grasp. Belief or *emunah* is a personal gift given to us by our Creator. It is the ability to have faith in Hashem beyond reason or logic, based purely and simply on the truth that our *neshamah* holds within.

Hashem puts each of us through challenges and tests in life. Each test is not a random occurrence but tailor-made by Hashem in perfect order to help us achieve our spiritual development and elevate us to a loftier level. Every *nisayon* (hardship) teaches us that Hashem is with us and we should trust that all of our needs are being provided by Him.

The *Chovos Halevavos* teaches us that the stronger our attachment to Hashem, the greater the supervision (*hashgachah*) that we will experience. Those living a life devoted to Torah have a crystal clear vision of *hashgachah Eloki* (Divine providence). They merit having a personal close relationship with HaKadosh Baruch Hu and seeing His guiding hand

---

37   *Tehillim* 55:23.

In memory of Michoel ben Kayla z'l (14 Shevat) Dedicated lovingly by Frannie Schmerling

in situations which they or others might otherwise have missed.

When natural law contradicts our *emunah*, we must strengthen our hearts and remain strong and steadfast under all circumstances. Even if we find ourselves in dire straits, we use our strength to pray to Hashem and invoke *rachamei Shamayim*. After praying with all our strength, we can cast away our burden. *Chazal* teach us that everything a person needs is in front of him and all he has to do is pray and wait for Hashem to open his eyes and see it.

GETTING PRACTICAL

Next time we find ourselves experiencing a hardship, let us imagine the following parable: A person is carrying a heavy load on his shoulders yet alongside he is pushing a carriage. Wouldn't it be easier to put the package in the carriage as opposed to lugging it along? This is likened to casting away our burdens onto Hashem. Ask Him to help you haul your load.

Ahh…. *menuchas hanefesh* — calmness of the soul.

Emunah is the tool that we need to weather the storms of life — to survive inevitable trials and tribulations without losing our sense of purpose. *Emunah* is the comfort of knowing that however intense the storms, we can rise to the challenge with the requisite strength. No matter what happens around us, we remain centered and balanced. Despite the hurricane, we feel safe.

Struggles and challenges are inevitable because the *neshamah* needs them in order to work and achieve rectification. Hashem designs particular spiritual tests precisely geared to what we need to work on in this world. Though they may arise in different forms, they are all targeted to generate spiritual growth in key areas of our lives.

We need to live life while awake — spiritually awake and attuned to what is going on around us and inside of us. Rather than ignoring our conscience and intuition, we need to tune in, listen, feel and act on those nagging thoughts urging us to act or make a change. Although difficult, by embracing our inner voice of truth we know we have chosen the path of truth and will ultimately experience true inner serenity.

But how do we identify this hidden, inner voice of truth? *Hisbodedus*, personal secluded one-on-one prayer with HaKadosh Baruch Hu, offers an ideal time to contemplate these emotions! Initially, it may feel odd or uncomfortable. But with practice we can increase our ability to sense Hashem at our side, guiding us to the path of truth. The certainty and sta-

In honor of Jonathan and Sara Kowal's 33rd Anniversary Dedicated lovingly by Kayla Krauss

bility achieved through regular *hisbodedus* enables us to feel habitually calm in the face of turmoil, to feel true peace of mind.

GETTING PRACTICAL _____

True peace of mind is going within — to our inner conscience and intuition. This will guide us in the face of turmoil. Regular hisbodedus is the way to get us there. We train ourselves to trust in Hashem, and to calmly do what He wants.

Hashem Loves the Humble

Hashem loves the humble. The attribute of humility contributes to a serene life. It is acknowledging that all that transpires is the will of HaKadosh Baruch Hu. There is thus no room for expectations and also no disappointments. Hashem carves our destiny in alignment with that of the entire world. *Emunah shleimah* brings with it tremendous freedom and joy because we know we are being cared for. Consequently, we can truly sing as we see ourselves part of the grand plan called *tikkun olam* (rectification of the world).

Dovid HaMelech experienced many victories. He could have easily felt it was his own "strength and might" responsible for these achievements. However, he did not allow himself to think along these lines. He lived with a profound awareness of Hashem's Presence, attributing every occurrence to Hashem's will.

Rabbeinu Yonah brings down that the principle behind attaining genuine humility is when a person realizes his true worth. When we recognize our true value — who we are and what we can achieve — our potential is endless. However, this greatness ought to be tied to the One who gifted it to us — Hashem Yisbarach.

The humble demonstrate flexibility when dealing with others, a pleasant manner and tone and genuine modesty. Rather than seeking respect, they see their own flaws before they see those of others. The humble person doesn't suffer from an inferiority complex and therefore does not need to belittle others in order to feel superior. He does not need to be in the spotlight or inflate his presence. He is

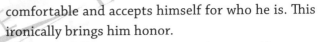

comfortable and accepts himself for who he is. This ironically brings him honor.

The soul, which is a part of Hashem, enables us to achieve an inconceivable exalted level of spirituality. Our soul aspires to conquer every aspect of greatness in serving Hashem and He awaits us to fulfill that mission which was tailor-made for us to accomplish.

GETTING PRACTICAL

The true catalyst for achieving humility is appreciating what we are and how much we can achieve. We are indeed great — it was Hashem who made us so. Let's work toward our eternity!

Hashem Controls and Is Above Nature

The golden rule of *emunah* is the belief that Hashem provides us with exactly what we need. This core belief must be apparent and palpable to us each and every moment. Everything comes from *Shamayim*.

Our generation is not worthy of open miracles. Therefore, we are obligated to exert effort into life so that every miraculous act of creation is veiled behind our hard work. The word *hishtadlus* means to put forth effort in order to yield results. However, though we are instructed and obligated to work, our effort does not create the results achieved. If we trust in anything outside of HaKadosh Baruch Hu as producing the results, He will actually remove His Presence and we will be left in the hands of whatever we trusted in — including ourselves!

In other words, if we believe in the power of our *hishtadlus* in its own right, we enter into the realm of *hester panim* (the concealment of Hashem). In such cases, any successful solution will be an accident of fate rather than directly from Hashem. Hashem treats us *middah keneged middah* (measure for measure), so when we attempt to approach life through natural means (i.e., relying on others, investing excessive amount of effort, etc.), He allows us to fall subject to the forces of nature. In contrast, when we live with the *emes* (truth) that all is from Hashem and He doesn't need any help from us in order to bring about results, He treats us from a higher, supernatural place.

The false belief that we have contributed to the outcome of life's events is actually caused by a weakened level of *emunah*. Thus, our devotion and efforts should be geared toward increasing our *emunah* rather than our physicality. Practicing *emunah* reminds us that increasing our efforts will not help us accomplish more than what has been decreed.

Hashem created nature and controls nature. He is therefore above nature and He relates to His people from above the natural law. Whatever Hashem "plans" for us will materialize. It makes no difference whether His solution conforms to nature or seems impossible. Hashem is *"Kol Yechol"* (He has the ability to do it all). If it is in our interests, He will make it happen as long as we exercise our free will and choose Him over nature; because ultimately, He is all good.

GETTING PRACTICAL

Nature is a "mask" created by Hashem, behind which He conceals His Divine hand. Practicing emunah helps us remember that our efforts at material creation are necessary only because Hashem instructed us to do them, but that only Hashem controls the results. Next time we are tempted to label something as "natural" let us remind ourselves that Elokim = Nature.

Shema Yisrael

The message of the *Shema* prayer[38] is to love Hashem and to teach this love for Hashem to children. Everything we have comes from Hashem out of His endless love which He wishes to shower upon us. Being aware of His infinite kindness motivates us to tell others to love Him as well and sing praises of thanks.

In her book, *The Hidden Beauty of the Shema*, Dr. Lisa Aiken notes that the profound *Shema* prayer literally accompanies us from cradle to grave. One of the main reasons why it is so central to our *tefillos* is due to the fact that we need constant reminders that we are part of Hashem's chosen people and that He loves us.

In His infinite knowledge of what is best for us, Hashem provided reminders as a vital spiritual compass to help us navigate our path and focus on our life's mission. Repeating these messages daily assists us to attach ourselves to Him and implants within us *emunah* in Hashem. We are constantly reminding ourselves that there is one G-d who cares about us and is always involved in the details of our personal lives.

Yet, even if we ourselves love Hashem in our hearts, do we teach this love of G-d to others? Every day, we encounter endless opportunities at work, on the bus, at synagogue and on the road. In each encounter, directly or indirectly, we affect (positively or negatively) others' outlook on Hashem. When meeting another, do we leave them with a stronger sense of His Presence?

In memory of Yisrael Reuven ben Meir Wolff z'l (9 Adar) Dedicated lovingly by Marcia Levy

---

38   *Devarim* 6:4.

Saying the *Shema* reminds us that our thoughts, speech and actions affect the entire universe. That, in turn, encourages us to live with ongoing devotion in our service of the Ribbono Shel Olam. When we keep His *mitzvos* we are drawn near to Him and feel His love.

GETTING PRACTICAL

Reciting the Shema twice a day implants emunah within us. There is one and only one G-d who cares about, and is always involved in, the details of our personal lives. Ingrain this message every time you say the words of this powerful prayer.

In *Olam Hazeh* (this world), the one thing that never changes is the fact that things always change! We often sense this as a feeling of lack of control and uncertainty. Even when we overcome one trial or tribulation, another challenge inevitably looms ahead like a cloud on the horizon. Stability and constancy may be comforting, yet change is inevitable.

The Baal Shem Tov teaches that whenever we find ourselves asking why something happened, we should answer "that's just the way it is." In Hebrew the word is *kachah,* taken from the *pasuk* in *Tehillim,* "*Ashrei ha'Am she'kachah lo* — Happy is the people for whom it is so."[39] Why is this happening to me? *Kachah!* This is what Hashem wants and that is the way it is meant to be!

For some of us with questioning minds (okay, many of us with Jewish minds!), this *Kachah* philosophy may initially appear frustrating or limited. It doesn't really answer the question, does it?

That is the point. The *Kachah* philosophy does not symbolize resignation. On the contrary, it reflects a humble acceptance, an admission that only Hashem is in control of our destiny.

Sefer Devarim states, "*Tamim tihiyeh im Hashem* — Be pure in your faith with Hashem."[40] Rashi explains that our relationship with the Ribbono Shel Olam should not be arrogant. Rather, it should reflect that He knows best and is the Master of the world. We should learn to accept whatever transpires with a pure, accepting and open heart.

---

39   45:1.
40   *Shoftim* 18:13.

Even though life is filled with ups and downs — and many curves in the road — by attaching ourselves to the Melech HaOlam we regain complete constancy and certainty in an uncertain world. Ah... what a relief!

GETTING PRACTICAL

The goal is to trust in Hashem. This world is a training field to learn that whatever Hashem wants for us is what we should want for ourselves. When attempting to complete a task and it doesn't go "our way," let's practice accepting it as it being the best way — Hashem's way.

Building Emunah Through Tefillah

Our interaction with the everyday world may extinguish our spiritual fire. So much of our lives seem non-spiritual. We can begin to forget that there is more than the physical. Torah, *tefillah* and *mitzvos* serve to remind us of Hashem and to connect us to Him. In our daily lives, we are constantly moving from the physical realm, such as eating, drinking and working, to the spiritual realm, such as *mitzvos*, Torah learning and spiritual deeds.

Tefillah is one of the most powerful ways to ignite the spark of our *neshamah* with the fire of *emunah*. It realigns us with the *emes* (truth) of Hashem because the act of prayer functions as an acknowledgment that we are completely dependent on Him. While all *mitzvos* serve to connect and demonstrate awareness of Hashem, by its very nature, *tefillah* humbles us and therefore has the ability to more greatly enhance our *emunah*.

The *tefillah* of *Shemoneh Esrei* is the climax of our connection with Hashem. We outline our requests in front of the *kisei haKavod* (Hashem's holy throne). Yet, if Hashem knows and gives us exactly what we need and what we are lacking, then what is the purpose of davening? *Tefillah* has many purposes, but perhaps its central one is for us to internalize — with our hearts, souls and resources — the idea that we are dependent on HaKadosh Baruch Hu for everything. In acknowledging that we cannot change things but He can, this process builds *emunah* in His *hashgachah* (Divine providence).

We tend to reach out in prayer to Hashem in times of hardship. Yet, if Hashem knows what's best for us,

In memory of Channah bat Esther z'l (28 Shevat)

what use is there in asking Him to change our situation? One answer lies in the fact that Hashem is kind and merciful. Rather than wanting us to endure any pain, He knows the best thing for us is a close connection with Him. Thus, He places us in the *nisayon* precisely so that we will daven. He "desires" that we reach out to Him in acknowledgment and for support and He "knows" that through the difficulties we will more likely call out to Him. In this way, *tefillah* becomes the all-mighty way to bringing us closer to the All Mighty!

GETTING PRACTICAL

Speaking to Hashem instills emunah in our hearts. It is a potent way of fostering a direct connection to the Borei Olam as we acknowledge that only Hashem controls the world. Speak to Hashem as a child speaks to her loving father. Such prayer builds connection and makes emunah tangible to grasp.

Face to Face with Hashem

Tefillah allows us to come face to face with HaKadosh Baruch Hu — it is only us and Him. Prayer is a living conversation with Hashem. It can take us to a place where we are removed from our body and are only soul. *Tefillah* can strengthen our life-force if we understand its value. However, this level does not come naturally. Rather, we are required to constantly train the mind to perceive the reality of Hashem. Ultimately, this mind training should enable us to live close to Hashem without exerting too much effort. The very act of trying to connect to Hashem will bring us to actually perceive Him.

The Rambam teaches that there are five things that prevent us from entering the realm of *tefillah*.[41] Four of these are physical things such as washing one's hands, covering one's nakedness, praying in a clean place, going to the bathroom, and the fifth is intent of the heart.

In addition, there are eight physical things a person should do while davening. These include standing, facing the direction of the Beis HaMikdash, holding proper posture (head facing downward, feet together, hands close to the heart, body bent forwards slightly), dressing properly, davening in a proper place, speaking in a proper voice, bowing low and, last, prostration.

Following the Rambam's advice will clear the spiritual channels and bring us to a loftier level. These requirements for davening also suggest that we are able to access our intimate spiritual connection with Hashem through our physicality.

---

41   *Mishneh Torah, Sefer Ahavah, Hilchos Tefillah.*

Ultimately, *tefillah* regulates our level of *emunah* because the process of davening represents a humble admission that we are dependent on HaKadosh Baruch Hu. The Sfas Emes teaches that prayer is not about presenting a wish list to Hashem but a process of awakening our hearts with *yirah* (awe) and *ahavah* (love) for Him.

He brings this point across by way of his commentary on the *pasuk* in *Tehillim*, "*Tachin libam, takshiv oznecha* — Guide their hearts, let Your ear be attentive."[42] The goal is to stir our heart with a desire to feel Hashem's closeness. Becoming one with the words we utter elevates our *tefillah* to a level beyond compare.

GETTING PRACTICAL

Tefillah is derived from the word pallel, to think. To pray reflects the act of making oneself think and thus declare the fundamental truths about Hashem and our relationship with Him. We were created in His image and through tefillah we stay close and devoted to Him. Something to think about the next time we pray.

---

42   10:17.

The *Metzudas David* explains that the blessing of building a *bayis ne'eman b'Yisrael* refers to the formation of a lasting, enduring home.[43] A home filled with peace. A home fashioned out of unity of different souls.

The key principle to building such a home is by emulating Hashem through the unconditional giving of oneself. Each partner must emphasize giving pleasure to the other without expecting anything in return. Giving 100% means giving completely and unconditionally, regardless of what the other gives back. Our pleasure lies in making the other happy. When one partner is happy, by default the other will benefit from their happiness.

However, each of us has different tasks to complete in life. For instance, in the physical realm, when we wish to clean our home, we divide the chores amongst everyone. One cleans the windows, while the other washes the floors and yet another washes the dishes. The overall goal of tidying the home is only achieved when each individual works at different but vital tasks. If we all washed the dishes, then the rest of the housework would suffer and the running of the house would be incomplete.

Similarly, man and woman have different spiritual strengths and roles within the home. However, they do share one goal — to create an abode which welcomes the presence of the *Shechinah*. If man and woman can work on their individual tasks with harmony, then together they can achieve the same objective — an emotionally healthy and harmonious place to live and bring up Jewish *neshamos*.

---

43   *I Melachim* 11:38.

Dedicated to the Werth Family (Tu B'Av)

Essentially, both parents impart Torah values to their children in order for them to absorb Torah's beauty and recognize its irreplaceable quality of life. Ideally this influence will motivate the children to build their *bayis ne'eman b'Yisrael*. We pray they will cherish Torah guidance to ensure that their own homes also become a *bayis ne'eman b'Yisrael* which can weather all storms.

GETTING PRACTICAL

Let us embrace our differences in marriage. A marital bond can be strengthened by understanding that our spouse may have different characteristics from us. Hashem deliberately chooses the perfect spouse for each of us — a spouse with different qualities perfectly complementary to ours to allow us to work and grow together. We can view our partner's contrasting strengths, roles and personalities as a necessary requirement for building a complete and lasting Jewish home.

Hashem gives Klal Yisrael the gift of Shabbos to be experienced only at a certain time of the week.

The Arizal points out that many people fail to feel spiritual delight on *Shabbos Kodesh* because they do not adequately prepare for it or anticipate it. Shabbos should be ingrained in our minds all week long, particularly on Thursdays and Fridays. Craving and anticipating Shabbos is a precondition for reaching a spiritual high on this holy day. The process of looking forward to Shabbos reflects our general longing for Hashem in our lives.

However, the *yetzer hara* knows about the importance of preparations in enhancing the holiness of Shabbos and may attempt to thwart us as a result. The Arizal explains that the *yetzer hara* is responsible for many mishaps that occur from mid-Friday until Shabbos. Yet, being aware of this tendency may help us better control our reactions. A main part of our *avodah* before Shabbos enters is to restrain ourselves from losing control by reacting to these annoying things that happen.

Hashem is aware of this challenging battle and grants us Divine assistance from mid-Friday to help us overcome these challenges. However, this assistance is only available to those who reach out for it. Learning Torah, particularly on Thursday evenings, strengthens our ability to grasp Hashem's helping hand and outwit the *yetzer hara* on Fridays.

Every deed conducted before the onset of Shabbos contributes to the holiness of Shabbos in the home. Women welcome the *Shechinah* in physically via carrying out domestic preparation tasks at

In memory of Sara Liba bas Moshe Eliyahu HaKohen z'l (27 Nissan) Dedicated lovingly by the Margolis Family

home. Men can welcome holiness into the home for Shabbos by immersing in the *mikveh* which separates the working week from the *kedushah* of Shabbos. These acts free up the necessary inner space for the holy light of Shabbos to move in.

GETTING PRACTICAL

The kedushah we experience on Shabbos is based on the level of our preparations. Our Shabbos will shine with splendor to the degree that we prepare emotionally and physically. Beware of the yetzer hara's attempts to thwart us on Friday afternoon. This can help us avoid reacting to this challenge.

Never Give Up Hope

In chapter 42 of *Tehillim*, a vivid image of a lonely man who lives with *emunah* is portrayed. His soul thirsts for Hashem. Although he is steeped in difficulty, he still desires to continuously cling to his steadfast trust in Hashem's compassion. Dovid HaMelech describes his feeling of abandonment, "When will I come and appear before Hashem?"[44] He describes the joyful memories when the *Klal* elatedly went up to the Temple and could readily feel Hashem's Presence.[45]

However, he now experiences such intense distance, cast as it were into an emotional exile. His anguish is so vividly felt. Nevertheless, he doesn't abandon his *emunah*. This lesson can easily be applied to many of us who endure hardships. We too can empathize with such emotions; the sense of feeling fragile, alone and confused, even abandoned by Hashem.

Later in the *perek*, water is illustrated as a destructive force[46] far different than initially described in the beginning of this *perek* as a source of nourishment for the deer. Here, the water sweeps over Dovid HaMelech and causes him to be lost. It is as if his inner voice yells out, "Where are You Hashem? I am frightened and need You."

Yet at the end of this *perek*, Dovid HaMelech regains his strength and states confidently, "I will **yet** praise Him." This hints to us the best possible response to distressful events in our lives. We must pour our hearts out in honesty, without reservation

---

44   *Tehillim* 42:3.
45   42:5.
46   42:8.

5 Cheshvan:
Ariella Rivka, z'l,
bas Avraham.
May her light
continue to
shine in this
world through
all who were
zoche to know
her. Lovingly
The Horenstein
Family

and not deny our pain, although at the same time not question Hashem's master plan.

Rather, just as Dovid allows himself to experience human pain and suffering, he also broadcasts confidently that he does not give up hope. Why? "*Ki od* (yet)…*" There is a future that has yet to be openly revealed. The exile will end and all will be clear.

GETTING PRACTICAL

"I will yet praise Him" — in spite of my current pain, weakness and overwhelming sadness of the present day, I am assured that all is good and I will merit seeing it, baruch Hashem, b'rachamim, b'karov, Amen!

Live as an Alien |

Chazal teach that although we reside in this world, we are also meant to live in this world as aliens on foreign land, viewing it only as temporary lodging. Even though it feels as though our stay here is long-lasting, we are advised to avoid becoming heavily involved with materialism.

To achieve such a mindset, we are taught to live with the keen awareness of Hashem's Presence everywhere. Ironically, if we view ourselves as aliens in this world, Hashem will thus become a resident. Conversely, if we make ourselves into residents in this world, overly attaching ourselves to non-spiritual pursuits, the Borei Olam will *chas v'shalom* become an alien in this world!

Thus, we should adopt the mindset that this life is a temporary abode, a place to accumulate eternal possessions for our souls' everlasting life span. In order to adopt such an attitude, we need to believe with a deep, internal faith in the World to Come, and that this is our main purpose and goal. While we are in this world, this requires *emunah* rather than logic. Turning to *emunah* rather than intellect takes patience, strength and a deep willingness to fulfill Hashem's will despite our circumstances.

Of course, we are entitled to and we should do our *hishtadlus* — that is, including investigating our circumstances to logically understand why and how they have occurred and to help us join with Hashem to circumnavigate the challenges we face. Yet, our work and investigation needs to be accompanied by an attitude of acceptance. We cannot rely on our intellect alone because *emunah* begins where intellect ends. *Emunah*

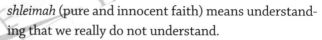

shleimah (pure and innocent faith) means understanding that we really do not understand.

Emunah is a belief that Hashem oversees all of life's minute details with our benefit in mind. Challenges are part of HaKadosh Baruch Hu's master plan put in place in order to achieve certain goals and a long-range purpose, whether or not we can recognize that purpose and those benefits from our vantage point in this world. Ultimately, struggles can help us achieve our purpose and maximum pleasure in both this world and the World to Come, as long as we keep in mind *Chazal*'s teaching that this world is merely temporary, not only in time but also in significance.

GETTING PRACTICAL

We are taught to see life in this world as a transitory hallway. Rather than becoming overly attached by what we see and experience, it is important to remind ourselves that we are on a journey, having yet to arrive at our final destination in the World to Come.

Putting Hashem in Our Yiddishkeit

Our forefathers, great sages throughout the ages, and millions of simple Jews all had a personal relationship with Hashem. They spoke to Him on a daily basis. He was a reality in their lives. The Baal Shem Tov refers to this type of bonding with Hashem and calls it *d'veikus* (cleaving).

Unfortunately, this type of bonding with Hashem is not as common today as it once was. Many of us do not regularly stop to think about Hashem and strive to establish an intimate relationship with Him. Interestingly, R. Ariel Bar Tzadok of www.KosherTorah.com reflects that although Torah learning has increased in recent years, the awareness of the need to bond with Hashem has decreased.

This lack of *d'veikus* within Klal Yisrael is disheartening. This is the work of the *yetzer hara*. The scheming ways of the evil inclination is to cool us down by making us feel that we are "okay" and that there is no need to strengthen our *Yiddishkeit* (practice of Torah). It constantly reassures us by whispering, "You perform *mitzvos*, you learn and dress modestly, that is surely enough."

Yet, the goal of all *mitzvos* is to attach ourselves emotionally to HaKadosh Baruch Hu, otherwise they are likened to routine habits, a body without a soul. The word mitzvah embodies the meaning *tzavta* (companionship) implying the main goal in fulfilling *mitzvos*.

The Baal Shem Tov provides a heart-warming analogy[47] that may inspire us to cleave again to Hashem on a daily basis.

In memory of Sabale' Aaron ben Yitzchok z'l (7 Tishrei) Dedicated lovingly by the Picker Family

---

47   *Sefer Baal Shem Tov, Noach 7.*

When a father wishes to teach his toddler son to walk, what does the father do? He stands his son up and places him before him. He stretches out his arms to the sides so the child does not fall. Thus, the child will walk between the two supporting arms of his father. When the child reaches the father, the father then moves back a little bit so that the child will again move forward and come close to the father; each time the child does more. In this way, the child learns to walk correctly, for if the father would not back up, the child would have no place to move forward. This then is the way of the Holy One, blessed be He with His creation. When a person strongly desires to bond with Hashem, Hashem removes Himself a bit. If not for this, a person would never develop strength and continuity in their bonding. However now, as Hashem backs up, the individual needs to strengthen himself more and more. Thus one grows in strength.

GETTING PRACTICAL

Craving a loving relationship with the Melech HaOlam is the fundamental precondition to fulfilling all the other mitzvos. Let's buck the modern convention and remind ourselves each day that Hashem is here with us, side by side, hand in hand and cheek to cheek! By talking to Him on a daily basis, we will once again let Him into our lives and acknowledge Him as the source of everything that happens the rest of the day.

Natural vs. Supernatural

After the sin of Adam HaRishon, confusion rained down onto this world. We could and can no longer directly feel or experience Hashem's Presence. Rather, we struggle to feel HaKadosh Baruch Hu. The Hebrew word for world, *olam*, is derived from the word *he'elem*, that which is hidden. Our lifelong task is to reveal HaKadosh Baruch Hu in everything. This world hides Hashem; it is our mission to uncover and increase the awareness of Him and His proximity.

On the one hand, we are required to observe the natural laws of this world. Yet, let's realize that Hashem hides behind this mask of nature. Hashem gifts us with countless opportunities to honor His will and bond with Him. He created this world with a natural order; we are required to act within the laws of this system. By acting in this way we are actually fulfilling His will and thus bonding with Him.

Both the natural and supernatural worlds reflect Hashem's will. The difference is that His Hand is concealed in the natural world. In the supernatural world, it is openly revealed. The natural world is dangerous because we are at greater risk of feeling independent; erroneously assuming that our efforts (*hishtadlus*) are what causes results. This is the *nisayon* (test and challenge) of *emunah*.

Torah and *mitzvos* are essential reminders or flag posts that bring our consciousness back to Hashem and His hand in everything that occurs in this world. We pray that whatever the outcome may be it will be best suitable for us.

Tefillah is the highest form of *hishtadlus* that we should devote our time and effort to. It is an action that highlights the true reality of our complete dependence on Hashem. In turn we are spiritually realigned by recognizing that we are in Hashem's hands and are being lovingly taken care of by Him.

GETTING PRACTICAL

Adam's sin caused Hashem to hide His Presence in this world. The punishment is that it becomes tempting to attribute outcomes to our own actions. Let's try to remind ourselves that any results in this world are not due to our own efforts, but only from Hashem. Torah, mitzvos and particularly tefillah draw us back to the true reality of HaKadosh Baruch Hu and our dependence on Him.

Dynamite! | DAY 46 ◄

R. Shimshon Dovid Pincus teaches that *tefillah* is compared to dynamite. When combined together with *ruach haKodesh* (Divine inspiration), the little letters in the *siddur* which make up our daily *tefillos* can break down spiritual walls just as the little particles of dynamite have the power to break down physical edifices. Wow!

The way to release the immense power of prayer is to first realize how much *koach* (power) the *tefillos* hold. These days, many of us underestimate the potency of *tefillah*. This may stem from the fact that we daven for something and seemingly are not answered, or because davening has become habitual for many. Yet, though small, these words have within them the spiritual ability to cancel harsh decrees, essentially moving mountains! Our words of *tefillah* set once-frozen things in motion.

One immense benefit of davening is to remind us that we could not do anything without the help of HaKadosh Baruch Hu. Often our *yetzer hara* tries to convince us that our accomplishments are due to our own efforts and hard work. Davening dismisses this mindset and maximizes our humility.

Tefillah also increases our *emunah*. We can extract true benefit from our davening by uttering such words as, "You know what is best for me and how to provide for me. I do not express my needs to You to make You aware of them, but so that **I** be made to realize my dependence upon You, reinforcing my trust in You."

Finally, we can view davening as a free therapy session with none other than the One who created us and all our issues and dilemmas in the first place.

In memory of Mordechai ben Rachamim z'l (22 Kislev) Dedicated lovingly by Mehran and Sepi Manouel

This creates tremendous peace of mind and adds to our total sense of well-being.

It's a time to talk it out one-on-one with the One Who is in charge.

GETTING PRACTICAL

The capability of tefillah lies in our believing in its power — to remind us Who is in charge, to increase our humility and to give us a chance to share our dilemmas with the Creator of all things. Now that is dynamite!

Hashem's Love Will Always Be

We must never let go of the thought that we are Hashem's children. Fix it in our minds and engrave it in our hearts. Like a father who loves his children, Hashem's love will always be. As it is written in *Yeshaya*, "Listen to me House of Jacob, and the remnant of the House of Israel, those who have been carried [by Me] since birth and supported since leaving the womb. Until you grow old I will be the same, when you turn gray, it is I who will carry (you). I was the Maker and I will be the Bearer; I will carry and rescue you."[48]

Mark Twain also noticed the unique existence of the Jewish people.

> Many people have wondered how it is that a small people can be scattered among the nations, persecuted, killed, decimated, exiled again and again, and still remain true to their heritage! For that matter, they wonder how we could continue to exist at all! There is no other culture in the world that has matched this feat.

The Torah has sustained our existence and through it we merit eternal life. The *Midrash Vayikra* teaches that the Torah is our marriage contract with Hashem — a token of His love for His people. It is difficult to love someone you don't really know. The Rambam teaches that the key to loving Hashem is by getting to know Him through studying His Torah and performing the *mitzvos*. Torah is likened to a personal letter written by HaKadosh Baruch Hu for Klal Yisrael. By learning Torah we are able to glimpse the

In memory of Baila Devora bas Sara z'l - Bella Resnicoff Dedicated lovingly by Allen and Susan Black

---

48   46:3.

essence of Hashem and "get to know" Him. The more we learn, understand and know about Hashem, the more we will come to love Him and the more we will understand how much He loves us.

It may be difficult to understand the concept of Hashem loving us unconditionally. What does this mean? This type of love implies that Hashem demands nothing in return, that He loves us purely for our sake, not for His own sake and that His love for us is not dependent or conditional on our behavior or anything else. Admittedly, Hashem does get "angered" when we are disobedient, similar to that of a rejected lover. However, this is simply because He knows it is for our own sake that we love Him and do what He prescribes is best for us.

GETTING PRACTICAL

We are Hashem's chosen people, His special children. It is so reassuring to remember that He will never leave us. The gift of His Torah enables us to know Him and realize how much He loves us. The next time we open up to learn, think about the remarkable privilege we have been given!

On *erev Shabbos*, a sukkah of peace spreads over Klal Yisrael and over Yerushalayim. Shabbos spreads out and protects the Jewish people just as a mother bird protects her little ones. Shabbos is the source and everything is in Her.

A famous Midrash discusses how Shabbos "spoke" to Hashem asking Him who will be its partner. Hashem responded that "the bride is the collective souls of Am Yisrael." Thus, as the Jewish people, we are the partner of *Shabbos Kodesh*. We can prepare ourselves and our home to honor Shabbos and bring joy to our eternal partner who is joining us. If we observe Shabbos properly, we will also merit being its companion in the World to Come.

Rabbi Shimon Bar Yochai teaches that when Am Yisrael brings in *Shabbos Kodesh* with the *tefillos* of *erev Shabbos*, a Heavenly voice emanates proclaiming, "Happy are you, Am Yisrael, for you offer your blessings below so that the holy camps may be blessed on high. Happy are you in this world and in the World to Come!"

Quoting Dovid HaMelech, Rabbi Shimon Bar Yochai also sheds a fascinating light on the well-known teaching about a husband returning home from shul on *erev Shabbos*.[49]

> *When one returns home from synagogue on Shabbos eve, he is accompanied by angels on either side, with the Shechinah arching over all, like a mother bird encompassing her*

---

49   Shulchan Aruch 262:1, quoted by the Tur in Gemara Shabbat 119b

children. At that moment, "a thousand may fall at your side and ten thousand at your right hand; but it shall not reach you. Only with your eyes shall you see and witness the recompense of the wicked. Because you too Hashem, my Refuge, the Most High as your haven, no harm will befall you, no disease touch your tent." All this is true when one joyously returns to his home and receives his Guest in joy. At this point the Shechinah sees the candles lit and the table set and the family in joy, and she says, "This household is mine."

All of our weekly blessings flow from *Shabbos Kodesh*. When the table is adorned with scrumptious food and delicacies on *erev Shabbos* and Shabbos day, the same table receives *berachah* every day of the week as well. The Arizal brings down that whoever consumes all three meals of Shabbos feeds himself with complete *emunah*.

GETTING PRACTICAL

Let's welcome the Shabbos Queen as our special guest. Let us await her arrival with a warm smile and a joyous home. We can then relish in the tranquility of envisioning the wings of the Shechinah embracing our homes every Shabbos.

I Want Hashem!

Everything is a *nisayon* (test) in life. The Ribbono Shel Olam provides us with these *nisyonos* in order to grant us the opportunity to make a decision and declare "I want the Borei Olam!"

Choosing between spirituality and base yearnings can be a difficult test. Interestingly, even seemingly unchallenging decisions represent a test and an opportunity to choose Hashem.

For example, we may be hungry and required to choose between eating kosher and non-kosher foods. Even if our *kashrus* beliefs are solid, and it may appear natural for us to choose the kosher food, nevertheless Hashem has still placed us in a situation of choice. We can bring this decision-making process into our consciousness in order to actively proclaim, "I want Hashem. I have a choice and I am choosing to do the will of Hashem Yisbarach."

Recognizing that we are choosing to become closer to Hashem creates a relationship with Him. It evokes an abundance of *rachamei Shamayim*. It also demonstrates how much significance Hashem places on even the smallest gestures that may seem undeserving of reward or recognition. Hashem treasures even those instances where no difficulty lies in fulfilling His will. This is a great *chesed* that Hashem gifts us with.

Often in life we are faced with opportunities to listen to our inner good or dismiss it. Whether it is difficult or relatively easy to make the choice to do Hashem's will, it still counts as a choice for which we are rewarded to attain closeness to our Creator.

In memory of Shulamit bat BenZion Mordechai z'l (23 Iyar) Lovingly remembered and deeply missed by her daughter

GETTING PRACTICAL

Hashem cares so much about us that He "yearns" to have us choose His will over our animalistic will. He even throws us freebies just to have the opportunity to grant us reward! Even the simple choices we make can bring us closer to Hashem.

"From the Depths I Have Called You"

We all have an innate closeness to HaKadosh Baruch Hu which we inherited at Har Sinai. This means that every Jewish soul emanates from the highest realm in *Shamayim*. This intrinsic spark causes our souls to yearn to fulfill Hashem's will.

However, material pursuits cloud this natural state and distract us from this true path. Our faith is often hindered by these material aspirations. According to the Rambam, material desires hamper the yearning for spirituality.

In *Tehillim* it is written, *"Mi-ma'amakim kerasicha Hashem* — From the depths I have called You, Hashem."[50] This touches on our struggle between spiritual and earthly pursuits. Specifically, Dovid HaMelech describes it as the spark of G-dliness hidden under layers of desire for materialism and worldly pleasures.

When we recognize the spark and the fact that it is so deeply buried, we can call out to Hashem from a place deep inside us. This process of calling out to Him will assist in uncovering the spark and bringing us closer to Hashem. No matter how far we have traveled Hashem will surely assist us in our return. When our point of faith deep within experiences turmoil and we fall spiritually, from those depths we call out to Hashem and rise once again.

Another way to bring out this spiritual spark is to invest effort in attaining a greater understanding of Hashem's ways. We have the ability to understand through Torah learning that Hashem's goodness is

*In memory of
Chana Toba bas
Dovid Shimshon
z'l (27 Tammuz)
Dedicated
lovingly by
Rivki Weiner*

---

50   130:1.

constant and to stay focused on His "desire" to impart good even when we incur difficulty in comprehending how an event is good.

The deeper our perception of Hashem, the more we love Him in our hearts. By getting to know Hashem, we will be able to appreciate His greatness and His benevolence, thereby enhancing our spirituality.

GETTING PRACTICAL

Each of us harbors a deep spiritual spark within us that connects us to Hashem. Material pursuits may cause us to lose our sense of spiritual purpose. Strive today to use your material acquisitions to elevate your spirituality and see them as a means to an end.

Daily Date with Hashem

The Rambam writes that each person must pour out his heart to the Borei Olam. Before the Men of the Great Assembly instituted the *tefillos* written in the *siddur*, the main form of prayer was *hisbodedus* or personal prayer. *Hisbodedus* was the original form of *tefillah* which emanates from the depth of the heart — in the language that each of us individually understands best.

The holy Chafetz Chaim teaches that *hisbodedus* was the way of our holy ancestors.[51]

> *All the troubles that befall us and which continue to plague us come about because we do not cry out to G-d and beseech Him over and over again to deliver us from them. If we would pour our hearts out to G-d, He would certainly not ignore our prayers and requests. A person should not be satisfied with praying Shemoneh Esrei three times a day; rather, he should pour out his heart, speaking in his own words, in his own home, several times a day.*

Personal prayer is an exalted time. It is a time to reconnect to our inner core, to tell Hashem how much we love Him in our own words in a way which cannot be substituted. This form of prayer infuses holiness into all of our needs. It is also a priceless opportunity to contemplate the endless list of gifts that we were given that may otherwise go unnoticed.

Ideally, *hisbodedus* should be practiced every day. It is the time to ask Hashem for everything, whether it be basic needs such as food and clothing or anything

---

51   *Likutei Amarim*, ch. 10, pg. 47.

else we may need in life. HaKadosh Baruch Hu provides the needs of every living creature from the tiny flea to the elephant. Yet, if we don't ask for it we are no different from them.

An ideal way to begin a personal prayer session is to offer words of gratitude for all of the kindness that Hashem has shown us. We should not hold back any feelings or requests. Rather, we should let our mind open in honesty over every single need. Spill out what is in our hearts; both our fears, worries and frustrations and also our feelings of gratitude and love.

Sometimes, we may find ourselves battling obstacles that attempt to stop us from making time for these personal daily prayer sessions. This is the guise of the *yetzer hara*, trying to stop us from connecting to the Source of all things. Yet we must not give into the *yetzer hara* because this personal prayer session is too valuable. Alternatively, when we speak to Hashem we may sometimes feel that we are not being answered. However, Hashem always hears us. He often speaks back to us through the thoughts that seemingly pop into our mind, or through a feeling of warmth and peace in our heart.

GETTING PRACTICAL

Let us think of hisbodedus as a daily date with HaKadosh Baruch Hu, a time during which we are embraced by the Shechinah. Let's see it as a special gift, our chance to request, to thank and to connect with our Creator.

How Hashem Talks to Us

How do we address Hashem in the most meaningful way?

Hashem desires our heart. Empty *tefillos* laced with beautiful words will not aid our emotional or spiritual well-being and development. Rather, we should recognize that we are limited in our ability to get through life on our own; we need His help.

We should continuously entreat *rachamei Shamayim* and see ourselves as helpless if not granted with *siyata diShmaya* (Divine assistance). These prayers must come straight from the heart just as a beggar solicits money for a long-awaited meal. The Borei Olam reads the feelings that lay in our hearts. We cannot "sell" him hollow supplications. We can only genuinely communicate with Hashem via our heartfelt words.

Hashem uses everything in this world to serve as facilitators to influence us and draw us closer to Him and to our purpose in life. It is therefore vital for us to ask ourselves many times a day, "What is Hashem telling me?" and "Why is this happening now and not yesterday, next week or last month?" and "How should I respond?" and "What would Hashem like me to do right now?"

Hashem uses many ways to "talk" with us, for example, we may suddenly notice a truck passing by with a sign on it that says "*Ein Od Milvado* — There is nothing else but Him"; this may be a signal from Above telling us that we are not in control and need to remember that there is nothing except Him. Even when a neighbor casually mentions in passing that she just returned from an amazing Torah *shiur* where they spoke about *Ahavas Yisrael*, this encounter is intended to ring an inner bell and reawaken our consciousness to the importance of interacting with our fellow brethren with unconditional care. Possibly we were overly self-absorbed at that moment and needed to be reminded of our task to care for others.

Striving to live life "awake" is one of the most important tasks in a Jewish person's life. It doesn't matter if Hashem talks to us through a rabbi, neighbor or book that someone handed to us; the idea is to see Hashem in everything and know that He is constantly connecting with us.

GETTING PRACTICAL

Today, let's take a single occurrence and try to translate the message from Hashem hidden within. What does Hashem want to tell us? What would He like us to do? Heed the message and act on it.

We Want Geulah - Now! |

The wonders of *yetzias Mitzrayim* (the exodus from Egypt) are often considered the archetype of the *geulah* (redemption). R. Aaron Fink recently wrote an article that explains how Moshe Rabbeinu taught *Bnei Yisrael* that the *geulah* is dependent upon their desire to be closer to Hashem. This suggests that redemption is dependent on our own actions. We give ourselves and our love to Him. He, in turn, gives Himself and His love to us. This giving and receiving is the essence of *ahavah* (love). *Shir HaShirim* states, "*Kol dodi hinei zeh bah* — The sound of my beloved! Behold, he is coming."[52] The fact that He is still waiting for us, His beloved, is both valuable and reassuring.

So, if redemption is up to us, which "enzymes" can we release to hasten the process?

The first step is to yearn for redemption with all our soul. Admittedly, we may pray for the *geulah* every day, begging, pleading or singing to be rescued from our troubles and pains. Yet, we can do even more. We ought to ask ourselves whether we fulfill the mandate of *tzipita li'yeshuah* — anticipating salvation as much as we possibly can.

The Gemara in *Shabbos* writes that the word *tzipita* is defined as anticipating, as opposed to merely waiting.[53] Its root is *tzofeh* — to be on the lookout and await its arrival on the horizon. This does not refer to an intellectual waiting, but rather a very real and active process of anticipation. Imagine waiting to see your loved one after a long period of absence. This is how we should view redemption.

---

52 Shir HaShirim 2:8
53 31a.

No matter how many delays we have endured, we never give up. In fact, we are closer to redemption than ever. Klal Yisrael has shed so many tears of pain, hope and desperation and *baruch Hashem* we are now at the entranceway of redemption. More and more Jews are back in Eretz Yisrael. More and more Jews are learning Torah. We are so close to the final *geulah*!

Each morning, the sun rises after an entire night of darkness. We expect it to shine and light up the day — every day. In the same manner we should expect and anticipate the *geulah* after the *galus* (exile). This is *emunah*. The more darkness we see, the more trust we have that the light of redemption will surely follow. We need to continue to yearn for the redemption — to desire it.

The second thing we need to do is to elevate ourselves and reconnect to Hashem as much as possible. The more we want Him in our lives, the more He will allow us to feel His Presence.

GETTING PRACTICAL

Our actions, thoughts and feelings determine when and how geulah comes — for our own lives and Am Yisrael. Imagine what redemption would be like until the thrill reverberates through you.

Don't Worry, Be Happy |

What does it mean to be truly happy? How do we create wholeness from within?

In *Pirkei Avos*, our sages teach us the following:[54]

> This then is the way of Torah: Eat your bread with salt, drink water in measure, sleep on the floor, live a life of difficulty and place your efforts in the Torah. If you do this, happy will you be and it will be well with you. Happy will you be in this world and it will be well with you in the World to Come.

What does this mean?

Life is transitory. So are our worldly possessions. *Chazal* teach us the importance of detaching ourselves from them. All the material toys of this world are short-lived and we should limit our involvement with them. Overeating, indulgent drinking, and ostentatious living are inadvisable because they may cause us to forget our inherent spirituality.

Still, we are not instructed to live a harsh life! Pleasure is good! G-d created a beautiful world for us to enjoy. Instead, we are directed to use material things for the right reasons. HaKadosh Baruch Hu hands us a prescription for a balanced, happy life in the form of His *mitzvos*. Keeping the *mitzvos* leads to a moderate and thus more emotionally harmonious life. Fostering the correct balance in life will help prevent us from being side-tracked from life's true purpose — serving the will of the Ribbono Shel Olam.

If we were offered a choice between a life of riches and a life of poverty, our choice should be simple and

In memory of Chaya Bracha bas Chaim Yaakov z'l (13 Elul) Dedicated lovingly by Bat Sheva Haber

---

54   6:4.

obvious. Anyone choosing poverty is either a fool or a liar. Poverty is not a sign of blessing from Hashem. All of our Patriarchs were wealthy individuals yet their wealth did not interfere with their spirituality. They chose to live their lives as simple shepherds in the desert with their sheep.

Still, many of us are imprisoned by our desires, slaves to our affluent lifestyles and captivated by our possessions. We may view our current way of living as moderate. Yet, such a concept is subjective — what is moderate to one is luxury to another. For instance, some Jews may refuse to move to Israel because of their need to maintain their current state of prosperity.

The key lies in the term "need." We often use the terms "want" and "need" interchangeably, yet they are vastly different. *Baruch Hashem*, most of us have everything we need. Anything additional merely represents something we want.

GETTING PRACTICAL

Practically speaking how can we objectively decide what we need (as opposed to what we want)? Try to list every item necessary for a newly married poor couple to start life together. The items compiled on this list are the only things a person truly needs; every other item constitutes a "want."

Shabbos Without Distractions

Shabbos invites us into a new place in time and in mind. We are given a chance to remove ourselves from our private internal world and instead enter a world where we become engrossed in a sense of unity with Klal Yisrael. On Shabbos, we stop everything and can experience our true essence without distractions. Without these outside interferences, we can come into contact with our true selves, our divine souls.

Shabbos involves a severance from the materialistic world. Though the food and *zemiros* (spiritual Shabbos songs) are means to delight, our true pleasure comes from bonding with Hashem, feeling His closeness and living in His reality. By shutting out the lies and falsehoods of this world and the distractions that come in the form of mundane vanities, we are able to feel the truth of Hashem's reality. This is the definition of what *Chazal* call *oneg Shabbos* (delighting in Shabbos). Shabbos is the only place where we can touch eternity and connect to our infinite soul, our *chelek Eloka mi-ma'al* (holy spark of G-dliness).

In order to tap into infinity, we ought to let go of our ties to this world. We should strengthen ourselves and not be tempted to speak of mundane matters during Shabbos but rather focus only on what contributes to our eternity. For instance, we can avoid thoughts and words such as "*Oy*" and "What will be?" or "I need to drive to such and such place on Sunday," etc. On Shabbos, we are "on strike" from the world and our minds need to totally disconnect in order to immerse ourselves into the realm of infinity.

In memory of
Yosef ben Levi z'l
(5 Tishrei)

Tehillim teaches, "*Kol Hashem ba-koach* — The voice of Hashem is in strength."[55] Hashem gives us strength through the gift of Torah study. Where is Hashem's voice? The commentaries write that Hashem's voice can be heard only by those who exert themselves to listen, those who shut out the disturbances that cause static on the phone line with Hashem. Hashem is speaking to us always, but can we hear Him? It is up to us whether we allow distractions to prevent us from listening to His voice. There is much noise and endless hissing and static on the line due to *our* interferences. Shabbos is the connection to enable us to cut out the noise.

GETTING PRACTICAL

Letting go of our ties and distractions to this world enables us to tap into the beauty of Shabbos and hear Hashem's voice calling to us. Find that quiet within and connect to Shabbos from that inner place of peace.

---

55   29:4.

"*Ashrei ha-am she'kacha lo, ashrei ha-am she'Hashem Elokav* — Happy is the people for whom this is so [who live with Hashem], happy is the people whose G-d is Hashem."[56]

Hashem gave us His Torah because He loves us. Torah is our manual and guide for life, complete with detailed instructions and definitive ways on how to understand our obligations. Klal Yisrael is fortunate to have Torah as a guidebook for success in life! Knowledge is power. Jewish knowledge (and thus power) comes from the Torah. Hashem set down rules to protect us from harm and poor decision-making, thereby demonstrating the way to live a happy life.

"For the commandment is a lamp and the teaching [Torah] is light".[57] Life can be confusing. At times, many of us may feel in the dark. However, life becomes much less difficult at such times when there is light and the unknown is revealed and exposed. Instead of creating something new or fighting the darkness, light simply serves to illuminate what is already there.

Hashem gave Klal Yisrael the Torah precisely to reveal the concealed, that is, by acquiring knowledge of Hashem's Presence. In our generation, where the *hester panim* (the concealment of the Divine Presence) is more profound than ever, we need the light of Torah more than ever!

In memory of Yossef ben Bitiyo z'l (14 Tishrei) Dedicated lovingly by the Ibragimov and Mirzakandov Families

---

56   *Tehillim* 144:15.
57   *Mishlei* 6:23.

GETTING PRACTICAL

Turn on the light! Let's view Torah as a flashlight that lights up our life with the knowledge and direction required on gloomy days. Hashem gifts His people with happiness by providing us with the guidance and certainty of the Torah.

Can We Feel Our Emunah?

Do we have tangible, living *emunah*? *Emunah* which pulsates through every fiber of our being? Are we loyal to Hashem's will and His Torah? Do we trust Him enough that we perform the *mitzvos* even if we don't understand them, in keeping with the proclamation, "*Na'aseh v'nishma* — We will do and then we will hear"?

Emunah is accepting that we don't comprehend everything, yet we remain faithful to Hashem and His Torah precepts nonetheless. True *emunah* is tested in the darkness when our future path is unclear. As Dovid HaMelech writes in *Tehillim*, "*L'hagid ba-boker chasdecha v'emunasecha ba-leilos* — To speak of Your kindness by day and Your *emunah* at night."[58] When doubt and confusion fill our mind, we need effort to chase them away, continuously reminding ourselves that Hashem loves and cares for us and does everything for our ultimate good.

Emunah is true living energy from which we draw vitality to do and act. Living means connecting to and fuelling the source of life, our *neshamah*. We accomplish this by "keeping in touch" with the Borei Olam through every thought, speech and action. It is inviting the *Shechinah*, the Presence of Hashem, to be there side by side with us throughout our every move. It is like giving a hug to Hashem... and Him hugging us back!

This focus on *emunah* requires dedication and constant daily work, in preparation for facing inevitable *nisyonos*. The effort it entails is very individual — no two people face the same level or type of *avodah*

---

58   Tehillim 92:3

In memory of Mordechai ben Yeshu'a z'l (4 Elul) Dedicated lovingly by the Mirzakandov Family

necessary to bring out and strengthen their *emunah* — but each and every one of us can do it. We can all, without exception, deepen our *emunah*.

GETTING PRACTICAL ⎯⎯⎯⎯⎯⎯⎯⎯

We cannot understand Hashem's ways, however this should not serve as a barrier to fulfilling His will. Next time we need to take a certain medicine which we know heals, let us internalize that although we do not understand its chemical make-up we still take it since we believe in its ability to alleviate our pain. So, too, should we trust in Hashem that He is looking out for our ultimate best.

Emunah is not a new concept that must be taught to Klal Yisrael. It is hidden in every Jewish soul; all we are required to do is uncover it. *Emunah* is not logical. It even seems irrational by the world's standards. *Emunah* is a commitment, individually and collectively as a nation, to stand by the words of the holy Torah even when it might seem old-fashioned. It may often require that we go against society's "acceptable terms of living" in order that we remain loyal to the *sefarim kedoshim* (holy Torah books). By its very nature, *emunah* dictates a mindset of accepting that which we do not understand.

"*Na'aseh v'nishma* — We will do and we will listen." We made a promise at Har Sinai. We promised Hashem that we would abide by His commandments, even without understanding them. Our *neshamahs* spoke and heard Hashem's words and they are ingrained in us. This was our commitment and remains so until the end of time. *Emunah* extends beyond the logic of our minds.

Nonetheless, *emunah* is not *blind* faith. We *know* the truth. It originates from our soul. Our *neshamah* is *chelek Eloka mi-maal* (a part of HaKadosh Baruch Hu from the higher realms) — the most reliable source of *emes* (truth). The trouble is that often this knowledge lies deep inside. It is a matter of peeling away the layers which hide this truth of Torah.

Jewish mystical teachings explain that our soul bears a complex number of layers, some of which reside in the upper realms. Therefore when it becomes difficult to uncover our inner G-dly core, we receive

In memory of Rachel bat Chana z'l (12 Tishrei) Dedicated lovingly by the Mirzakandov Family

help from Above, from that part of our *neshamah* that connects with that Above.

Using our intuition and going deep within helps us listen to that real inner voice which resonates with the voice of truth. In order to do this, we are encouraged to abandon our obsession with worldly pleasures. Life is wonderful, but physicality should not be our focus. It is time to return to Hashem!

GETTING PRACTICAL

Our inner core is filled with the light of truth which calls from deep within. Its message may go against what is defined as rational, yet it is eternal truth. Unpeel the layers, search inside yourself for your intuition and listen to the voice of emes, the truth of Hashem.

Just Stop | DAY 59 ◄

In *Likutei Halachos*, Rebbe Nachman teaches us that redemption will be brought through prayer. It can break through all fifty gates of holiness and surround us with a shielded fortress to protect us from the rough elements of life. Just as the world was created with words, our personal words of prayer can shield us from the antagonistic powers of the world.

The words of personal prayer are unique and heartfelt. They are deliberately not written down because they stem from the heart and a place of truth. Personal prayer provides an individual, tailormade, innovative pathway of achieving attachment to the Borei Olam. Every time we pray from our heart we embark on a new path. Depending on our feelings and experiences of the day, each session is different from the previous one.

Some days we may feel lost. Our feelings and emotions may be buried in the fast pace of life. Or the intensity of our own personal life may feel all-consuming. Or we may be completely immersed in routine or its reality. We rarely take the time to stop and just think. Why? What happens when we cease our activity and breathe? What surfaces?

It may be scary to confront the hidden identity discovered when we are alone. Stopping can be fearsome for we never know what is lurking inside until we sojourn and let the feelings surface. Yet, it is essential to distance ourselves from the ostrich approach whereby we bury our heads in the ground and refuse to face reality. In reality, all of our innermost feelings, both conscious and unconscious are already known by our Creator anyway.

In memory of Mazal Tov bat Chana z'l (17 Tamuz) Dedicated lovingly by the Mirzakandov and Ibragimov Families

We can avoid ever reaching a state of despair by reaching out to Hashem. He craves to ease our pain and have a relationship with us. This connection will imbue us with *emunah* and *chizuk* (strength). *Tefillah* in the form of personal prayer changes us and it also changes nature, though not necessarily in the way we anticipate. This personal prayer will leave us happier, more tranquil and more secure.

GETTING PRACTICAL

Every time we have a personal talk with Hashem we uncover hidden emotions. This requires courage, but the reward is immeasurable. We emerge with strengthened emunah and ammunition to battle life's challenges.

Marriage and Emunah

The building blocks of *emunah* begin at home. Home is the place to perform acts of kindness, express appreciation and practice unconditional giving. A marriage requires that we unconditionally fulfill our obligations to our spouse, just as *emunah* requires from Klal Yisrael to follow the Torah instructions — even if we do not "agree" or fully recognize the reasons why.

Marital struggles mainly arise when each partner focuses only on him/herself instead of on the other. Empathy is an essential ingredient when building any relationship. The ability to go outside ourselves and feel what the other is going through opens up our heart to giving to others.

The Torah requires us to perform *mitzvos,* which are essentially bonding tools to help us create an eternal relationship with Hashem. Our obligations to our spouse also bind us to them and create connections. We perform *chukim* (*mitzvos*/obligations without logical reasons) just because Hashem commands us to, not because we necessarily understand why. It is precisely this selfless approach that allows us to grow in our relationships.

We need to continue this selfless, *emunah*-based approach ("just because he/she said so") throughout difficulties and turmoil. Remaining loyal to the mitzvah of building a *bayis ne'eman b'Yisrael* (a loyal, faithful home in the nation of Israel) should motivate us to keep the relationship alive.

Marriage is the training ground from where we can both practice and acquire *emunah* and realize our potential. The Gemara writes, "*Kol tikunei ha-bayis*

For Yaakov ben Benjamin and Shevach bat Pinchas on occasion of their anniversary (21 Adar II) Dedicated lovingly by Devorah Ohayon

180 Degrees in 180 Days 155

heim tikunei haShechinah — All of the fixings of the house are the fixings of the Divine Presence."[59] The harmony of the house lies behind the scenes. Hashem brings together a husband and wife in order that they both experience growth, often through their differences. Yet, just like a seed, growth begins in the ground invisible to the naked eye. It requires digging, planting and nurturing in order to flourish.

Have *emunah* that growth in your relationship is happening. But remember: like in any rewarding relationship, it is a slow, effortful process.

GETTING PRACTICAL

A marriage provides a perfect feeding ground for the cultivation of emunah. Just as with our relationship with Hashem, the foundation of any marriage should be based on loyalty and trust. Both require unconditional love, repeated efforts and time to grow and develop stronger connections. Deepen your relationship to your spouse — and to G-d.

---

59   *Sotah* 17a, commentary in *Tomer Devorah*, ch. 6.

Where Am I?

I'm hanging the laundry,
Folding pants, ironing shirts,
Putting neatly arranged clothes into their drawers.
All the while,
My thoughts drift far from an orderly closet...
I'm with You.

I'm cleaning the kitchen,
Washing dishes, pots and pans
Sorting utensils, scrubbing the sink.
All the while,
My thoughts drift far from organized tableware...
I'm with You.

I'm cooking dinner,
Cutting chicken, peeling onions,
Throwing salt and spices into the pot and onto potatoes.
All the while,
My thoughts drift far from a fancy menu...
I'm with You.

I'm standing with my siddur
Saying praises, giving thanks,
Making requests for family and friends.
All the while,
My thoughts drift far...
To the laundry that awaits me
To the mess in my kitchen
To the food not yet prepared
When all the while,
I should have been with You.

Poems by Leah Rubabshi, copyright 2015.
Used with permission.

Mashiach   I Await Him Every Moment

We should refer to the coming of Mashiach Tzid-keinu in a manner that indicates our belief that his arrival is imminent and that we are anxiously anticipating him. Whereas words such as, "...Until Mashiach comes... *oy*! It'll take forever" refers to a distant future, we should hope for his speedy arrival that is about to happen.

Some of the prophecies regarding the events that will transpire before the coming of the arrival of Mashiach as described in the Talmud[60] include:

- Disrespect will increase and honor will dwindle;

- The government will turn to heresy and there will be none to offer them reproof;

- The wisdom of the learned scribes will be degraded;

- Fearers of sin will be despised and the truth will be scarce; and

- Youth will put older men to shame — the old will stand up in the presence of the young, a son will scorn his father, a son will not feel ashamed before his father.

These prophecies are unraveling before our very eyes! Disrespect is widespread in all cultures, disregard of the elderly has become a norm in most homes and many Torah scholars are experiencing extensive degradation.

Those who live in doubt of Mashiach's arrival rely on their sense of reason. They may consider it impossible

---

60   *Sotah* 49b.

for Mashiach to rule over the mighty nations that possess nuclear arsenal that can destroy the world. Yet, *emunah* in *divrei Chazal* (the holy words of our sages) requires the opposite of rationality. We should believe because these are the words of the Boss, the Designer of the world.

Every day in our morning prayers (*Az Yashir*) we remind ourselves of the exodus from the mighty empire of Egypt and the extremely harsh punishments to which Hashem subjected the Egyptians. The exodus can also serve as a reminder that the all-powerful HaKadosh Baruch Hu will send us Mashiach in a similarly awesome way.

In *Sefer Shemos*, it is written that "Hashem shall fight the war for you, and you shall remain silent."[61] Hashem fights our wars. He is leading us to our final redemption. Human eyes cannot see this, only eyes drenched in *emunah*, love and hope for an end to all suffering.

GETTING PRACTICAL

A major part of our avodah of emunah is the belief in the imminent coming of Mashiach. We are required to believe in Hashem's power to override the nations of the world. Let us live in that reality today!

---

61   *Beshalach* 14:13–14.

The Time-Out of Shabbos Every Day!

When we ask Hashem, "Where are you?" Hashem answers, "I am here... can't you hear me?"

Often we honestly cannot hear Him because of all of the disruptions of life that cause fuzziness on the phone line. Shabbos represents a time-out in order to delve inside and reconnect. As parents know, a time-out essentially requires taking a moment to recollect thoughts and realign actions. Entering Shabbos requires us to let go, make space and allow Hashem to enter.

However, this special time-out of Shabbos need not be limited to one day a week. We can also celebrate Shabbos during the week by practicing time-out on a regular basis. In other words, we can transform every day into a *Shabbos katan* (micro-Shabbos) by practicing *hisbodedus* — private *tefillah* with Hashem. By entering our own personal space and pushing aside the worldly distractions (such as telephones, errands, tiresome thoughts), we may eventually find ourselves more available to ourselves.

This quiet, reflective time may allow us to discover all of the things that hold us back. It may involve asking ourselves the tough, deep questions such as, "What do I want to do when I grow up?" or "What is stopping me from achieving genuine happiness?" It is a time to explore fundamental, soul-searching questions about ourselves that we may not have been able to identify due to the external distractions and noise. In this way, the term "Shabbos" becomes a euphemism for self-reflection and being in touch with the holiness within, a revelation of who we really are and who we really can become.

In memory of R' Kehas ben R' Avraham Yitzchak z'l (8 Elul) Dedicated lovingly by Fayge Parker

Many of us may avoid this challenge, preferring instead to continue on the path of life without stopping to think. Admittedly, delving inside and actively seeking out our true core selves (including our strengths and weaknesses, our potential and our hidden G-dliness) can be emotionally draining or daunting. It may be painful to dig within and find out who we really are, perhaps because it may involve a reassessment of our choices, or a revisiting of moments of struggle and trauma.

However, if we courageously choose to enter this space, we will ultimately be gifted with the ability to hear our inner voice. This voice will help guide us to make the right choices and choose the correct paths in life, chanting to us where to go and what to do. Gradually, the veil of confusion will begin to lift. We will begin to understand our true selves better. Ultimately, we will reach a place where we are able to give ourselves unconditionally to others and thus feel more fulfilled and at peace — a true Shabbos experience.

GETTING PRACTICAL

The time-out that comes with every Shabbos gifts us with space to recollect and realign our thoughts. Ask yourself questions such as, "Where am I heading?" and "How can I get there?" We are able to answer them with greater clarity when we remove ourselves from worldly distractions. In this chunk of time, we can experience the "shalom" of Shabbos.

Torah Reveals Hashem's Hand

The *Torah HaKedoshah* teaches us that all is Hashem and Hashem is everything. Hashem wants us to understand, as is told in the verse, "*V'yadata ha-yom v'hasheivosa el levavecha...* — And you should know today and set it firmly in your heart that Hashem is the One and Only Master of the Universe."[62]

Though Hashem is truly everywhere, the *Shechinah* (Divine Presence) is hidden and there are times and places that we cannot feel His Presence. Thus, the Jewish people were appointed to bring G-dly consciousness into the world.

One of the key ways to reveal G-dliness in every earthly particle and creature is by learning Torah. By learning the various *halachos* of the four kingdom worlds from lowest to highest — inanimate, plant, animal and human — we connect their essence to their Divine source, thus tightening the mindset of "*Ein Od Milvado* — There is nothing else but Him (Hashem)." Learning Torah bonds our minds and hearts with Hashem. Through Torah study we "take" Hashem and delve into understanding His infinite ways.

In the *Shema,* we are instructed to implant love of Hashem into our hearts. Living and studying Torah is a way of carrying this love for Hashem from our mind down into our hearts. Learning Torah enables man to glimpse the reason why Hashem created the world. In turn, this can inject us with deep fulfillment and a force of vitality; enabling us to better fulfill the commandment to love Hashem and helping us transform our *emunah* into *bitachon*.

---

62   *Devarim* 4:39.

Learning Torah provides delight and pleasure, the most Heavenly experience possible. Subsequently, Torah scholars are infused with a spiritual light, radiating to others and injecting this world with Hashem's Presence.

GETTING PRACTICAL

Though Hashem is everywhere, His Presence in this world is sometimes hidden. Learning Torah enables us to reveal G-dliness in this world and to implant love for Hashem into our hearts. Let's delve into Torah's wisdom and remember that we are thus lighting up the world with Hashem's Presence.

Cleaving to Hashem through Davening

Among the many *mitzvos* that we are commanded to keep is that of *d'veikus*, cleaving to Hashem. In *Sefer Devarim* it is written, "If you will keep the commandments of Hashem your G-d and you will walk in His ways and... cleave to Him."[63]

The commentators offer many explanations of this mitzvah.

The Rambam explains that "to walk in Hashem's ways" means to act in a manner that corresponds to the conduct that is ascribed to Hashem; to follow the Divine attributes mentioned in the Torah as a model for us to follow.[64]

The Ibn Ezra brings down that *d'veikus* comes at the end (after loving Hashem and following in His ways) and is a "great secret."

In contrast, the Seforno interprets this verse to mean that when we do all that we can to fulfill the Borei Olam's will, we are in a state of cleaving to Him.

R. Aviner explains that there are three main ways to establish *d'veikus* with Hashem.[65]

1. Torah learning enables us to cleave to Him via our minds.

2. Performing *mitzvos* enables us to connect through our bodies.

3. *Tefillah* — using our words — enables us to connect our souls to Him.

*In memory of
Yisrael Aryeh ben
BenZion Zev z'l
(16 Elul)
Dedicated
lovingly by the
Margolis Family*

63   *Ki Savo* 28:7–9.
64   *Sefer Hamitzvos*, based on the *Sifri*, *Devarim* 11:22.
65   Commentary on the *siddur Tefillas Amecha* #40–41.

The main purpose of learning Torah is to get a glimpse of Hashem's wisdom. This knowledge kindles awe of His grand creation in our heart and thus draws us closer to Him. Yet Torah learning is incomplete without prayer. Words ignite the soul's fire and allow for deep bonding with Hashem. Utilizing the precious opportunity to speak to Hashem and let go of our emotions is a sure way of attaching ourselves to the Borei Olam, the Source of all good.

GETTING PRACTICAL

Complete unification with Hashem is the overall purpose of existence. Practice aligning your thoughts, actions and words to those of Hashem's. This gifts us with the present of d'veikus, a most exalted pleasantness that is incomparable to any other experience here on earth.

Miniature Sanctuary

The meaning of the traditional Hebrew word used for the wedding ceremony, *Kiddushin*, promotes understanding of the Jewish view on marriage. *Kiddushin* comes from the root word "*kadosh*," meaning holy. Marriage is holy since Hashem unites a couple in their goal to achieve harmony, joy and peace in their home. Man and woman marry for the holy purpose of continuing Jewish existence. Torah values and traditions are practiced and preserved within the sacred walls of the Jewish home.

A Jewish home is a *Beis HaMikdash Me'at* (a miniature sanctuary). A married couple is required to build an atmosphere of respect and kindness toward one another. In doing so, they sanctify their home, "inviting" the *Shechinah* to dwell there and open themselves and their home to spiritual and material blessings.

Both partners enter marriage with imperfections and blemishes. However, Hashem has precisely matched them together in order to build on their deficiencies and ultimately blend into one complete whole. The Vilna Gaon taught his disciples that the core purpose of Jewish life is to perfect our inner flaws and build our character.

In order to be worthy enough for the Divine Presence to dwell within their home, each partner needs to work on his or her individual *middos*. Home is the place to do this most important work of refining our character traits. Whether it is elevating ourselves from haughtiness to humility, selfishness to generosity or sadness to happiness, our home is a training camp to strengthen our G-dliness.

*In memory of
Avraham ben
Zelig z'l (6 Av)
Dedicated
lovingly by the
Gerowitz Family*

Peace depends on love in the home. Unfortunately, we may have been misled by Hollywood's definition of love which differs immensely from Torah tenets. Hollywood's values are purely illusory — not showing the process, the self-discipline and the elevation of character by means of bonding to Hashem.

Yet, it is never too late to adjust our thoughts, speech and actions and create a home of *kedushah*. The founding Torah principle for successful *shalom bayis* is hinted to in the Hebrew word for love — *ahavah*. The root of the Hebrew word for *ahavah* is *hav*, to give. The Torah thus considers love as the outcome of giving. The more each individual spouse gives to each other, the more love in the home and the more peaceful the family.

GETTING PRACTICAL

Home is where the heart is. Let's adorn it with Torah values of kindness, compassion and love and thus allow our home to become the dwelling abode of the Shechinah.

Nature Has No Place

A high level of *emunah* is defined as centering one's thoughts on Hashem and living with a tangible belief that He guides everything at every moment. Nature has no place in a mind filled with this level of *emunah*. Unfortunately though, the moment we let our thoughts stray from Hashem, nature takes charge and we begin to be governed by it.

In the *Nefesh Hachaim*, R. Chaim of Volozhin (the foremost student of the Vilna Gaon) expounds on this profound lesson. He reminds us that in times of difficulty, we are summoned to collect our thoughts and focus on HaKadosh Baruch Hu and His Divine providence, which will guide us through struggles directed by Him.

The *tefillah*, *Kevodo Malei Olam* — His honor fills the universe (recited by the Chazzan during the *Shabbos Musaf* service) indicates that Hashem's glory envelopes the entire universe. Our belief in this fundamental teaching guides us to the understanding that Hashem is everywhere and intimately supervises with loving care all that occurs in our lives.

Put simply, Hashem rules the world. Repeating these unpretentious words brings love and devotion to Hashem down into our hearts. Concentrating on this basic principle will pave the way through difficult travails. If we force ourselves to suspend logic and instead internalize the idea that any form of hardship is for our own good, we merit the feeling of Hashem's Fatherly embrace. By placing ourselves on a higher spiritual plane of existence above nature, we are gifted to inhabit this lofty place beyond nature, measure for measure.

GETTING PRACTICAL

Rather than relying on nature, we should keep our thoughts on Hashem and the fact that there is no other power apart from Him. Internalizing this message will guide us through difficulties in life. When we suspend the laws of nature, we are gifted with the laws of nature being suspended for us!

Fear G-d and No One Else!

Living with fear is a leading cause of stress.

In contrast, living with *emunah* imbues us with positivity, confidence and hope, despite inevitable daily challenges.

Rabbeinu Yonah teaches that when one trusts in HaKadosh Baruch Hu, they are rewarded with a bonus sweetening of Heavenly decrees. Thus, not only does having *emunah* support us through *nisyonos* (trials and tribulations), it changes our fortunes too! Since everything that happens to us is worked out by Hashem to the exact measure, if our level of *emunah* and *bitachon* ascend beyond the realm of nature, HaKadosh Baruch Hu will ensure our problems are taken care of through supernatural means as well — measure for measure.

The Rambam teaches us that we merit *hashgachah pratis* (Divine providence) to the exact degree that we devote ourselves to attaching ourselves to Hashem. The more we notice Hashem's presence, the more we will merit seeing His Divine hand in our lives. How do we increase this awareness? By thinking about Hashem and seeing Him in every little thing — from the cup of coffee in the morning to the trip home without traffic in the evening.

Actively attuning ourselves to His everlasting care and the constant good He does for us attunes us to His infinite and constant kindness and *rachamim* (compassion). This allows tranquility to flow, which in turn will both lead to further *hashgachah* moments and allow us to more easily identify them.

Dovid HaMelech instructs us to "Cast away our burden unto Hashem."[66] A daily practice of

In memory of Bachmal bat Chana z'l (8 Shevat) Dedicated lovingly by the Mirzakandov Family

---

66   *Tehillim* 55:22.

consciously handing over our intense emotions to Hashem will surely help us reap the benefits of *emunah* on a practical level.

Another benefit of trusting in the Borei Olam is that it creates a solid, loving relationship with Him. This bond guides us through *nisyonos* and helps us make correct choices. Fear One and then you shall fear no one.

GETTING PRACTICAL

Trusting in the Borei Olam reduces anxiety because of the inner awareness that He is in control. It helps us get through life's challenges but also sweetens our decrees. It helps us notice all the good that Hashem bestows on us, which enhances the aforementioned benefits of trusting in Hashem. What burden can you hand over to G-d? In what challenging area in your life can you increase your trust in Him?

Dawn Is Coming

Dovid HaMelech cries, *"Penei eilai v'choneni, ki yecheed v'ani ani* — Turn to me and show me favor, for I am alone and afflicted [lit., poor]."[67]

Often, when we do a self-accounting of our deeds we reach a candid place where we come to realize how alone and helpless we truly are. Our *zechuyos* (meritorious deeds) are in short supply, and our future rests only on *rachamei Shamayim* (Hashem's compassion). Consequently, we may feel "alone and afflicted." It dawns on us that there is no one to rely on other than on our Father in *Shamayim* (*Ein al mi l'hisha'en ela al Avinu she'baShamayim*).

However, once we have entered deep into the mindset of how much we depend on HaKadosh Baruch Hu, and daven from the depth of our soul to Him, we can be assured that He will show His kindness and help us. As it says, *"Ba'erev yalin bechi, v'la-boker rinah* — In the evening one lies down weeping, but with dawn, a cry of joy."[68] In the evening, when we face hardships, we go to sleep weeping and experience a negative mindset. "But with dawn" — when good fortune appears on the horizon — we cry tears of joy and we see everything in a positive light.

Life may feel like a rollercoaster; sometimes good times and sometimes bitter times. When we experience smooth sailing, it is relatively easy to think positively — everything is good and will be good. Yet, the opposite is true as well. The trick is to avoid this rollercoaster by constantly reminding ourselves

In memory of Ziva bat Aaron z'l (17 Sivan) Dedicated lovingly by Betty Bendavid

---

67   *Tehillim* 25:16.
68   30:6.

— particularly during the tough times — that everything is for the good. When we think rosy, things become rosy.

No matter how tough or negative a situation appears, we should revitalize ourselves to stay positive in our thinking. We can actively search for every minute benefit that may accrue from that situation, no matter how small or far-fetched. The impact of our mindset is more powerful than we can fathom. As someone once said, "Life is all about perception. It is not what it is — it is what we think it is."

GETTING PRACTICAL

The experience of feeling "alone and afflicted" can serve as a motivator to turn to Hashem and daven with full intent. If we use this negative situation to connect to Hashem, we are creating the most positive benefit imaginable. Let's make a conscious decision to wake up and look for the rosy dawn. It is more powerful than any change in the external situation because it affects our mindset and perception of the world.

Shabbos Is Here, Now All Is Good!

Shabbos is a day which is all good and overflowing with joy. However, we cannot experience this joy fully if we are tied down by worries and anxiety from the mundane world. Self-absorption and our attachment to this world make it extremely difficult to spiritually nurture ourselves.

We direct so much of our efforts on the game of physical survival that we are distracted from focusing on spiritual pursuits. Throughout the work week we may be weakened by the disappointments of life — our regrets, unmet desires, unrealized opportunities and unfulfilled aspirations. Yet, the core of our being, our *neshamah*, is still patiently waiting to be actualized.

In *Likutei Moharan*, Rebbe Nachman teaches that it is only the all-giving part of us, the portion free from self-indulgence, that delights in *Olam Haba*. In other words, it is the humbled fragment, the spiritually cleansed and elevated piece of our essence that will enjoy the World to Come. This piece is revitalized through both the process of self-accounting during the week, and immersion in the delight of *Shabbos Kodesh*.

What can we do to strengthen our soul and thus enjoy Shabbos to the fullest? During the week, we should work toward cleansing our souls via a process of self-accounting, involving private time to examine one's deeds, words, actions, thoughts and emotions. This evaluation quiets our ego down. Our weekday self-accounting practice represents the necessary preparation required in order to completely submerge ourselves in Shabbos mode.

In contrast, on Shabbos it is vital to talk only of life's blessings. This dual practice enables us to rebuild our soul, arming it with new energy to pursue its eternal goals. After our weekday self-analysis, let's release any judgment or evaluation and cast our burdens on to Hashem. It is essential to leave our troubles, weaknesses and sins behind, viewing ourselves as having completed our task to that point.

On Shabbos we are fully present in the moment; no unfinished business or future concerns can impede our joy on this special day. Shabbos is here — now all is good!

GETTING PRACTICAL

Though it may appear insurmountable, we can let go of the nagging daily concerns in honor of Shabbos Kodesh if we regularly reach out to the Borei Olam and entreat help from our Father who loves us.

Awe and Fear

Tehillim states, *"Ivdu es Hashem b'yirah v'gilu b'ra'adah* — Serve Hashem with fear, and rejoice with quaking."[69]

Yirah does not just mean fear, it also means awe. In his commentary on *Mishlei*, the Vilna Gaon teaches that *yirah* (awe) serves as a basis for joy.[70] He instructs that we ought to begin by "serving Hashem in awe," and ultimately build up to attaining the level of "serving Hashem in joy."

Serving Hashem with awe can be interpreted as a sense of reverence and fear of missing the opportunity to connect to Him. The ideal way to serve Hashem is to make His will our will, thereby subsuming our ego with His. This may feel like a daunting task. Many of us strive to control our lives in order to feel secure. Yet, despite our best efforts, any security we achieve remains false because we actually have very little control over what happens to us.

Ironically, giving over control to Hashem should instill the greatest levels of security, for instead of mortal man being in charge, we cast our burden onto our Father who has complete power and kindness. The only true control we have is over the extent of how much control we give to Hashem.

Once this message is internalized we can proceed to understand *"v'gilu b'ra'adah,"* serving Hashem with joy. By understanding the eternal reward of serving Hashem and attaining *yiras Shamayim,* we can now rejoice in living a life of meaning with Hashem, Torah and His *mitzvos*. The greatest joy one can experience

In memory of Chana bat Dvorah z'l (16 Tamuz) Dedicated lovingly by the Mirzakandov Family

---

69   2:11.
70   21:17.

is the serenity that flows when there is no internal conflict between our will and His.

This joy is born from a sense of awe toward the Borei Olam in that we submit ourselves before Him and appreciate the greater purpose in serving Him. Allowing ourselves to be completely absorbed in the Presence of Hashem instills *simchah* into our lives, particularly when we are beset with difficulties. Ultimately, the tighter our connection is with Hashem, the brighter the Divine light which illuminates our soul's true path.

GETTING PRACTICAL

Today, try to allow Hashem's plans be your plans. Formulate an idea with the mindset that it may not come to fruition as intended. Work toward accepting the outcome with a full heart and without stressing over it.

Mashiach's Arrival

Am Yisrael has currently reached a very low point, both morally and ethically. Despite this (or perhaps because of it!), we must wait for Mashiach like we would gaze at the horizon to witness its new phases in the sky.

Rebbe Nachman of Breslov teaches that immediately before Mashiach's arrival, real *emunah* will be scarce. True believers will be scant. He considers that "praiseworthy are those who hold onto faith in these times... Many will be selected, whitened and refined like ore (smelting) in this test of faith. He who merits passing the test and remains with his faith is praiseworthy and will merit all the good that will come to us... It will be a great test... There will be great battles in their minds... This has been foreseen."

In *Sichos HaRan*, the following is said about Mashiach:[71]

The Rizhiner Rebbe described the time before the coming of Mashiach as being as difficult for the Jews as scaling a straight wall.

The Slonimer Tzaddik predicted that before the coming of Mashiach, the Jewish people will lose patience.

The Alter of Kelm, R. Simcha Zissel reminds us that when *Bnei Yisrael* left Egypt, they were not worthy of being redeemed. Rather, they merited the *geulah* due to their faith. Thus, we can gain insight into the future and final redemption by reading and immersing ourselves in the story of *yetzias Mitzrayim* (the exodus from Egypt).

Instead of instilling despair, these messages can serve to forewarn us and thus strengthen our *emunah*

In memory of
Pincus David
ben Gedalya
HaKohen z'l (23
Tevet)
Dedicated
lovingly by Jaci
Nadav

---

71   Essay 220.

in the face of the great tests ahead. These words can help us view difficulties as a necessary precondition of Mashiach's arrival, and serve as a reminder to hold fast to our *emunah*. It may also be comforting to recall the words of Chabakuk that "even if [the Mashiach] tarries, wait for Him for He will surely come."[72] Never lose hope! He *is* coming!

GETTING PRACTICAL

The time immediately before Mashiach arrives will be extremely challenging. Let's remember this and thus hold on even tighter to our emunah.

---

72   2:3.

Have No Fear

Trust, *bitachon*, is characterized by an overall feeling of calm and serenity, based solely on the belief that you are being guided and nurtured by Him, rather than by rhyme, reason or logic. It is the result of knowing that Hashem is good and He's the only one in charge. Consequently, there is no room for worry or anxiety.

A simple way of understanding the difference between *emunah* and *bitachon* is that *emunah* resides in the realm of thought and emotion, whereby we know and feel Hashem's Presence. *Bitachon* is when we take this awareness and carry it over to the realm of action. With *bitachon*, all my deeds are affected by the knowledge that Hashem is present always; thus allowing me to relinquish control and maintain inner composure.

Bitachon is outside the realm of the rational. It is seeing things as being good and living with a positive attitude deep within our soul. This core belief is not affected by the whims of reality. Rather, *bitachon* is the prism through which we see reality, as being aligned with Hashem's master plan and the *emes* (truth) of creation.

There are varying degrees of *bitachon*. At certain times, one may be on a level whereby he believes things will become good eventually, although things right now are not good. A higher, more exalted level is the belief that everything (right now!) is already good — even when it looks terrible superficially.

Sometimes, situations arise that seem impossible to surpass via any natural means. At that point we need to press the *bitachon* button in order to reawaken the awareness of Hashem's guiding hand. Rather than saying, "Woe is me! Who can help me?" our inner recording should play the tune that says, "My help is from HaKadosh Baruch Hu, Who makes heaven and earth, and therefore can do whatever He wants." Hashem created the situation and will see me through to its solution.

Healing will come through a good doctor and profit will come through better business tactics; yet the doctor and the tactics are only channels for the real healing and profit that come straight from Hashem's benevolent hand. *Bitachon* is finding comfort beyond natural means because Hashem is above nature and our *yeshuah* (salvation) always comes through Him.

GETTING PRACTICAL

Emunah is needed in order to acquire bitachon. We cannot act with trust if our emunah is built on shaky grounds. A simple exercise to strengthen bitachon is to repeat the words "Ein Od Milvado — There is no other existence but Him (Hashem)" until you feel enveloped with a blanket of calmness and inner composure.

Speak and He Will Open the Channels to Your Heart

The Rambam teaches us that when we contemplate Hashem's greatness, we immediately feel awe for Him and yearn to know His great name. We fall in love with Him and yearn to connect with Him. Once we have that yearning, how can we actually connect to Him?

In *Sefer Devarim*, the question is presented, "For what nation is there so great that has G-d so near to them whenever they call out to Him?"[73] This reveals that in order for us to feel closer to Him, we must call out to Hashem.

Rebbe Nachman teaches us that the idea behind *hisbodedus* — personal secluded one-on-one prayer with Hashem — is to intimately involve Hashem in our everyday life. Any and all forms of speech that we use during our *hisbodedus* session will bond us to Hashem. Whether we express gratitude, make personal requests or share our intimate thoughts, our heartfelt words communicate and create a strong relationship with the Melech HaOlam.

But how do we speak to a Supreme entity that we cannot see? By making the effort to speak to our Creator even if it seems forced or strange or stilted at first, Hashem will open the channels to our heart. We will suddenly find ourselves not talking to ourselves but rather truly sensing Hashem's Presence and feeling that He is listening to us. We may even begin to notice the various clues indicating Hashem is listening to us and is right there with us during every minute aspect our lives. Any dark, lonely or stuck places

*In memory of
Baruch ben
David z'l (24 Av)
Dedicated
lovingly by the
Gerowitz Family*

73   *Devarim* 4:7.

will subsequently dissipate and be replaced by feelings of HaKadosh Baruch Hu's love enveloping us.

Rebbe Nachman suggests that part of our *hisbodedus* session should be geared toward areas of our life in which Hashem is waiting for us to improve; for instance, anger, *simchah*, thinking good and holy thoughts, *shalom bayis*, spiritual connection to Hashem, *emunah*, etc. We can also use this time to beseech Him for whatever it is in our life that we feel we need.

However, we have to remember to apply humility and admit our limited understanding. When entreating Hashem, we ought to remember that a request that we feel will benefit us may actually be detrimental. We can exercise humility and let go of the results by leaving an opening for Hashem's infinite wisdom to enter, accepting with *emunah* that His decrees are brought about through His endless compassion.

GETTING PRACTICAL

It is a heartwarming notion to consider the idea of Hashem "longing" to draw close to His nation. We have a remarkable opportunity to be embraced by His loving care and form an unshakable bond by emptying out our mind and pouring out our feelings. This is the founding principle to forming all relationships; it is no different with Hashem.

Believe and Anticipate!

We are not aware of Mashiach's exact time of coming and must not attempt to calculate a date for the redemption. However, we are required to wait, believe and anticipate his arrival. By exploring the signs leading up to the coming of Mashiach as predicted by *Chazal*, we can more easily anticipate and perceive his imminence.

In *Iggeres Teiman,* the Rambam writes that Mashiach will first reveal himself in Eretz Yisrael, as it is written, "And the L-rd whom you seek will suddenly come to His Temple and the messenger of the covenant whom you delight in; behold he comes, says the L-rd of hosts."[74] The Mashiach will be proven through the open miracles that he will perform. All the people of Israel will gather together in Yerushalayim.

Sefer Yeshaya dictates that the land will widen from east to west until it reaches Yemen and India. The ground will be blessed and be reinstated as in the days prior to the *chet* of Adam HaRishon. The choice to do good will be natural because there will be no desire for sin. Though the process is complex and will occur in stages, man will eventually be free of internal conflict and will return to the original state that he was in before the sin of Adam.

R. Dessler explains that there are two possible ways in which Hashem can bring about the Mashiach. If we are a worthy nation the coming of Mashiach will be as if "the son of man comes with the clouds of heaven."[75] Alternatively, if we are not meritorious

---

74   *Malachi* 3:1.
75   *Sanhedrin* 97b.

chas v'shalom, "the king comes to you lowly and riding upon an ass." This lowly state depicts a nation that cannot cover up for their evil dealings and feels helpless when attempting to overcome their temptations. They need Hashem to remove them from their depraved place.

Jews who are far removed from Torah life and have forgotten their Jewish roots will repent because they will acknowledge the need for salvation. Practicing Jews should also repent and humble themselves, acknowledging their dire need of Hashem's salvation as well.

Either way, when Hashem redeems us it will be out of love, not because we are deserving of it. Due to His mercy and unconditional love, He will shield us from shame and bring the *yeshuah* to make it appear as if we did in fact merit the *geulah*.

GETTING PRACTICAL

Just as we are sure that the sun will rise tomorrow, so we should anticipate the absolute arrival of Mashiach Tzidkeinu, bimheirah b'yameinu, Amen.

Hashem's Light

For a Jew, life's greatest joy is to live with *emunah* and be connected to the Borei Olam. From such a vantage point, we do not need to worry about physical or material problems because we realize that everything that happens is truly according to Hashem's plan and is therefore for the best. As R. Pinchas of Koretz states, "When you believe that everything is from Hashem, blessed be He, then there is no evil or bad at all. There is only all good."[76]

In contrast, living without a personal bond with Hashem inevitably leads to misery. The Jewish soul is sustained by the light of Hashem. Naturally, separating from Him and His light leads to depression, anxiety and worry. It is therefore vital to rekindle our relationship with Him if we want to feel that light again.

What obstructs Hashem's flow of light to us and brings about distance? Our transgressions create a distance since our sinful actions demonstrate a lack of trust that Hashem loves us and is giving us exactly what we need at all times. If we fully internalized this *bitachon*, we would follow the Torah to the letter and avoid transgressing.

An analogy can be made to two items that cannot stick to one another with glue unless both items are completely free of dirt. The slightest trace of dirt impedes the glue's adherence. Transgressions are the dirt that "sticks" to our *neshamah*, preventing it from bonding to HaKadosh Baruch Hu. Often this leads to a slippery slope, as a person who feels distant from Hashem starts doubting His care or even existence —

In memory of
Perel Malka bas
Aryeh Leib z'l (11
Adar)
Dedicated
lovingly by
the Berenstein
Family

---

76   *Tosefta l'Midrash Pinchas* #187.

a further transgression. The channel is thus almost completely blocked, allowing only a small light to shine through.

If we, *chas v'shalom,* experience such a blockage, we need to search for this small beam of light. Yet, paradoxically, this light can only be found when one is in a state of happiness! Somehow we need to lift ourselves up to a state of joy even if our actions of joy do not radiate inside at first. The Torah teaches, "Open for Me an opening the size of the eye of a needle, and I will open for you one the size of a hall."[77]

When it comes to serving Hashem we should do the very best we can, given whom we are, our position in life and our strengths and weaknesses. But even when the best we do falls short of what the circumstance requires, this still counts for much more in the eyes of Hashem. As a result of our state of joy, Hashem then allows us to recognize the *teshuvah* we need to do in order to remove the obstructions. Gradually, the light beam will intensify, connecting us more strongly with Hashem.

GETTING PRACTICAL

What are the impediments that hide Hashem's light in your life? We all make mistakes. Spend a few minutes to analyze what is holding you back from fully experiencing G-dliness.

---

77   *Shir HaShirim Midrash Raba* 5:2.

The Redemptive Power of Shabbos

Shabbos is the one day of the week when we are required to relinquish total control over human creativity. We must not contribute any significant change to our material environment or demonstrate our mastery over nature in any way.

In *Tehillim*, Dovid HaMelech writes, "*Hakshivah el rinasi ki dalosi me'od hatzileini mi-rodfai* — Hearken to my cry for I have become very low; save me from my pursuers."[78] The Sfas Emes explains that this verse refers to Dovid HaMelech's request to break away from the constraints of the six days of the working week.

On Shabbos, our *neshamah* is transformed. We are freed from the bondage of and attachment to this mundane world. We receive a boost of renewed energy from this spiritual day in order to reconnect to our true purpose. As Rabbi Dr. Abraham Twerski points out in his "Growing Each Day" column on Aish.com, though Hashem wants us to engage in work during the week ("Six days shall you work"[79]), we should feel like a person away from home on an assigned duty, longing to return home to our loved ones.

Though the six days may have flooded us with misery, Shabbos holds in it healing of all ailments. Feelings of despair are replaced with Divine, life-giving energy. A person can be uplifted from his state of distress and be awash with a fountain of hope. No matter what state of brokenness one is in, he can be rebuilt.

---

78   142:7.
79   *Shemos* 20:9.

When Hashem created the world, the initial light was said to be so radiant it was too intense for man to bear. It was hidden in this world and appropriately named *ohr ha-ganuz* (the hidden light). One portion was hidden in the Torah only to be discovered by those who study it with a pure heart. Another portion of the light was hidden only to shine on Shabbos.

For example, the *sefarim ha-kedoshim* teach us that Shabbos can be seen as a force of Divine light. This light represents the Presence of the *Shechinah HaKedoshah* (Divine Presence) which our souls should yearn for all week long.

GETTING PRACTICAL

Shabbos is unique. Unlike the other days, it is a day when we relinquish complete control and creativity. If we experience Shabbos correctly, we can bask in Hashem's radiance on this day, and yearn for it the rest of the week. This Shabbos let us try to not make any plans that pertain to weekdays and focus solely on this one holy day.

Love Is Sacrifice

How can a person judge how much he is loved by someone else? Sacrifice. The extent to which one is willing to sacrifice their own comforts and material pleasures for someone else shows the amount they love him. Love is sacrifice. Love involves doing something for someone else, especially at those times when it's uncomfortable and inconvenient.

For instance, if someone asks their spouse for a cup of water just as they are about to sink into the couch, that is a test. By fulfilling and nurturing their need with a genuine smile despite the inconvenience, a sacrifice has been made. That sacrifice is love.

We are placed in a world which demands sacrifice. We are required to channel our animalistic desires and sacrifice physical pleasures in order to satisfy our higher soul and perform the Divine will. Love is loyalty and is expressed when we commit ourselves to others through action. It resides in the heart but manifests itself through the behaviors that we do.

Our love is clearly apparent when we invest ourselves in another in spite of our lack of understanding why. It is a commitment whether it is comfortable, convenient or difficult. It is no different with our love to Hashem.

Our love for Hashem should not be limited to words, but should include action. Fulfilling Hashem's will by keeping Torah and *mitzvos* and refining our character traits to emulate G-dly attributes is testimony to our love, particularly when it is challenging.

In memory of
Naftali Lipa ben
Shmuel Halo z'l
(5 Elul)
Dedicated
lovingly by Sara
Stobezki

GETTING PRACTICAL

It is our lifelong task to give our heart and emotions to Hashem. This comes in the form of sacrifices that we make in our daily lives. Our actions form the framework of a loving relationship between us and our Creator. Today, do a small deed just to show how much you love Hashem.

Visit Hashem Once a Day

Just as we don't wait for a crisis to visit the doctor and should check in with him regularly and not visit only when we are unwell, so should we "visit" Hashem once a day to maintain our emotional and spiritual well-being. During these visits, we should express ourselves in our own words and use this precious time to draw closer to Him. It is a time to open up with honesty, tell HaKadosh Baruch Hu all that happened throughout the day, and make requests for all of our needs. There is nothing too big or small.

Secluded prayer raises us to a very spiritual place and is delightful to Hashem. Even if we are unable to bring ourselves to the right words or any words, the fact that we yearn to speak serves in and of itself to increase our attachment. This is because as human beings we possess the highest of the five soul levels, due to our ability to talk. Speech is the only differentiating factor between animals and human beings. The more we speak to the Melech HaOlam, the higher we elevate ourselves in our *avodas Hashem*.

In *Tehillim*, Dovid HaMelech refers to the fact that "*Shivisi Hashem l'negdi tamid* — I have set Hashem before me at all times."[80] These words can be fulfilled by impressing Hashem's Oneness in our mind and heart via regular communication with Him. The Rambam explains that the commandment of *avodah she'ba-lev* (work of the heart) is prayer. The words written in the *siddur* are a holy vehicle to reach Hashem. True communication of the heart should also include one-on-one personal and individual pleas from the heart to the Borei Olam.

---

80   16:8.

This contemplative, secluded prayer to Hashem is formally called *hisbodedus*. It is the pathway to strengthen our *emunah*. By practicing this lofty form of prayer, we welcome the Borei Olam into every aspect of our day — whether it be discussing, seeking advice, strength or clarity on all of the issues that arise in our lives.

GETTING PRACTICAL

Hisbodedus, or contemplative, personal communication to Hashem is a daily chance to connect with Hashem and maintain our well-being. It is a priceless opportunity; call today 1-800-ALMIGHTY.

Happiness Is Medicine for the Heart

In *Mishlei* it is written that "a happy heart is as healing as medicine."[81]

Many doctors call this generation the "Tylenol generation" because many of us unfortunately run to take pills to whisk our pain away. For instance, though a doctor may operate to remove his patient's inflamed appendix, we rarely examine the source of the inflammation. Thus, we take care of the symptoms without exploring the cause.

In this day and age, it is our hearts that need healing. So what is the cause of our inflamed hearts?

R. Avigdor Miller was known to teach that "a person who is sad has a lack of *hakaros ha-tov* (appreciation) for what he has been given." It is often easy to overlook our blessings and take them for granted. Modern media may attempt to convince us that happiness equates with extravagance and luxurious items, however, being aware of the great value of being alive and the absolute treasure embedded in every second of life is a powerful balm to a wounded heart. Being grateful with what we have can motivate us to utilize each moment to its fullest, and avoid feeling downhearted.

Our greatest blessing is that we have all been hand-picked and chosen to be Hashem's children and that He loves us no matter what! Remembering our special, unique status is an initial step toward strengthening our *hakaras ha-tov*. When we know that Hashem loves us and is taking care of us, we have no alternative but to be happy.

In memory of Rafael ben Mazal Tov z'l (8 Tevet) Dedicated lovingly by the Mirzakandov and Ibragimov Families

81   17:22.

Hashem, the King of Kings, the Master Planner of the world, the head of all corporations, the chief *Shadchan*, the Head Doctor — is our Father! We are truly blessed.

GETTING PRACTICAL _____

Today, let's appreciate and pay particular attention to each life-giving breath we take. Treasure the sun, wind, stars and nature — and appreciate each of these as a special gift to us from Hashem!

Giving and Taking

Hashem loves us more than we love ourselves. This principle is the cornerstone of *emunah* — we can only trust Him if we know clearly that He loves us. What is the essence of this love?

The Torah teaches us that our bodies are created to be takers whereas our souls are naturally givers. Even during those times when our bodies give, they give with the ultimate intention of receiving. Egocentric people give as well but they do so in order to receive twice back. For us to reach the highest form of emulating Hashem, we ought to learn to give unconditionally, without expecting anything in return (*chesed shel emes*). That is our *tzelem Elokim* (Divine image).

One example of giving unconditionally (as depicted by *Chazal* as true *chesed*) is attending to the needs of the deceased. When we give to the deceased, we give without expecting anything in return. This illustrates the highest form of giving.

The essence of love is in the giving, not in the taking. This is the key to understanding our relationship with Hashem. Our holy sages teach us that the purpose of creation is in order for HaKadosh Baruch Hu to bestow His endless kindness on those He creates. By virtue of His giving, we are showered with His love, yet He benefits by being able to give to us. Similarly, He wants us to be givers so we can benefit in the same way!

Sometimes, though, it is right to take, as well. The Sfas Emes teaches us that we should take in order to give; that is, to offer the giver the opportunity to

*In memory of
Leah bat Joya z'l
(9 Tishrei)*

gain the *chesed* from giving to us.[82] In this way, our taking is in essence really giving. For example, when we receive a homemade present from a child, we take pleasure in witnessing their happiness at our taking. We may even exaggerate our joy at their "practical" gift in order to maximize their pleasure. This is the way of Hashem who "takes pleasure" when we enjoy His gifts and express our appreciation for them. By doing so we are actually giving Him the opportunity to give to us.

This ricochet effect of giving and taking, where our taking enables Him to experience pleasure, and our giving enables us to experience pleasure, which in turn enables Him to experience pleasure, sheds a beautiful new light onto the essence of giving, taking and loving-kindness.

GETTING PRACTICAL

Our loving relationship with others ensures that we gain pleasure from seeing them gain pleasure at our taking. Let's learn to give more — and sometimes take — for the sake of giving!

---

82   Sfas Emes elaborates on this teaching of taking for the sake of giving in his commentary on the verse in *parashas Terumah*, "Take for Me a contribution from everything."

Day and Night

Our souls' true desire is to speak to Hashem, to constantly connect with His constant Presence. But the disparities of life, uncontrollable circumstances and our moods may cause us to interact with HaKadosh Baruch Hu differently each time we pray. Whereas we may sometimes reach angelic heights with our *tefillah* and cleave to our *Abba she'baShamayim*, at other moments, we feel uninspired or pray only out of obligation. This is certainly in line with human nature.

Dovid HaMelech suggests that the time of day we pray influences the type of connection we have with Hashem. Whereas evening is a time of darkness, of great uncertainty and of the unknown, daytime is a time of hope and brightness. "One may lie down weeping at night, but with the morning dawn, there is great joy."[83]

R. Samson Raphael Hirsch elaborates on this distinction.[84] He teaches that after we recite the *Shema* in the morning, we say *Emes V'yatziv* (true and upright). However, in the evening we recite *Emes V'emunah* (true and faithful). Similarly, during the day we can look up and see the light of *Shamayim*. It is easier to feel positive because we can see far into the distance. In contrast, at night we cannot see into the distance as our light source is only the dimmer moon and stars. We must therefore more heavily rely on our faith to reassure us that HaKadosh Baruch Hu is still guiding us.

References to day and night are allusions to good and bitter times in life. We are human. We all face

In memory of Miriam bat Rivka z'l (12 Adar) Dedicated lovingly by the Riter Family

---

83   *Tehillim* 30:6.
84   Hirsch on *Tehillim*.

difficulties and dark times that may drag us down. We can use our "daytime moments" — when things are light and clear — to boost our *emunah*. We can rely on this storehouse of trust during the difficult, darker "nighttime moments" of life, to breathe new life into our *emunah*-hungry souls.

GETTING PRACTICAL _____

It is natural to feel closer to and further from Hashem at different points in life. We each experience lighter, happier moments signified by clear, positive light of day, and darker more difficult times of "night" during which we more heavily rely on our emunah. Try to boost your emunah during "daytime moments." That helps create a storehouse for the night time.

A Pure Heart

In *Sefer Tehillim*, we read the *pasuk*; "*Lev tahor bara li Elokim, v'ruach nachon chadesh b'kirbi* — Create for me a pure heart, Hashem, and renew a steadfast spirit within me."[85]

Dovid HaMelech requests a change of spirit, as opposed to a newly created soul. Why?

Though our *neshamah* is embedded in holiness, sometimes we fall out of touch with it. It is natural for all human beings to feel more and less in touch with their spirituality, their soul. Though eternal and accessible, there are times when our *neshamah* may seem unreachable. At those moments we need to beseech Hashem's *rachamim* to lead us to greater heights. Despite our feelings, the *kedushah* remains and can be accessed any time we desire it.

We need to engage in *tefillah* always. We are required to even daven for the strength to daven because nothing is handed to us without working for it. Hashem desires our hearts. Rebbe Nachman teaches that it is not the words of the *tefillos* that actually ascend to *Shamayim*, but the burning desire of the heart that rises before the Holy Throne. Pouring out our heart before HaKadosh Baruch Hu helps us reach the exalted sacred level and feel our *neshamah* again.

It is written in *parashas Nitzavim*, "Hashem will circumcise your heart and the heart of all your offspring to love Hashem with all your heart and soul in order that you may live."[86] Our hearts are often enveloped in *klipos* (shells or husks). These layers block our ability to

In memory of Roni Yosef ben Moshe z'l (28 Nissan) Dedicated lovingly by the Hayon Family

---

85   51:12.
86   *Devarim* 30:6.

speak and act with *kavanah* (proper intent), hence distancing us from fully connecting to Hashem or others. We create this foreskin surrounding our hearts either unconsciously or consciously in order to protect our hearts from feeling pain. But this barrier blocks love from flowing too.

A quick remedy to solve this is to visualize Hashem's prevailing love that He wishes to bestow on us, and allow His love to melt into our hearts. This will assist us to shed the layers over our hearts and awaken our souls which are burning eternally inside of us.

GETTING PRACTICAL

We all have a pure heart burning within us. However, the extent to which we are in touch with our spiritual neshamah fluctuates over time. We often cover our heart with layers to protect ourselves. Let's uncover these layers using passionate heartfelt davening to Hashem.

Prepare for Shabbos

At Har Sinai we lived in Hashem's tangible Presence. We were adorned with crowns on our heads and were illuminated with Hashem's holy light. The Midrash teaches that this light was essentially the light of consciousness. We entered a place of spiritual perfection, intrinsically aware that Hashem was with us always and would never leave us.

Every Shabbos we can be blessed again to be adorned with these precious crowns and luminous light. We have the *zechus* to marry Hashem again and sense His immediate Presence.

Our Shabbos preparations enable us to ready ourselves for this intimate meeting with Hashem. Just as *Bnei Yisrael* prepared themselves before receiving the Torah, we elevate ourselves and our material possessions for the encounter with Hashem on Shabbos by infusing them with the intent that it is all in honor of the Shabbos Queen. We are entering that same place of love that we experienced at Har Sinai.

Though Shabbos brings with it a surge of *kedushah*, our bodies and material possessions need to be prepared in order to receive this radiant holiness. It is therefore important to separate clothing, tableware, specialties and other objects and designate them solely for Shabbos. It is customary to say the words, "*L'kavod Shabbos Kodesh* — In honor of the holy Shabbos," when preparing food delicacies and other specialties for Shabbos. With these words, Hashem will sprinkle *mahn* into our dishes, submerging them with a spiritual spice.

In memory of Pnina bat Shimon z'l (23 Shevat) Dedicated lovingly by Lirit Adam

GETTING PRACTICAL _____

As we did at Har Sinai, we can experience Hashem's Presence tangibly right now every Shabbos! This Shabbos, let's undertake special, separate preparations to enhance the Shabbos kedushah and thus prepare for this weekly connection with Hashem.

Breaking Down Fortresses

Sometimes, we may find it difficult to speak or connect with HaKadosh Baruch Hu. It may feel like there are walls surrounding our hearts.

One reason for such barriers is our transgressions, which can cause distance between us and Hashem. This is hinted in the Hebrew word for transgression, *aveirah* (*avar-ka* — on the other side of Hashem). Our *aveiros* create layers blocking our heart. These layers may serve to numb us. Another possible barrier to our connection with Hashem may be caused by emotions such as stress or anxiety. Stress is a negative emotion that can affect our productivity and capacity to tackle life's challenges.

What should we do when faced with such barriers? Pray. It is recommended that we move our lips and speak to Hashem, even in absence of feeling (*kavanah*). The point is to avoid distress and rather begin to speak. As it is written in *Sefer HaChinuch*, "Acharei ha-maasim nimshachim ha-levavos — Our hearts are influenced by our actions."[87] Through our prayers, we can beg Hashem to reveal His Presence in our lives. Calling out His name over and over may assist the walls around our hearts to crumble and flood us with true emotion.

If our barriers have frozen up our words, perhaps we can write down our thoughts and read them out to Hashem. A benefit of such personal prayer is *yishuv ha-da'as* (inner composure, peace of mind). This process reminds us of the goal of living. When we remember that the purpose of life in this world is to

In memory of Safta Esther bat Jamilla z'l (30 Cheshvan) Dedicated lovingly by the Hayon Family

---

87   Mitzvah 16.

build *netzach* (eternity), we may feel more tranquil and accepting, which may help break down barriers caused by stress or tension.

What happens if we still find ourselves incapable of speaking, despite trying to pray? Rest assured that even this silence is valuable. Hashem notices the mere fact that we have a desire to connect to Him and overcome our silence, and He will thus assist us in stirring emotion and the connection we crave.

GETTING PRACTICAL

Breaking down the barriers that prevent us from connecting our hearts to Hashem requires effort. Tefillah is our most powerful chisel to perform such a task. When we talk to Hashem we instill His Presence readily in our lives, reassuring us that we are never alone. Just Do It: Open your heart.

▶ DAY 85 | Humility and Independence

In Torah, humility (*anavah*) is considered one of the most outstanding character traits. *Chovos Halevavos* teaches that "humility before Hashem" is the foundation on which all other character traits are based. A humble person recognizes that all of his achievements and also all of his failures come from Hashem. From a moral viewpoint, a humble person believes that he is not superior to others.

Humility does not mean a feeling of lack of self-worth or self-effacement. Rather, it is the ability to avoid feeling superior in the face of success. We should be grateful for our ability to achieve, and simultaneously recall our failings as well. As we are generally able to identify our own strengths, actively attempting to focus on others' strengths and our own weaknesses evens up the score card.

Generally content with their lot, humble people are able to perceive whatever they receive as an unexpected gift. The Rambam teaches that humility leads to the path of *yiras Shamayim* (fear of Heaven) as is written, "Through humility there will emerge in your heart the virtue of reverence for you will consider always from whence you came and where you are going... And when you will think of all of this, you will fear your Maker and you will avoid sin."[88] Reflecting on this fact enhances humility.

When a person embraces and works on this quality of *anavah*, he may find himself more able to do the following:

- Forgive others who have wronged him

In memory of Saba Natan ben Gittel z'l (13 Adar) Dedicated lovingly by the Riter Family

---

88   Quoted by the Rambam in *Hilchos De'os* 2:3.

- Accept Hashem's decrees with love

- Avoid pride in his heart when people honor him

- Avoid feeling superior for his wisdom, wealth or other traits

- Admit his faults and do *teshuvah* without delay

- Humble people also have the courage to remain loyal to their convictions rather than feeling peer pressure to buckle and compromise their religious and moral standards.

R. Nissim Yagen teaches that a humble person respects the *Shechinah* (Divine Presence) rather than the *shecheinah* (neighbor). He identifies with *emes* (words of truth) and therefore places his needs secondary to the importance of sanctifying what the Torah teaches is the right thing to do. Remaining unmoved by the dictates of society or what others might think or say, humble people live by their beliefs. This recognition of Hashem gives him genuine independence which ironically paves the way to far greater honor.

GETTING PRACTICAL

Humble people recognize that we are each allotted our own gifts based on the individual missions we must fulfill in this world. Instead of looking down on or judging others, those with humility accept that Hashem granted each of us different strengths necessary to fulfill our individual life purpose. Instead of following what is socially accepted in order to seek honor, let's be humble enough to seek Hashem's approval.

DAY 86 | **Kindness: The Result of Trust**

It is written, "*Ha-boteach b'Hashem chesed yesovevenu* — The one who trusts in Hashem, kindness will envelop him."[89] Why?

First, Hashem does not want to disappoint those who hope and display their reliance on Him.

Second, measure for measure — when we entrust ourselves only in Hashem's hands without any rhyme or reason attached to it, so shall our *yeshuah* (salvation) come about through surprising means. Let us not be confused — surprising is not miraculous. It is simply a way in which we hadn't realized the *yeshuah* could occur.

Lastly, measure for measure — because I allowed myself to trust in that which I cannot see, my *yeshuah* will not be shown to the Heavenly prosecutors that may dispute my worthiness in receiving it.

Sometimes, we still feel, though, that we are undeserving of a *yeshuah* due to our transgressions. Yet, if we closely read the *pasuk* above again, we shall see that Hashem's kindness embraces us as a result of our trust, not our worthiness. It is appropriately named *chesed chinam* (undeserving kindness).

So what am I hoping and trusting in Hashem to do? To steer me away from anything that is not beneficial for me in this world. I do not want to travel on an unsafe road. Hashem is my "tour guide" in this world and I am but a tourist needing Him to show me the way to the most exalted lofty places!

In memory of Kochava bat Esther z'l (5 Sivan) Dedicated lovingly by the Hayon Family

89   *Tehillim* 32:10.

GETTING PRACTICAL

When we hope and wait for the yeshuah, we essentially cuddle into Hashem's arms and are embraced by His kindness. Hashem wants to shower us with good. Keep hoping. This opens the channel for the yeshuah to arrive.

Someone Pushed My Button!

We crave control because we dislike being dependent on others and want to know what is coming next. Controlling our lives provides us with a sense of security. We therefore seek involvement and having a say in everything that occurs in our lives.

One of life's major challenges is accepting the fact that we have little or no control over our lives. Hashem controls everything. Any sense of control is just an illusion. Since this sense of control is just a delusion, the process of overcoming this *gaavah* (arrogance in assuming that we are in control) actually involves training the mind. Our generation today faces the challenge of rectifying this negative character trait by relinquishing control and surrendering our will to HaKadosh Baruch Hu.

Hashem interacts with us through the circumstances of our lives. For a clue as to what we should be working on, focus on the next time you feel you are losing it! Others often push our buttons and trigger our animalistic drives. By overcoming our natural tendencies to react, we experience empowerment and strength far deeper than mere physical strength. That is how Hashem helps us to grow greater than we were.

Yet, though we are to accept the smallness of ourselves in order to overcome this trait of arrogance, we must also treasure the little acts of goodness and acts of self-discipline that we do perform in order to move forward and avoid despair. We can exercise healthy control in the realm of our reactions to the events that occur in our lives. We can exert control over our instinctive, knee-jerk reactions to negative events.

In memory of Tuvia ben Natan z'l (26 Tishrei) Dedicated lovingly by the Riter Family

Rather than responding instinctively or with extreme emotions, we can hold back and accept our circumstances. We can do this by reinforcing the fundamental belief that everything in our lives is from Hashem, Hashem loves us and it is all tailor-made and good for us. This is the healthy, beneficial way to exert control.

GETTING PRACTICAL

We crave control because it provides a sense of security. In truth, however, the best way to exert control is by managing our reactions to events, rather than the events themselves. The growth from this process of holding back and accepting that Hashem is in charge is liberating. Obstacles increase stamina and strengthen our ability to meet life's struggles with ease. Try it.

Sensory Emunah

Two of our main organs that are capable of perceiving the *emes* of *emunah* are the brain (i.e., the mind) and the heart. *Emunah* of the mind is named intellectual *emunah*. It is encapsulated in the obligation set upon every Jew to acknowledge the existence of HaKadosh Baruch Hu. To know that He was, is and will always be.

The Rambam teaches that we must realize intellectually that Hashem is totally perfect — we cannot doubt His existence for a moment.[90] He created the world and continues to place His Divine *hashgachah* on every minute detail of our lives. From the bounced check to the insult that hurts.

One way to strengthen intellectual *emunah* is to study Torah sources discussing HaKadosh Baruch Hu's kingship. This enhances fear of Heaven, *yiras ha-Romemus*. The more we seek this intellectual knowledge, the more readily we will find it.

However, the Steipler Gaon (R. Yaakov Yisrael Kanievsky) teaches that intellectual *emunah* alone is incomplete.[91] We are also required to bring this *emunah* down into our hearts so that it affects our feelings and emotions. Every decision and movement we make should ideally be colored by *emunah* of the heart, which also can be called heartfelt or sensory *emunah*.[92]

How can we enhance our sensory *emunah*? One way is to avoid sin because sin and *emunah* have an inverse relationship. The Mishnah teaches that the

---

90   *Sefer Hamitzvos*, first positive mitzvah.
91   *Birkas Peretz, parashas Noach.*
92   The Steipler refers to this as *emunah chushis*.

result of one sin is another one.[93] Sinning clogs the spiritual arteries of one's heart and makes it easier for them to reject holiness the next time they have the opportunity to learn a new Torah insight.

Another practical way to stir our hearts and feel Hashem is by paying attention to His endless love and kindness. Most of us take life for granted and do not strive to increase our sense of gratitude. However, the more we become aware and recognize, for instance, the amazing powers of the human body, the more we will acknowledge the gift of health that Hashem gives us each day as something precious.

GETTING PRACTICAL

Intellectual emunah is necessary but incomplete. We also need to draw this emunah down into our hearts; that is, to develop sensory emunah which colors our decisions and emotions. One way of enhancing sensory emunah is to avoid transgressions which have a long-term impact on our ability to develop sensory emunah. Let's try to live a life with a genuine sense of appreciation. This also provides a powerful avenue to feeling closeness to Hashem in our hearts.

---

93   *Pirkei Avos* 4:2.

Teshuvah and the Frog

In the book *Shivhei HaBesht* (depicting stories from the life of the holy Baal Shem Tov) it is told that the Baal Shem Tov was once taking a stroll through a deserted place when suddenly he saw a huge frog. He asked the frog who it was. The frog explained that he was a transmigration of the soul of a former scholar. His original soul had done so many sins that he was forced to wander in the desert. The rabbi asked about his sins. The frog explained that when he was in human form, he had once carelessly washed his hands without *kavanah*. Though this in itself wasn't a terrible sin, he failed to do adequate *teshuvah*. Subsequently he was tested with further challenges and failed these tests. Eventually, he became relaxed in fearing Hashem and soon became a great sinner.

When he died, the Heavenly court decreed that his *neshamah* (soul) transmigrate to the form of a frog because his original sin had to do with water. He was sent to a deserted place to minimize the chance that a Jew would come along and say a blessing in his presence, as that would elevate his soul and free him from this transmigration. The Baal Shem Tov said the necessary blessings and praises to *Hashem* in the frog's presence which enabled the frog's soul to be saved.

This story teaches us that one sin leads to another, and from here we can also learn that by contrast one mitzvah leads to another. Even the sinful frog placed way out of the way in the desert was able to hear a *berachah* and be saved. After long and hard cries, he was released from his suffering state.

The *yetzer hara* wants us to despair that there is no rectification for our weaknesses. It fills us with doubts and makes us lose hope of improvement or change. Or it attempts to convince us that no one else succumbs to their desires as we do. However, *"Ein yeush ba'olam klal* — there is no room for despair in this world." Hashem has given us all the great gift of *teshuvah*. Even before the world was created, the concept of *teshuvah* was implanted into the world's DNA.

GETTING PRACTICAL

Hashem has granted us an inbuilt system of rachamim and compassion. We can always return and renew our relationship with Him; no matter how far we have strayed.

Shabbos Kodesh - Are You Prepared?

Though we are busy and trying to do our best, we live most of our workweek in a state of semi-darkness, awaiting the light of Hashem to be revealed. Then, with the moment of candle lighting, the light of healing arrives. The radiance of Shabbos brings comfort and warmth from the inevitable pains and suffering of the week.

Shabbos brings with it the heart and soul of all reality since it realigns us with the truthful reality of why we are here on earth. We become centered and whole once again by focusing on the purpose of our existence. Embedded in Shabbos is a powerful reminder of the divine life-force that surrounds us and lies within us.

However, there is a catch!

This holy energy cannot be felt by those who haven't adequately prepared themselves to absorb it. Are we ready to contain the Shabbos holiness? Are our bodies, our vessels, in a place to receive it?

Just as only a skilled musician can hear the off notes on the instrument that he professionally plays, only a holy *neshamah* who has trained itself can tune into the vibrations of *kedushah* that fill the world every Shabbos.

Although each Jew experiences the holiness of Shabbos differently, generally it is uniquely dependent on each person's *avodah* that he has done to prepare himself for his encounter with the Borei Olam. For that reason the ability to tap into the *kedushah* of Shabbos is essentially connected to the preparation one has made throughout the entire workweek.

Though we must engage in the natural order of the world all week long, the focus of our mind should be on strengthening our vessel in order to receive and contain the holiness we are given every Shabbos.

GETTING PRACTICAL ⸺⸺⸺⸺⸺⸺⸺

How do we view our responsibilities during the week? Does our mind remain focused on the seventh day or do we prioritize something else? Let's make Shabbos the goal — the workweek is merely part of the journey to reach that goal.

Heavenly Art

Wisps of pink on powder blue
The clouds move slowly by
Above horizon's golden hue:
A painting in the sky!

What calming tones the heavens hold
A masterpiece of art
As different colored scenes unfold
Then slowly drift apart.

How beauty reigns so unaware
Majestically on high
While here on earth there's much despair
Beneath the untold sky.

Perhaps it's sent from G-d above
Who saves the tears we cry
And paints us healing hues of love
Across the canvas sky.

Poems by Leah Rubabshi, copyright 2015.
Used with permission.

That Yetzer Hara What a Joker!

Chazal teach us many valuable tools to achieve the goal of attaching to Hashem with purity and increased *emunah*. One important *middah* to foster in order to minimize transgressions (and thereby improve our *emunah*) is self-discipline, otherwise known as *gevurah*.

We are all born with innate desires, thoughts and tendencies. These desires need to be harnessed in order to achieve our maximum potential. *Chazal* set boundaries to safeguard us from sin. For example the laws of *yichud* (prohibition of seclusion between man and woman) build definitive borders that should not be passed as precautionary measures.

An acknowledgment of human frailties, these borders serve to prevent us from entering a dangerous situation from which retreat will be virtually impossible. Whereas individuals may move borders to suit their ever-changing wishes or desires, respecting the sages' wisdom about human character and weaknesses and their methods for safeguarding us helps us stay on the right path in moments of weakness.

Often, we may feel that we cannot control our thoughts because they are involuntary. Yet, the very act of refusing to act on a thought represents the epitome of self-discipline and holiness. Rising to the challenge of refusing to bow to our temptations leads to tremendous spiritual rewards. Rebbe Nachman teaches that controlling one's urges creates a conduit for receiving *berachah* into the world. Ultimately, restraining from following our desires ultimately makes us feel good. Deep down, our souls know we are making difficult yet wise choices.

Yet, not only can chasing after non-spiritual pursuits be dangerous, it is ultimately futile. Rebbe Nachman teaches that the *yetzer hara* is like a trickster who runs around with its fist closed asking people, "What do you suppose I have in my hand?" Each person imagines that the closed hand contains exactly what he most desires and runs after the *yetzer hara*. Yet, when they reach the *yetzer hara*, its hand opens to reveal... nothing! This is the way of the evil one. The *yetzer hara* lures us into sin without ultimately fulfilling any of our desires!

GETTING PRACTICAL

Self-discipline is an important middah which enables us to avoid sin. Chazal place boundaries around the laws to help ensure we avoid temptation. Avoiding acting on our thoughts or desires is praiseworthy. In contrast, following our base temptations not only leads to sin but is ultimately unfruitful. Next time you are inclined to say something harmful about someone else, restrain yourself. You will feel empowered by your ability to control your base impulses.

It All Depends on Where the "Me" Is

In order to achieve a close relationship with HaKadosh Baruch Hu, controlling our ego is vital. Humility is a key *middah* which requires constant work. Selfish desires can be removed by replacing them with noble ones. It is essential to train ourselves to work against self-centeredness because of the harm an over-inflated ego can cause. The stronger our desire to free ourselves from vanity, the more *siyata diShmaya* we will receive in order to overcome it.

The reason for the importance in conquering our ego is that only through emptying the "me" can we raise ourselves to a level of consciousness where we can clearly see Hashem. When I am consumed by my ego my view of the world will be tainted based on whether my life feels wonderful or miserable to me. The better I feel life is treating me, the closer I will feel to Hashem. The more horrible I feel my life is, the more estranged my relationship with Hashem will feel.

From this we can learn two different, but equally valuable ways in which to bond with Hashem.

The first way is the path carved with the feeling that Hashem loves me and all is good in my life. I am then filled with immense joy and gratitude for the kindness Hashem has bestowed upon me.

The second way is by connecting to Hashem when we are struggling to wipe away the feeling of being treated unfairly and not earning Hashem's special attention. By crying out to Hashem and asking that He help wipe out the egoism causing us to feel deserted and unloved, we can also rise to a

Refuah shleimah to Chaim ben Tzipporah and hatzlocha to the entire Cohen Family

higher level of closeness to Hashem. It all depends on where the "me" is.

The process of removing egoism from ourselves helps us emulate Hashem in our thoughts and actions, as Hashem pours His compassion and goodness endlessly just for the sake of giving. By lessening the focus on "me," I am able to attach myself to eternity and to infinite greatness. The intentions behind my actions will be pure because I will see anything I do receive as a gift, as a favor and a special service over and above what I deserve. The more credit I give to Hashem for everything good that does happen, the more readily I will give myself over to do His will with a full heart.

GETTING PRACTICAL

It is important to nullify our ego in order to bring ourselves closer to Hashem. We can do this by expressing gratitude and joy for everything we do receive and by distancing ourselves from the selfish "me" when things don't go our way. How? Let's loosen our ego's grip by doing mitzvos just because Hashem wants us to, and for no other reason.

A Bit of Mashiach in Every Jew

Our generation is being tested much more than previous generations. We have easy access to the most immoral places. The *yetzer hara* knows its days are numbered and will soon be eliminated, and is therefore barraging us with every weapon in his arsenal. We need Mashiach right away to save us from further deterioration.

Our holy sages explain that the war before the coming of Mashiach will not be a mere physical battle, but also a battle of *emunah*.[94] There will be confusion and turmoil. It is our very faith in Hashem that will be tested.

Yet, the time of Mashiach is the time when Hashem's true unity will be revealed. The purpose of creation is Mashiach. The Torah is the blueprint of creation and therefore Mashiach is in everything that was created. *Emunah* means internalizing that we live in a world on the crux of revealing Mashiach and thus reaching its ultimate goal.

The *Meor Einayim* teaches that there is a bit of Mashiach in every Jew. The more we are in touch with our inner *neshamah*, the more the coming of the Mashiach will seem a reality. The belief in the Mashiach is not merely the belief in the possibility of his arrival, but rather the knowledge that he **is** coming. Our duty is to have *emunah shleimah* (complete faith) that the world cannot exist without Mashiach and that he **must** come.

In order to hasten the Mashiach's arrival, each and every one of us should strive to look at the world through "*geulah*" lenses. We can actively do so by

In memory of Aryeh Leib ben Shepsel z'l (22 Elul) Dedicated lovingly by the Berenstein Family

---

94   *Metzudas David* in his commentary on *Zechariah* 9:10.

learning in depth about the *geulah* and Mashiach. We can also recognize the daily opportunities to bring G-dliness into the world.

This may include going beyond our natural tendencies of giving to others. Or it may mean not holding a grudge toward someone who you ordinarily would have done so. Or it could include spending extra time thinking about those less fortunate than us, really feeling how difficult it must be for that person sitting in the hospital and davening with the same heartfelt *kavanah* for them as for ourselves, were we in need.

GETTING PRACTICAL

Mashiach is coming. We can hasten this process by rolling up our sleeves and bringing G-dliness into the world.

A central idea in *Yiddishkeit* is that there is purpose to all that happens in our lives. Whatever we choose matters to Him and has profound meaning and effect on the entire creation. However, at times we may find ourselves asking, "Why me"?

In this world, there are no clear answers to this question. Asking "Why?" places us in denial of the true reality of life. It demonstrates a distorted view of life such that we think that we are in control or can understand the full picture.

However painful it may seem, we ought to submit and fully accept the will of Hashem. We can pray, "Please Hashem make my will to do Your will." The concept of submission of our will to Hashem's will requires *mesirus nefesh* (self-sacrifice). For instance, some *mitzvos* may be extremely difficult for us to perform, but we carry them out because we honor HaKadosh Baruch Hu and wish to cleave to Him through them.

We have G-dliness in each of us. Therefore let us believe in ourselves and the lofty heights that we can reach. What a gift to be created in the image of Hashem! Each of us houses within us a reflected piece of Hashem. Therefore, we must believe in our self-worth as much as we believe in Him. We have Divine worth but need to work to bring it forth. Yet, with all of our endless potential, we are just human. We are finite beings placed in this world to learn and experience. Growth is dependent on our ability to forgive and be tolerant of ourselves — and others.

The Borei Olam cares and loves us. He walks with us through life; through our ups and downs. He delights in our desire to attach ourselves to Him because He knows it is the ultimate pleasure. We can replace the question "Why me?" with the thought, "You believe in me and know that I can handle this. Stay with me and never let me go!"

GETTING PRACTICAL

Our finite intellect cannot grasp infinite wisdom. Asking "Why?" only serves to further distance ourselves from acceptance and brings us to doubt Hashem's direct providence on life. Let us reach within to find Hashem's love and care as a Father to His child. Emunah is the answer to all of life's questions.

I Have No Time! |

Time is both a privilege and a responsibility. Time is a privilege in the sense that it is a commodity to be cherished and not taken for granted. Time is a responsibility because we are accountable for the way that we spend it, benefit from it and use it to assist others.

Time teaches us patience. Can we wait to see what will evolve through time or are we in such a rush to get immediate results? Unfortunately, when we identify with the term "time," we may zoom into the future and forget the "now." Some of us feel uncomfortable in the present because we want — or feel an obligation — to be somewhere or someplace else. However, Hashem has gifted us with each moment and we are therefore obligated to live in the present time frame and deal with what we are doing and where we are right now.

We only have now. If we spend our present time fretting about other things we either should have done or should be doing, we are not giving our full attention to what Hashem wants us to do right now. This is essentially the *yetzer hara* working to prevent us from getting things done. So let's ask ourselves, where are we right now? Can we focus just on today... or on this moment?

The famous saying "I have no time" is a figment of our imagination because we actually create time by dedicating it to what is important to us. If something is urgent enough, we would do it straight away. Time is something we use to prioritize what we view as important. After all, if we had to go to the doctor we would certainly find the time to do so.

Even if we failed to make the right choices in the past, we have been granted the present moment to do *teshuvah* and begin again. In the blessings before *Shema* we recite, "*Mechadesh b'chol yom tamid maaseh Bereishis...*" Just as Hashem recreates the world anew every moment, so do we have a chance to start afresh every moment. Our pasts do not need to dictate our futures. For instance, if until now our spouses, children, family and friends have only seen our backs because we have not had the time to make eye contact with them, we can begin to do so right now... because we have "now."

Emunah is intertwined in the concept of time. A common scenario which happens in most of our lives is when we attempt to create time to do *chesed*, go to a *shiur*, attend a *simchah*, etc. It may happen that our plans do not come about after we exerted genuine effort in trying to do so. We need to accept that this is precisely the way the Borei Olam willed for it to be.

The priorities we set create the structure for our personal time management. Making time to strengthen our *emunah* is of great importance and should be incorporated into our daily schedule.

GETTING PRACTICAL

Time management has become a challenge for many of us in our generation. Our minds are time and again looking back to the past or toward the future. Relish in the moment right now and you will see what a "present" it truly is.

Working on Our Middos

It is difficult for *tzaddikim* — let alone us — to judge objectively our own spiritual *madreigah* (level) unless we are immersed in our *avodas Hashem*. The harder we work to change our *middos* (character traits), the more we are capable of understanding our own spiritual selves.

Avodas Hashem involves work and struggle to establish a bond with HaKadosh Baruch Hu. During this contemplative process, we may discover how dependent we are on Hashem for everything. We may even begin to experience a sense of helplessness because we are letting go of our own perceived power over situations. Yet, this helplessness is a great step in our spiritual path for it is humbling and ideally will lead us to seek *rachamim* from Hashem from the depths of our being. Our heart may begin to soften, and from this state of weakness we can emerge strong and optimistic.

This new perspective can only eventuate as a result of hard work and *siyata diShmaya*. To reach such a level, we ought to put in effort of the heart. We should beseech Hashem and plead with Him to help us improve our *middos* and thus change our ways. *B'ezras Hashem* this heartfelt prayer will open up the channels from Above and lead to success. However, we must remember that we cannot achieve anything without Hashem's will.

As we begin to see a change in ourselves, we experience great joy. There is no greater pleasure than knowing we have worked hard on ourselves in the right direction and brought ourselves closer to Hashem as a result. This joy is a genuine happiness that comes from well-deserved hard work and a resulting feeling of the honor of serving HaKadosh Baruch Hu. On this level, the greatest effort we expend feels sweet and enjoyable.

Emunah can then begin to saturate every thought and action. This level of *emunah* originates from a renewed perspective on the way we look at ourselves. Through the light of truth, we can now see ourselves as a vessel in Hashem's hands. Gradually, we begin to witness that nothing exists other than Hashem's will. This process is part and parcel of our lifelong journey for spiritual growth.

GETTING PRACTICAL

We all have a tendency to see things subjectively, including our own middos. However, spiritual growth is primarily dependent on honesty and objectivity. To achieve this, we are in need of G-dly vision and perspective. Let us use our prayers to ask Hashem to help us see ourselves clearly so we celebrate our strengths yet work to improve our weaknesses.

Shabbos Nourishment

Shabbos is the source of nourishment from which we draw strength for the rest of the week. On Shabbos we are commanded to withhold from creating. Why? Because on Shabbos we are required to avoid the physical and material spheres, and thus should not involve ourselves with physically creative activity.

All week long, we are heavily involved in our physical existence. On Shabbos, we let go of our constant thoughts and actions which connect us to our bodily existence. Instead, we focus on the spiritual. We thus become better attuned to the needs of our *neshamah* when we stop being enslaved by our material side.

However, in actuality we do not avoid the physical on Shabbos. Rather, through the physical act of preparing ourselves to enter the holy day of Shabbos, and by enjoying the physical pleasures of food, beauty and order we transform the ordinary into *kedushah*. Consequently, all the physical *oneg* (pleasure) that we involve ourselves with even on Shabbos becomes spiritual in nature and is no longer weighed heavily in its material form.

Our superficial life of the workweek is compared to a spiritual death which numbs our spiritual senses and needs to be renewed and brought back to life on *Shabbos Kodesh*. How is this done? An interesting lesson is learned when we take the letters *lamed* (30) and *tes* (9), which represent the *lamed tes melachos* (thirty-nine prohibited creative acts on Shabbos) and change their order to *tes* and then *lamed*, forming the word *tal* (dew). On Shabbos, the mundane and materiality many of us are immersed in during the week

In honor of Rabbanit Oshrat Elkin Dedicated lovingly by Lenore Richter

turn into a spiritual awareness as fresh and nourishing as the dew. It is this dew that renews our purpose of living, just as it will occur at *techiyas ha'meisim* (the resurrection).

GETTING PRACTICAL

Our attachment to materiality often makes it difficult on Shabbos to separate ourselves from thoughts that relate to the physical. By restraining from the thirty-nine melachos on Shabbos, we are creating "dew" which revitalizes us for the rest of the week. Let us aim to experience the revitalizing dew of spirituality this coming Shabbos.

Confronting Life's Hardships

In *Sefer Iyov*, it is written that "Man was born to toil."[95] Our efforts and hardships in this world earn us our place in the World to Come. It is essential for each and every one of us to strengthen our *emunah*, in particular when confronting life's tests. We cannot allow inevitable difficulties to uproot our deeply ingrained faith.

The central theme in *emunah* is having courage and being prepared in advance for inevitable struggles in life. A tzaddik lives with this understanding and is thus not discouraged by life's ups and downs. Understandably, the *beinonim* (average people) in Klal Yisrael find the concept of suffering difficult to accept. This is partly due to our under-appreciation of both the reward that awaits us in the World to Come and to the value of our suffering in this world. The Torah teaches that suffering in this world has a purifying effect that maximizes our reward in the World to Come.

Though we never truly know why Hashem sets a certain path before us, understanding the meaning behind our suffering will enable us to experience it with less difficulty and more equanimity. The following are some possible reasons for our suffering:

The Gemara teaches that the foremost reason for suffering is to atone for sin.[96] Consequently, we are advised to respond to our hardships by entering into a mode of self-accounting of our deeds.

The Rambam suggests that our troubles may be due to our own carelessness such as poor eating habits, careless spending, etc.[97]

---

95   *Iyov* 5:7.
96   *Berachos* 5a.
97   In his book, *Guide to the Perplexed*, 3:12.

Trials and tribulations may also be a sort of wake-up call to deter us from continuing on our current path.[98]

Tzaddikim often suffer to atone for sins of their current generation.[99]

Suffering in this world may be a *tikkun* (repair) for certain misdeeds from a previous life.[100]

Regardless of the cause or message, hard times should stir within us humility and a clear understanding of Who is in charge. Challenges in life are tailor-made for each individual in Klal Yisrael, and are aimed to benefit him.

GETTING PRACTICAL

Accepting that there is meaning and purpose behind our suffering helps us to respond with humility to the difficulties that we endure. Think about one difficulty in your life and decide not to complain about it.

98 *Berachos* 5a.
99 *Shabbos* 32b.
100 Arizal, *Gates of Reincarnation*, 22:3.

Humility Is Genuine Perfection

A generation's uniqueness is defined by its people's ability to focus their hearts on Hashem and exclusively honor His will. Every day Hashem recreates the world and everything in it. Pondering everything that occurs in this world and analyzing how it is a reflection of Hashem's will has a profound effect on one's humbleness and *yiras Shamayim*.

As the Rambam writes, "What is the path to love and awe of the Creator? When a person contemplates Hashem's wondrous deeds and creations, he will surely see infinite wisdom within them and become filled with love of Hashem and a strong desire to praise Him and to know His Name."[101]

Wisdom only begins by recognizing our nothingness in comparison to the infinity of Hashem. Thus, this level can be achieved only if humility is brought into the picture. By working toward total nullification of one's ego, we can begin to develop ourselves spiritually. The trait of humility is fundamental because it enables a person to fulfill Hashem's will wholeheartedly, free of one's own ego.

Reb Zusha used to say, "The more we make ourselves small, the less likely that we will delude ourselves in our *avodas Hashem*." One way to achieve this end is to attach ourselves to a tzaddik. By attaching ourselves to a tzaddik we imbue ourselves with his spirit of holiness and reach even higher spiritual levels.

Chazal instructs us to stand in awe of *talmidei chachamim* (Torah scholars), just as we do in front of the Borei Olam, as they represent the epitome of living a holy Torah-filled life. This connection to a *talmid*

---

101   *Mishneh Torah, Hilchos Yesodei HaTorah* 2:2.

chacham influences us and spreads holiness in and around us. The acknowledgment of someone else's greater wisdom and *middos* is a humbling experience. However, we can only grow and be affected by this experience if we empty our ego and make room for others' wisdom and holiness to enter.

GETTING PRACTICAL

It is humbling to ponder that Hashem is everywhere and He created everything. Humility is a crucial precondition of yiras Shamayim and serving Hashem. If we are "full" of ourselves, where can Hashem reside? Think about how 'great' great people are.

Our Perceptions Are Subjective

Our perception of the world and of reality is heavily filtered by our sensations and experiences. Other people's viewpoints will appear differently because their senses and experiences are different from ours. Our perceptions are therefore subjective. Thus, two people may experience the same situation but perceive it and relate to it in two contrasting ways. One may feel entrapped in darkness, while the other may be enveloped in tremendous light.

The extent to which we come away from a situation viewing the light rather than the darkness depends on the level that we sense Hashem's hand and His goodness in it. The greater the darkness one feels, the less recognition of Hashem's Presence and His goodness. In what way can we emerge from a thick film of darkness and weakened state of *emunah*? By using our *ratzon* (willpower) to break free of our current cycle.

For instance, reading a *sefer*, listening to a *shiur* or attaching ourselves to *limud Torah* can help us perceive a tiny ray of light, a weak observation of Hashem's Presence. Gradually, through repetitious contemplation of Hashem, we can then emerge from the darkness and begin to sense the light. Ultimately, we may even reach an advanced level of *emunah* whereby we welcome the inevitable moments of darkness because we understand that it is part of a spiritual elevation process and that we cannot appreciate light unless we have experienced a comparison of the feeling of darkness.

Another important piece of advice that enables us to see through "*emunah* eyes" is learned from

In memory of
Michla Seema
bat Kalman z'l
(29 Kislev)
Dedicated
lovingly by the
Gerowitz Family

the verse, "*He'emanti ki adaber* — I believed so that I spoke."[102] Speech can uplift, encourage and benefit ourselves and others. We speak what we believe, speaking about matters of spirituality has the power to strengthen our beliefs.

GETTING PRACTICAL

Hashem's goodness is perceived as light. When we live life with clarity and sense Hashem's compassion, we are essentially feeling His loving light. Seeing life's events through "enlightened" eyes takes practice paired with a strong will to view things differently. This process will eventually leave us bathing in the warm rays of Hashem.

---

102   *Tehillim* 116:10.

Developing Gratitude

The more our souls are revealed to us the more *hakaras ha-tov* (appreciation) we feel compelled to express. The less we feel our soul's presence, the more inclined we are to feel entitled to the many gifts of life.

The person who has a weakened connection to his soul will often shy away from expressing gratitude. He may come up with ways to reduce his need to ask for favors from others, thus avoiding his sense of indebtedness. He may also downplay the significance of the kindness extended to him therefore exempting himself from feeling a sense of appreciation. Yet another hidden method that he may employ is to use money and attempt to pay someone for the favor in order to release himself from feeling obliged to the other.

What a shame that we run away from prime opportunities to celebrate the priceless *middah* of humility whenever an occasion arises. Conveying gratitude to another and undoubtedly to Hashem moves us to become more caring and less self-centered individuals.

The teaching of "*Sonei matanos yichyeh* — He who spurns gifts will live," taught in the Gemara[103] causes many to misinterpret the idea of receiving. We certainly should limit our dependence on others and attempt to carry our own weight in order to also strive to be on the giving and not receiving side of life. However, if Hashem sends us His emissaries to bestow upon us His kindness, we should not refuse their benevolence because we wish to free ourselves of the obligation to express gratitude toward them.

---

103   *Chullin* 44b.

We cannot live in this world without a certain amount of dependency on others; this would break down the social fabric and cause intense separation between us. By design, Hashem created such a world to develop our ability to appreciate and love one another — and Him of course — by uttering the two simple, powerful words, "Thank you."

GETTING PRACTICAL

The nature of man is to shun expressing thankfulness to his benefactors since this seemingly displays that he could not have survived without their help. However, it is not enough to just say, "You are so kind and nice." Let's say the words "Thank you." This conveys the message that we truly value the assistance and serves to motivate the other to do so again in the future.

Pick Up the Phone

Tefillah is like picking up the phone and dialing 1-800-Almighty. The phone number is never busy or unanswered. The number is not only available to the righteous! It is the same phone connection for everyone in Klal Yisrael. All one needs is a heart filled with desire to attach to HaKadosh Baruch Hu. Hashem wants to hear from us every day, all day long.

One reason why we seem to lack things (be it money, a spouse or whatever) is to prompt us to call out to Hashem. He wants a deep, heartfelt relationship.

Yet, how do we daven?

Do we cry out from the depths of the heart? Or, rather, are we looking to just finish davening quickly, so we can be free? If so, we need to beseech Hashem to help us change our davening approach. The idea behind our *kavanah* (intent) in *tefillah* is to feel ourselves standing in front of the Borei Olam. Do we cry out with gratitude for everything, including our troubles? R. Dessler explains that when we pray, the most important aspect is to connect with Hashem in the deepest and most intimate way. One way to connect with Him is to contemplate all of His greatness and the kindnesses He bestows on us.

Life has a way sometimes of spinning things out of control and we may be left feeling that we have no way out. Yet there is a place we can turn to — Hashem. Everything can be undone. The salvation can be orchestrated at any moment. Don't let your tears fall down to the ground. Elevate them upward; send them to Hashem.

GETTING PRACTICAL

We should examine our tefillah and see if we are davening with the correct intent. Next time we daven, let us realize the power it has to realign our soul to its mission in life and remind us that we are never alone.

The entire *Sefer Tehillim* focuses on being G-dly. Dovid HaMelech advises that the real pleasure of living is experienced by those who live in accordance to Hashem's will.

Specifically, the first *perek* of *Tehillim* begins with the concept of *ashrei* (happy). It advises that we achieve happiness by avoiding the taking of advice from scoffers, imitating their lifestyle or becoming scornful like them. What should we do instead? The second *pasuk* then tells us that we should delight in Hashem by having a strong desire for wholeheartedly committing to the Torah way of life. Thus, it is the combination of avoiding those who are disrespectful of the Torah, and following Hashem's *derech* (way) which will ultimately lead us to happiness.

The third and fourth *pesukim* of this *perek* compare a tzaddik to a fruitful tree, planted by streams of water that cause it to grow. *Chazal* teach that man is like the tree of the field, firmly rooted and made secure by living a Torah life. The *pasuk* teaches that a tzaddik yields his fruit in season. Fruit is an allegory for a tzaddik's good deeds, which benefit others. The *pesukim* then contrast the tzaddik with the wicked who disdain the Torah, considering them to be "like chaff that the wind blows away." They are the empty husks, living a fruitless existence.

The righteous are protected by Hashem's care. This protection motivates them to remain loyal to the Torah way of life. The roots of the tree may be an allegory for *emunah* because roots are buried deep in the ground, serving to keep the righteous anchored despite strong winds and storms. The sap of a tree is its nourishment, which may be an allegory for nurturing the righteous person's steadfast faith and trust that Hashem will always take care of him.

GETTING PRACTICAL

This perek focuses on the importance of living by Torah values; it is likened to the lush greenery of a growing tree. Embracing Hashem's will as our own provides us with the necessary nutrients to live joyfully. Let us learn from the specific instructions on how to avoid negative spiritual influences and live as a righteous person.

The holiness of Shabbos connects us to something timeless. Just as Hashem is beyond time and space and not bound by finite rules, so too when we attach ourselves to Shabbos we are ultimately connected to endless and unworldly boundaries.

We may not be aware of the exalted spiritual transformation that occurs within each of us on Shabbos. Yet we actually receive a new vitality, a deep awakening of the spiritual senses that are often deadened by the mundane activities of the working week. On Shabbos, we experience *shleimus* (completeness) — derived from the root of the Hebrew word *shalom*. *Shalem* is a state of true perfection and wholeness.

Hashem is always present with us. However, during the week, His miraculous Presence is generally hidden under the guise of nature. In contrast, on Shabbos our soul level of consciousness is deepened. We experience a renewed perception of Hashem's Presence. Our mind becomes receptive to the *emes* of our purpose of existence and creation.

In total, our week is made up of both mundane working days and the holy Shabbos. Similarly, our bodies are comprised of mundane physical bodies and our holy *neshamah*. Our task is to infuse the two together, while allowing the holy side to have the upper hand. In other words, we should strive for our soul to govern our body and elevate Shabbos over the working week, and yet for both to co-exist in harmony.

Ironically, on Shabbos, our physical body is the very vehicle which we can use to gain a higher awareness of our spiritual soul! Instead of denying the physical, we can use our physical senses as a vehicle

In honor of Tzvi Hirsh ben Koppel z'l (2 Elul) Dedicated lovingly by Chaya Edelson

through which we can peel the outer body or husk away to reveal the fruit of our being — the sweet spiritual layer lying deep within.

GETTING PRACTICAL

We can become more attuned to the outpouring of spirituality on Shabbos. When lighting the Shabbos candles let us think about how we are being directed to a greater infinite light that will illuminate our path to completeness, where nothing is lacking. This spiritual revitalization can then spill over into the entire working week.

How to Attach Ourselves to the Tzaddik (Part I)

When we daven to the Borei Olam and make every effort to beseech His eternal compassion, our prayers are more likely to be answered for the very best if we are able to invoke *rachamei Shamayim*. One way of connecting to Hashem and achieving Hashem's mercy is by relying on the virtue of *tzaddikim*.

Many people pray in the merit of *tzaddikim*. This requires recognition that we have no personal merits upon which to rely. The more we believe in the worth of *tzaddikim* and attach ourselves to them through our thoughts and feelings, the more we will truly connect and awaken Hashem's *rachamim* in their *zechus* (merit).

One of the important effects of bonding to *tzaddikim* is the arousal of feelings of humility and an inspiration to turn to HaKadosh Baruch Hu in *teshuvah*. Our recognition of the holiness and purity of *tzaddikim*, and our shame over our own comparatively low level due to our many transgressions, can serve to make our prayers more likely to be accepted. We may feel our smallness next to their greatness and a lowering of ourselves in their presence. This aids to crush our egos and stirs an overwhelming feeling of awe. This evocation of nothingness may lead to a feeling of shame in the presence of Hashem's greatness and ideally inspire our *teshuvah*.

Our *emunah* may be strengthened when we visit the graves of *tzaddikim*, mention their holy names or light a candle in their memory. Such actions may serve to remind us of the importance of living a life of righteousness. We can strive to emulate the *tzaddikim*'s G-dliness by contemplating their ways and the Torah inheritance they left behind.

GETTING PRACTICAL _____

Hashem has given us a priceless gift in the form of the zechus of holy tzaddikim. We can pray in their merit to invoke humility in ourselves, inspire teshuvah, strengthen our emunah and ideally invoke rachamei Shamayim. How can you connect to a tzaddik?

How to Attach Ourselves to the Tzaddik (Part II)

When the soul departs from the body and returns back to its source, it enters a pure, spiritual state. One possible benefit of attaching our prayers to a *tzaddik* who has passed is that they may ascend to the higher planes as the soul of the *tzaddik* rises to the upper realms. We may then be gifted with the privilege of our prayers being delivered by the *tzaddik* before the Holy court.

Another possible benefit of davening in the merit of a *tzaddik* is being granted spiritual insights which enable us greater clarity in comprehending and accepting our difficulties. The extent to which we obtain this benefit depends on the extent of the connection and closeness we share with the *tzaddik*. The grander the arousal of abundant love and submission, the more we can draw down *siyata diShmaya* (Divine assistance). By clinging and connecting to the holy words and teachings of the *tzaddik*, we can capture the radiance of the *tzaddik*'s love and fear of Hashem.

When visiting the holy resting places of the *tzaddikim*, we may also be filled with a sense of *emunah*, which in turn may lead to a state of self-nullification. It may help us give over our entire being and pour out our words before Hashem from the depths of our heart. We may feel remorse over our enormous distance from HaKadosh Baruch Hu.

In a sense, this process may become circular because once we concentrate our thoughts on *teshuvah*, the love and fear generated in our hearts may also cause the *tzaddik*'s soul to be stirred. After visiting the *tzaddik*'s gravesite, we may consequently experience a new life from the light of the *tzaddik's* Torah and *avodah*. This occurs due to the aura of Gan Eden that encircles his place of burial.

GETTING PRACTICAL

Chassidus teaches that when a tzaddik passes he becomes more powerful in a spiritual sense, and thus more able to affect changes in this world than when he was alive. We should take advantage of any opportunity to pray at a tzaddik's grave and obtain the numerous consequential benefits of doing so.

G-d or Nature?

Divine decrees govern everything that transpires. Strong or weak, clever or foolish, rich or poor, the character of our soul and our physical appearance — it is all solely governed by Hashem. There is no other power or force that can affect our lot. For instance, if Hashem decides that something good should happen to a person, He orchestrates nature in such a way that this event happens. If harm is meant to come one's way, *chas v'shalom*, there are countless ways for Him to have it carried out. As we know, "*Harbei shluchim yesh la'Makom* — Hashem has many messengers [at His disposal]."[104]

Hashem runs the world with justice disguised into nature. Hashem gives us the right amount of space that we need so we can feel independent. But Hashem is always there. We are the ones who need to choose to look for Him and build a relationship with Him. The greatest challenge is to totally accept that Hashem's guidance is the only directive in man's life.

However, if one chooses to believe that only natural occurrences govern his life, HaKadosh Baruch Hu hands that person over to nature and allows nature to take over. Belief in chance distances us from Hashem. In turn, He will distance Himself from us.

What about Mother Nature? To bring clarity to this subject, let us begin by saying that nature is not our mother but only a method which Hashem chooses to use when He wishes to hide His intervention. Everything is from Hashem, however when we choose to think that nature is an independent entity that exists, Hashem allows Mother Nature to be His agent as opposed to Him directly guiding our way.

---

104 *Bamidbar Rabbah* 18:18.

Hashem's ways are always just, whether we merit understanding them or not. It is necessary to constantly remind ourselves that every creature and action in this world is governed by *hashgachah pratis* (Divine providence). There is no such thing as happenstance. Am Yisrael is above the *mazal* and we are personally led "hand-in-hand" by HaKadosh Baruch Hu through every circumstance.

GETTING PRACTICAL

Hashem governs every single thing that happens in the world and in our lives. If we choose to believe in the physical, financial and other laws of nature instead of Him, He distances Himself from us and lets nature take its course. Let's take on the challenge of finding hashgachah pratis and Hashem's hand in even seemingly "natural" events, until it becomes "natural" to do so.

Free to Do What We Want Any Old Time

We all have free will. Before a *neshamah* descends into this world, Hashem does not predetermine whether it will be righteous or wicked. Rather, Hashem grants us freedom to choose our actions and we are held accountable for the outcome of our choices. Consequently, choosing to sin is voluntary and if we do so we should repent and do *teshuvah*. As is taught in *Pirkei Avos*, "Everything is foreseen, yet free will is given. The world is judged with goodness, and all is according to the majority of deeds."[105]

Although Hashem's knowledge is not known to us and therefore does not affect our ability to choose, in some way beyond human understanding, HaKadosh Baruch Hu knows what we will choose in advance. Our finite minds cannot perceive the Infinite and how the Borei Olam has the knowledge of the future, yet leaves us with complete freedom of choice — but that is the case.

The purpose of the evil inclination is to provide us with opportunities to face temptations and overcome them. Through this battle, we spiritually strengthen ourselves and come one step closer to perfection. Free will can be exercised only at those points when we must make a choice between that which we imagine to be true but deep down know that it really is not.

Chazal explain how the *yetzer hara* craftily entices us to sin. The *yetzer hara* is known as "the sly one" because it deludes us into believing that Hashem accepts the fact that we sin. Yet, transgressing

---

105   3:19a.

HaKadosh Baruch Hu's will causes the lower levels of our *neshamah* to disconnect and distance from Him. Not only could this leave us exposed to the winds of chance, detachment from the Borei Olam is an unnatural state that affects us on many levels.

GETTING PRACTICAL

Hashem has gifted us with free will, though He knows in advance what path we will choose. The yetzer hara slyly convinces us that sinning will not distance us from Hashem. In truth, teshuvah is vital in order to reconnect to Him. Think about a sin you've done and how it has led you away from Hashem — and do teshuvah.

Emunah Peshutah (Simple Faithfulness)

"Many are the mishaps of the righteous, but from them all the Eternal rescues him. He guards all his bones; not one of them was broken."[106]

This *pasuk* can refer to *tzaddikim* who undergo misfortunes. Their trust in HaKadosh Baruch is so strong they need no explanation for any misfortune that befalls them. A *tzaddik* doesn't view anything in life as a mishap, but as being part and pair with Hashem's *hashgachah pratis* (Divine plan). This is called *emunah peshutah*, simple and innocent faithfulness. Their view is everything that happens is a result of Hashem's design and plan for creation. There is no happenstance. This is pure and simple *emunah*, not asking questions but accepting Hashem's decrees as being brought to us from the very best place.

Tzaddikim see themselves with no merits and are instead beseeching *rachamei Shamayim.* Their mouth speaks words of constant praise, thanking Hashem for all He does for them and praying for *siyata diShmaya,* Heavenly assistance.

In order to practice *emunah peshutah*, we need to nullify our ego. Discarding our self-interest grants us more success. The greater space we leave within (the more we empty ourselves of self), the more fitting we become for Hashem's light and blessings to shine upon us.

We need to rely on Hashem's past track record that He does everything for the best — for our ultimate best. *Emunah peshutah* comes from our hearts,

---

106   *Tehillim* 34:20–21.

In memory of Osnat bat Carmela z'l (29 Kislev)

not our heads, and directs our actions to be in sync with Hashem's will because our hearts know that He loves us — more than we can ever imagine!

GETTING PRACTICAL _____

Practice living with emunah peshutah in Hashem. Westernized sense of reason should not be the dictate of what makes sense. Accept that everything that happens is because of Hashem's will and that Hashem is perfectly good.

We Have Been Bribed!

There is a famous Torah saying, *"Shochad misan-ver einei chachamim* — Bribery blinds the eyes of the wise."[107] There are a few questions and insights that need to be addressed from this axiom.

1. What is bribery?

2. How can it blind the eyes of even the wise?

3. What is the consequence to enticement?

Bribery comes in various forms. In today's generation, bribery is masked in *gashmiyus,* materialism and physicality. The world offers us an exciting, colorful display of "worldly toys." Toys, you may say, are children's play. Correct, but many of us are children in adult's attire.

The latest electronic device, the trendy car, the expansive home, clothing and then some, a gadget to help us "save time," etc... These are but a few examples. You may ask, "What is wrong with wanting and/or owning some of these?"

Nothing, if you are not enthralled with having them. Everything, if you are.

The lure of material luxuries blinds us. They create diversions in our desire to live a life of meaning. In essence, they are band-aids that we shop for to cover our wounded heart that cannot find happiness and meaning. However, they are the wrong shape and size and will never adequately cover the boo-boo.

The only solution toward living a life of purpose is to reveal Hashem's purpose in placing us in this world. The *yetzer hara* does not want us to

---

107   *Devarim* 16:19.

stop and think. It encourages us to keep running the rat race of life so as not to pause and think about our existence. Why am I here? What am I supposed to accomplish?

The pursuit itself of materialism is the bribery in today's generation. The need to purchase unnecessary things[108] connects us to this world and distances us from Hashem. How does going to the mall and buying a shirt that I really want do that? Read on.

GETTING PRACTICAL

Take a deep look at your life and decide which of yours toys is unnecessary. What do you "need" and what do you "want"? There is a world of a difference between the two.

---

108   The definition of "unnecessary" will be discussed at a later point.

Charge Your Spiritual Energy on Shabbos

Do we live with an intense yearning to come close to Hashem?

While our soul yearns to cleave to Hashem, the physical world often acts as a barrier to achieving our soul's goal. Hashem therefore created Shabbos, a day of holiness which acts as a bridge between *chol* (mundane) and *kodesh* (holy). Attaching to Shabbos enables us to connect to HaKadosh Baruch Hu in this world since we are able to elevate the pleasures of this worldly dwelling in His holy Presence without any outside distractions.

With Shabbos being the center of Jewish life our home serves as a *chupah*, a wedding canopy. The decorating of our home with flowers, fine china and delicious food is part of the wedding reception. We light the candles eighteen minutes before sundown, and thus steep our homes with 'life' ('*chai*'), whose numerical value is 18. Shabbos is the time for the renewal of our *neshamos* — a giving of new life — which we are gifted with every week.

The *Me'or Einayim*, R. Menachem Nachum of Tchernoble explains that wherever there is *chillul Hashem* (desecration of Hashem's name), Hashem removes His Presence. The Jewish nation is a light unto nations and thus is obligated to fulfill the will of their Creator and be loyal to His commandments. One example of a *chillul Hashem* would be the failure to properly honor Shabbos.

Consequently, if Shabbos is not honored to its fullest, Hashem will withdraw His Presence, that is, His life-force. Since the influx of spiritual light we

In memory of Moshe ben Esther z'l (4 Kislev) Dedicated lovingly by the Hayon Family

receive on *Shabbos Kodesh* serves as a recharger for the entire working week, by us missing our weekly charge, we might find ourselves without vitality, feeling empty and lifeless for the rest of the week.

Honoring Shabbos creates an intimate bond between us and Hashem. The sense of distance that we experience due to the rat race of life thus lessens and we are able to feel so much closer to Hashem. Keeping Shabbos gifts us with spiritual sensitivity. Subsequently, our soul is revived and better equipped to face life's challenges.

GETTING PRACTICAL

Shabbos provides us with a special opportunity to enable our soul to cleave to Hashem. We cannot afford to miss out on this priceless opportunity to live with the revitalizing spiritual energy bestowed upon us every Shabbos. Let's take advantage and get our weekly spiritual injection.

Remove Our Ego, Feel Hashem

Contrary to popular perception, *emunah* is not blind faith. Actually, it is the opposite — *emunah* is defined as a clear perception of Hashem's existence. Our *neshamos* are actually *chelek Eloka* (a piece of HaKadosh Baruch Hu) and are always mindful of Hashem's Presence on some level. This *emunah* knowledge can buoy us with a feeling of strength, a link to eternity.

Why do most of us not consciously feel Hashem's Presence?

For some, it may be because we do not realize what we are missing so we do not start searching.

For those that do search but fail, the answer may lie in the purity of our yearning. If we are filled with self-centeredness (i.e., full of ourselves), we will be unable to allow Hashem's light into our consciousness. As R. Aryeh Nivin says, "ego" stands for "edging G-d out."

In other words, our need to seek physical pleasure in this world stems from our ego, which interferes with access to the Divine. *Chazal* teach us that through the process of selflessness, we will be able to open up our perception of the spiritual world beyond us. Without the distractions of this world, the spiritual world would open us up to feel Hashem clearly.

We can initiate this place of connection to Hashem by using our will to surrender our desires, and instead place Hashem's will above our own. This is called "*emunah* above reason." It requires a conditioning of the mind — to give ourselves to Hashem as a spiritual vessel which He can fill with G-dly sensitivity.

The way to expand our spiritual vessel is by overcoming the various hindrances that are placed before us. We all face numerous struggles which serve as distractions and may cause us to doubt our belief in Hashem. However, before the distraction arises, we need to deeply internalize the eternal truth that Hashem is in control and is enacting all events for our very best. If we understand and accept this truth deep inside, we can hold onto our *emunah* in times of trouble and may be able to enter a spiritual reality that was not known to us before.

GETTING PRACTICAL

The greatest concealment we sense in our relationship with Hashem is essentially created by us — in man's heart. The more we focus on "I" the less we see Hashem and the opposite. Let us teach the "I" that it needs Hashem and then its false sense of independence will cease to exist.

The road of life is often painful, tangled with hardships and disappointment. Nevertheless, let us internalize what is taught in the Midrash; there is "cause and effect" to every thought, speech and action.

In the *sefer Mesillas Yesharim* (*The Path of the Just*), the holy Ramchal teaches that "man has been put into a fierce battle. Whether good or bad, everything in the world is a test."[109] From this we can learn that life is full of difficulties that must be confronted. This is part and parcel of the Divine design. When faced with such challenges, we will be less likely to fall and lose balance if we adequately prepare by acknowledging that this is the path of life.

Though this may be uncomfortable to admit, facing this truth will help us understand that we may be the root cause of the problem, but that we can also help to fix it. On a certain level, our struggles can often be seen as a mirror image of our behavior toward Hashem. The Baal Shem Tov underlines this idea by teaching us that if a person looks closely at his difficulties in life he may be able to uncover a hint as to what *middos* (character attributes) might need improvement.

Therefore, we are required to always examine our deeds and seek to improve our *middos*. For instance, in the *sefer Shomer Emunim*, R. Yosef Irgas teaches us that if a person has sinned through his actions, his possessions may cause him suffering. If he has committed sins connected to his speech, others may speak ill of him. If he has contemplated sinful

Refuah shleimah to Aharon ben Henya Hadassah Dedicated lovingly by Amanda Goldman

---

109   Ch. 1.

thoughts, he will suffer through his children.[110] All occurrences are measure for measure.

Suffering may be incurred due to our weakened grasp of Hashem, which leads to the trials and tribulations that come our way. However, no matter how miserable the situation appears, Hashem instructs us that we are to maintain *emunah* that all is for the best.

In *Mishlei*, the *pasuk*, "*Eitz chaim hi la'machzikim bah* — It is a tree of life to all who grasp it,"[111] reveals the importance of holding onto Hashem. Hashem truly desires that we not sin in the first place. However, if we do sin, Hashem wants us to do *teshuvah*.

GETTING PRACTICAL

Our difficulties and challenges in life are often tests. Hashem interacts with creation measure for measure, just as a mirror reflects one's image. Therefore, just as we display steadfast unwavering emunah in Hashem, no matter what happens and seemingly beyond reason, so will He — measure for measure — go beyond logical and rational means to aide us through our difficulties. Think of a difficulty you are experiencing now, and trust Him.

---

110 *Ma'amar Hashgachah Pratis*, ch. 9.
111 3:17.

When we take a sincere look at life we may find that the central (yet perhaps subconscious) focal question of every decision we make is, "How much will I gain from this?" Many of us often erroneously assume that this world is our world and thus view everything from a "me" perspective. Hashem organized the world with this perspective as it is part of granting us free will.

Sacrificing our conveniences for the sake of benevolence is a lifelong battle, especially when the secular world feeds us a very different message. We are often programmed to seek out our own pleasures and occupy ourselves with our own interests.

However, this approach to life distances us from being givers because much of our motivation lies merely in meeting our own needs and wants. The challenge is to exert continuous effort and attempt to overthrow this selfish perspective, instead seeing the world through giving eyes. If we emulate Hashem in this important *middah* of *chesed,* we will begin to see Him more clearly in our daily lives.

How do we accomplish this lofty task? Daven — talk to Hashem and ask for His help. As in every aspect of life, we can first beseech Hashem and then physically act. This two-step process builds a vessel into which Hashem pours His Presence. It creates a partnership with Him which is more likely to lead to success.

To successfully be givers it is important to invest our energy on emotionally loving ourselves enough to ensure that we do not feel cheated or deprived when giving. Givers are not losers. In fact, they are winners

In memory of Moshe ben Neima (16 Sivan)

for they gain much more than they give. Givers gain a life bejeweled with purpose — strong enough to feel safe and healthy within themselves, and also by making a difference to others.

GETTING PRACTICAL

In order to give to others with a full heart, it is vital to work on feeding ourselves with love, recognizing our self-value and actualizing our potential. It is also important to realize that givers are winners because we gain a feeling of self-worth by realizing the difference we can make in other peoples' lives. See how you feel next time you give and experience the emotional uplift.

A New Vision

Living life mindfully (aware of what is happening around and within us) is certainly of important value to increasing our *emunah*; a big stepping stone. As we work our way to reaching a newfound expanded awareness, our minds quite naturally becomes attuned to a new way of thinking that never was before.

We begin seeing Hashem in places, people, objects and events, and a new vision of life begins to emerge seemingly out of nowhere. In spite of the fact that emotional work may require strength and effort, be assured that the outcome is irreplaceable — a polished point of view on life.

The goal in learning the significant value of living life awake and in tune with the world within is intended to transform our way of thinking on a deep, pure level. This delightful way of living brings with it a new experience when reciting the *berachah*, "*Baruch Atah Hashem...* — Blessed are You Hashem." We sense Hashem, Whose honor fills the world, even more closely.

Yes, this sounds like an unattainable level, but with *ratzon* (will) and practice this will naturally occur. Through the daily exercise of becoming cognizant of the messages in life, our physical eyes begin to see as our soul does. The soul indeed sees Hashem in everything but our bodies impede us from tapping into this lofty vision.

Being aware of Hashem's Presence in our lives exchanges our confused reality to a clearly painted, truthful reality. How can it not when the soul is at the forefront? Think of it as a spiritual GPS — if we turn it on we will hear the GPS voice talking to us when we take a wrong turn. We can then become aware of when Hashem is re-routing us to travel on the right pathway. It is all in the reception waves and whether we hear them clearly.

GETTING PRACTICAL

Today let us start to notice the small things in life and the way that Hashem is intimately involved in it all. Practice seeing Hashem in everything and everywhere; living in this mindset leads us to live in the truthful reality of "Ein Od Milvado — There is nothing else but Him (Hashem)."

Hashem Is Everywhere

Our higher soul yearns to cleave to Hashem, a world bursting with pleasure and without suffering. However, as soon as our *neshamos* are placed into this world, we immediately stop recognizing HaKadosh Baruch Hu. This lack of awareness creates free will, providing a choice as to whether we seek Hashem in every occurrence. Though tempting, choosing to hide ourselves from His Presence is an illusion since there is no place devoid of Hashem. The challenge to see HaKadosh Baruch Hu in spite of the (false) perception that He is not with us allows us to earn eternal reward and to bask in His Presence in *Olam Haba* (the World to Come).

At times, Hashem does gift us with an awareness of His Presence in order to reassure us that He *is* truly right here with us. In this world, the immediate reward of perceiving HaKadosh Baruch Hu is a unique feeling of calm and tranquility.

There are different methods to achieve this goal of tranquility stemming from feeling Hashem's Presence. One way to enter this state of awareness is to emulate Hashem's *middos* (character traits). The extent to which we are able emulate Hashem's *middos* is the extent to which we are able to feel His nearness.

Another way to experience inner calm is to delve into the understanding and purpose of life's challenges. By deeply comprehending the idea that difficulties wake us up from our spiritual slumber, promote self-analysis and improvement and lead us to embark on a new journey of *teshuvah*, we can spiritually elevate ourselves and develop *yishuv ha-da'as* (clarity; lit., stillness of mind).

In memory of Tova bat Avraham Moshe HaKohen z'l Dedicated lovingly by the Ledder Family

Though we would prefer not to endure hardships, it is often these challenges that drive us to the path of *teshuvah* which we may have otherwise avoided. As human beings, we naturally gravitate toward physical delights. In order to prompt our spiritual growth, Hashem must sometimes diminish our material blessings and thereby motivate us to change our direction.

When we readily feel Hashem close to us, we will cease to choose any other way of living since we have crossed the threshold into *emes* — that is, the truthful reality of Hashem. In a sense, we thus lose our free will because as soon as we readily feel Hashem, there is little choice but to make decisions which bring us closer to Him.

GETTING PRACTICAL _____

Hashem's nearness envelops us with inner serenity. Next time you find yourself in a place of distress, close your eyes and remember that you are not alone. Hashem is everywhere you invite Him in.

Hashem Wants the Heart

The Talmud teaches that *"Rachmana leebah bah'ay —* Hashem wants the heart."[112] Torah learning is the highest of the high and performance of *mitzvos* is vital. However, Hashem wants our hearts to fully belong to Him.

The essence of our *avodas Hashem* concerns working on our hearts. What are the true intentions behind our actions? The reason that it is so crucial that our heart's intentions be pure is because the heart directs all body parts and is thus called the "king of all bodily organs." When our hearts are spiritually healthy, we are then able to bond with Hashem which in turn cleanses our hearts even more.

However, this heart purification process involves a number of steps. First, we need to have a profound desire to cleave to Hashem. By jam-packing our heart with yearnings to connect to HaKadosh Baruch Hu, there will be no space for any interferences or distractions to enter and contaminate it. We are showing Hashem we want to connect with Him, that this is our ultimate goal and desire.

Second, we should put in the hard work to connect to Him. Refining our heart requires tireless and continuous effort. There will be obstacles that arise during this lifetime *avodah* (work), including internal conflicts between material and spiritual pursuits. However, this is actually a good indicator that we are on the right track — it symbolizes the *yetzer hara*'s 'give it all' fight to prevent us reaching the ultimate goal in life. It is not going to give up easily, and neither should we.

Hashem wants us to prove how much we really want this closeness to Him. The closer we get to

---

112 *Sanhedrin* 106b.

reaching a purer heart, the more intense the outside interferences become. At this point we can remember the teaching in *Pirkei Avos*, "*Lefum tzara agra* — according to the effort is the reward."[113] The degree that we strive and work to overcome the obstacles is the degree to which we will feel the reward.

In response to our efforts, Hashem will reveal Himself to us and essentially make it easier for us to overcome the worldly distractions by enabling us to feel His closeness. The distractions will not go away. But rather, we will find that our thoughts and actions will be conducted with inner composure and happiness. We will become more in-tune with ourselves and our mission. We will be able to enjoy life simply because we have transformed our selfishness to selflessness. Just as the Borei Olam created this world to bestow pleasure upon us, we will grow accustomed to bestowing goodness to others and in so doing, emulate Him in the greatest way.

If we continually work at elevating our spiritual side, we will ultimately be gifted with immense joy that stems from an open heart. We will have acclimated ourselves to the purpose of creation. It will not feel like a burden or a sacrifice to leave our worldly priorities behind, since we will have attained *da'as* (spiritual knowledge) and will thus not feel we are missing out in any way.

GETTING PRACTICAL

Once we fill our hearts with a desire to seek Hashem, and work hard at this relationship despite interferences, we will be blessed with a feeling of closeness to Hashem. That makes it easier to continue along this path in the future.

---

113   5:27.

The Rambam writes, "A person should love Hashem with a very great love until his soul is bound up in the love of Him."[114]

When two people are very close, it may be possible for them to communicate just by gazing into each other's eyes. Israel is likened to an *eishes chayil*, a woman of valor, and HaKadosh Baruch Hu to her husband. Shabbos brings us closer to Hashem, and returns us to the time of that holy meeting at Har Sinai where we as the Jewish people understood and knew precisely what Hashem expected of us. We passionately awaited the opportunity to follow His will.

A passionate longing to attach ourselves to Hashem is otherwise known as *d'veikus* (bonding). *D'veikus* on Shabbos results from intensive preparation invested throughout the week. On Shabbos, we cleave to the source of all good in its original form. Hashem's love is revealed in its entirety and any walls of separation between Him and us are broken down. On Shabbos, we should delight in drawing close to Hashem. On Shabbos, we become again united with the Borei Olam. On Shabbos, we merit to dwell in Hashem's palace.

Do we stand in bitterness and sorrow over the distance between us and Hashem during the week? If so, be assured that this sorrow is beloved to HaKadosh Baruch Hu and we shall merit being healed by His personal closeness. During the week we are distracted by artificial pleasures and far removed from Hashem's light. Therefore, during the

---

114   *Mishneh Torah, Yesodei HaTorah*, 2:1.

*In memory of
Leah bat
Rachel z'l
Dedicated
lovingly by the
Gerowitz Family*

week we should anticipate and savor Hashem's intimate closeness that is achieved on Shabbos. This will assist us in internalizing the teaching that "Hashem, the Torah and Israel are One."

GETTING PRACTICAL

Shabbos brings us closer to Hashem. Being in love with Hashem is easily achievable on Shabbos Kodesh and undoubtedly equates with delight!

If Hashem Will Not Guard a City | DAY 119 ◄

The first *pasuk* of chapter 127 in *Tehillim* tells us, "If Hashem will not build the house, in vain do its builders labor on it; if Hashem will not guard a city, (its) watcher keeps his vigil in vain." This teaches us that despite our hard work, we labor in vain if Hashem does not desire the end result.

In the following *pasuk*, Dovid HaMelech proclaims that rising early and staying up late and depriving ourselves of rest is useless and will have no ultimate effect on the results of our actions without Hashem's help. Hashem gives to those He loves "in their sleep." On a deeper level, this phrase could be interpreted to mean the inner serenity of living a life of *emunah*. Those who do not overly involve themselves in their *hishtadlus* but rather recognize that Hashem alone is responsible for any results are exercising true *emunah*, casting all anxieties onto HaKadosh Baruch Hu and leaving it to Him to grant what He thinks is necessary for their benefit.

An even deeper insight into this *perek* may suggest that as mere mortals in this world, we are not able to judge what is appropriate for us at a given time. Hashem often blesses us in very different or unpredictable ways. Thus, success lies not in our own hands, but only if and when our involvement is an extension of *emunah*.

For those whose foundation of life is *emunah* and attachment to HaKadosh Baruch Hu, the third *pasuk* points out, "Behold, the heritage of Hashem is sons, the reward is the fruit of the innards." Thus, His beloved ones are rewarded with the fruit of the Torah that is planted in their hearts and into their children's hearts. This is the inheritance that we are granted, after 120 years.

In the fourth *pasuk*, Dovid HaMelech states, "Like arrows in the hand of a mighty man, so are the sons of one's youth." Primarily offensive weapons intended to hit their target, arrows are carefully prepared and tested before they are placed. Those who have nurtured their children carefully have full confidence in their ability to fly straight and true, that is, to remain loyal to *Yiddishkeit* in the face of conflict. It is our hope that our children will defend Torah values in spite of social pressure.

The fifth *pasuk* states, "Praiseworthy is the man who has filled his quiver." We invest in our children, giving to them our energy, time and wisdom. It is our hope that just as the arrow is shot to hit a long-range target, so too our children will serve to carry out Torah values until the coming of Mashiach, Amen!

GETTING PRACTICAL

We exert great effort in building our home. It is important to "decorate" it with the finest prayers and illuminate it with exquisite Torah values. Yet, we also should request Hashem's blessing that it may be His will that our efforts merit success.

Getting to Know Hashem

Wouldn't it be special to feel close to Hashem all the time? He wants this. We want it. So why can't we? After all, our *neshamah* is G-dly and is housed right inside our heart.

The subject is very complex and deep but one reason we fail to connect is because of our intellect. Connecting to Hashem includes accepting the fact that although we comprehend an aspect of HaKadosh Baruch Hu, our finite minds cannot grasp His entire existence. Belief in Hashem thus transcends intelligence.

So how can we strengthen the connection to Hashem and thus lessen the distance? The solution is *emunah* — to train ourselves to seek out Hashem in life through those situations that seemingly just happen. We are commanded to delve into Hashem's Torah and get to know HaKadosh Baruch Hu in order to perform our *mitzvos* with greater dedication.

In the opening of his detailed work of Jewish law, *Mishneh Torah*, the Rambam writes, "The foundation of all foundations and the pillar of knowledge is to know that there is a Primary Existence who brings into being all existence."[115] We are commanded to attach ourselves to Hashem by learning from His infinite wisdom, revisiting every occurrence in our lives through the prism of acceptance and core belief that He is compassionate and good.

Thus, we do live with G-dliness inside of us always. Our *neshamah* is *chelek Eloka* — an actual part of Hashem — which is intimately bound to Him beyond intellectual understanding. But we have to

---

115   *Sefer HaMada*, ch. 1:1.

In memory of Label ben Zalman Halevi z'l (28 Tevet) Dedicated lovingly by Sora

uncover this *chelek*. We must work to suspend reality, overcome our intellect and instead trust that He loves and cares for us beyond our finite comprehension. This is our *avodah*, our regular required practice — to let go of what logic and our senses dictate and instead accept that all that He does is for our best, our eternal best.

The Torah teaches "*Karov ha-davar me'od eileichem* — It (the truth) is very near to you."[116] We can gain *chizuk* from realizing that we are natural believers. Housed within each of us, sometimes deep within, lies *emes* — the innate belief in Hashem's constant Presence that helps us forge ahead with this *avodah*. Just look within and you will find it!

GETTING PRACTICAL

We all house within us an actual piece, so to speak, of HaKadosh Baruch Hu. Yet, often we do not connect to it because this connection takes work. Let's make the effort and take the risk to overcome our intellectual resistance and reach deep inside ourselves. We will certainly have intimate access to Hashem Yisbarach, too.

---

116 *Devarim* 30:14.

Geula

Israel's Your beloved nation,
You're our King above.
Years of seeming separation
Did not affect our love…

All my days are filled with yearning
Night's a tearful song,
'Til you stop my heart from burning
Come back where You belong.

Come the day when You will face us,
And the world will see
Truth revealed as You embrace us,
The King of kings and me!

Every day feels like forever,
We'll no longer wait!
Klal Yisrael longs to be with
Her Eternal Mate.

Reveal Yourself, we've waited years!
Our lessons we did learn.
Please heal my heart and wipe our tears
I wait for Your return.

Which Level of Emunah Are You On?

"And you shall know this day and consider it in your heart that the L-rd, He is G-d in heaven above and on the earth beneath; there is no other."[117]

From this verse, *Chazal* deduce that there is a two-step process to belief in Hashem. First, we should strive to attain an intellectual belief that Hashem is the Creator of the universe. This is *emunah* of the mind. Second, we should plant this knowledge in our hearts. This is emotional, heartfelt *emunah*. This suggests that although it is necessary to do the intellectual work and understand that there is a Creator in our minds, it is not sufficient to just know He exists. We attain *emunah shleimah* (complete and pure faith) when this awareness affects our thoughts, speech and actions.

According to the Chazon Ish, there are four different levels of *emunah*: [118]

1. The lowest level is merely an intellectual acknowledgment of Hashem's existence, without it reaching our hearts.

2. The second level involves turning to HaKadosh Baruch Hu only in times of need, but not when the ocean is calm.

3. The third level is living with a yearning to be close to Hashem only when we are involved with Torah and *mitzvos*.

---

117 *Devarim* 4:39.
118 *Emunah and Bitachon,* Chazon Ish, ch. 2, "Bitachon."

4. The highest level is the ability to connect to Hashem in all matters and at all times. It is seeing Hashem in front of us... always!

This final level is exemplified in the famous words written by Dovid HaMelech, "*Shivisi Hashem l'negdi tamid* — I have set Hashem before me always."[119] Reaching this highest level of *emunah* is dependent on our capacity and choice to be aware of Hashem's continual Presence in our lives.

The Rambam teaches us that all is known before Hashem. He knows all the thoughts, speech and actions of all creatures. This concept is awe-inspiring. Contemplating the fact that if not for the will of the Borei Olam, the world and our entire existence would cease instantaneously can inspire heartfelt feelings of both fear of and closeness to Hashem. The entire universe was created through Hashem's utterances and He recreates the world every day.

GETTING PRACTICAL

Life is a combination of moments, one following the next. With each passing moment, we have the ability to grow, change and elevate ourselves. Take a moment to contemplate Hashem's continuous benevolence in recreating us and being involved in our every thought and deed. We can aspire to move from level to level on the emunah scale.

---

119   *Tehillim* 16:8.

Serve Hashem in Happiness

"*Ivdu es Hashem b'simchah, bo'u lefanav birnanah* — Serve Hashem in joy, come before Him with praise."[120]

This is a *mizmor* (song) written at the time of the Beis HaMikdash in honor of the *korban todah,* the thanksgiving offering brought before Hashem. Unlike other obligatory sacrifices, this voluntary *korban* could be offered whenever one was filled with gratitude for having experienced a miracle.[121] When we feel gratitude to Hashem, this chapter of *Tehillim* suggests we should proclaim that feeling by shouting out and thanking Him.

Developing the emotion of joy is closely interlaced with strengthening a sense of gratitude. Experiencing feelings of joy comes as a result of one noticing how beautiful and miraculous his life is. Interestingly, although we are commanded to love and fear Hashem, we are not commanded to feel gratitude toward Him. Why not?

Perhaps because appreciation should be part of the natural make-up of human beings and can be genuinely ignited when we witness the hand of Hashem personally in our lives. By abandoning the entitlement attitude and seeing life as a continuous free gift we will automatically instill our lives with appreciation and joy.

Why is it vital to serve Hashem with *simchah*? The Radak suggests we do so in order to show HaKadosh Baruch Hu that serving Him is not a burden.[122] When we perform our *avodas Hashem b'simchah* we are conveying the fact that it is a *zechus* to be an *eved Hashem*

---

120   *Tehillim* 100:2.
121   Rashi brings down in his commentary to *parashas Tzav* (7:12) that a *todah* offering is brought by "someone who experienced a personal miracle."
122   Radak on *Tehillim* 16:9.

(a servant to Hashem). Our emotions testify that we feel honored and blessed to have been chosen to serve the King of Kings.

But in essence, Hashem is commanding us to feel joy because Hashem knows what is best for us, better than we know ourselves. In the Torah, Hashem becomes angry with *Bnei Yisrael* when they become discontent and do not serve Him out of genuine happiness. One such example occurred while the *Bnei Yisrael* wandered in the desert thirsty for water. They experienced a period of decreased *emunah* and pleaded to Moshe for help, not trusting that Hashem would take care of them. Yet this was a test to increase their trust in Hashem's loving care; He didn't forsake them then nor will He forsake us now.

Hashem loves us. He wants us to actively seek *simchah* since it aligns our hearts with our actions. It proclaims that there is meaning to all that we do and creates a stronger connection to Him. *Simchah* provides a positive breeding ground for building a healthy emotional state, not just in our service to Hashem but in all areas of our life.

Simchah is a natural outcome of contemplating the endless list of gifts that Hashem bestows upon us daily. Focusing on Hashem's gifts in gratitude is a proactive way of enhancing these feelings of joy and appreciation, leading to a healthier heart and mind.

GETTING PRACTICAL

Joy is a critical ingredient in serving Hashem. Let's focus on appreciating all that He bestows on us. Thus we ignite our joy and enhance our service of Hashem and our lives.

In G-d We Trust

In G-d we trust… or do we?

Let's examine this question in more detail. Every *nisayon* involves a degree of suffering. The question is how much we are affected by it. Will we mentally give up? Or can we retain the comforting thought that Hashem is doing this for our ultimate best, no matter how difficult it might be to find the positive?

The Chafetz Chaim teaches that the only thing we can control in life is our outlook.[123] Everyone has a different level of *emunah*, which may vary during their lifetime. *Emunah* is like a muscle, it needs to be constantly strengthened and tested in order to grow. Two different levels of *emunah* are "*emunah*" (faith) and "*bitachon*" (trust).

R. Zachariah Wallerstein makes a classic distinction between *emunah* and *bitachon*. *Emunah* refers to the intellectual *da'as* (knowledge) that Hashem exists and the belief that everything that He does is for the best. *Bitachon* is the *ma'aseh* (the act) that we undertake based on this knowledge, extending *emunah* one step further by implementing it practically in one's life.

R. Wallerstein illustrates this distinction by using an analogy: Imagine there is a circus stunt man walking along the high wire above you. The man then dramatizes his act by riding his unicycle across the wire. He then offers to take someone to ride with him

---

123 The Chafetz Chaim teaches this lesson through his commentary on *parashas Bamidbar* 26:41. There he explains in depth the result of Yaakov Avinu's blessings for the tribes of Dan and Binyamin. He concludes that the only thing in our control is our ability to decide how to react ethically and spiritually over what happens in our lives. Everything else is in Hashem's hands.

on his shoulders across the wire. If he would then ask the audience members if they believe he would make it across safely, they may respond affirmatively because of the stunt man's solid track record. This belief reflects their *emunah* in his ability to complete the act. But you may be more reluctant to be the volunteer sitting on his shoulders! The volunteer, however, demonstrates *bitachon*. A failure to volunteer may highlight *emunah* that has not yet been translated into *bitachon*.

This story illustrates the point that *bitachon* is the physical act of living with *emunah* in practice. While *emunah* refers to the belief that Hashem is taking care of us, *bitachon* is applying that *emunah* in difficult times in order to avoid despair.

When faced with a *nisayon*, we can view each setback as a challenge, a test of faith and a chance to grow closer to Hashem. Or we can become angry, feel abandoned, picked on and treated unfairly. Although we cannot choose the circumstances of our life, we can choose how to respond to them. Do we choose anger or fear, or do we choose instead to trust Hashem to see us through each tight spot?

GETTING PRACTICAL

Bitachon is a translation of emunah into everyday life, a mindset or attitude adopted when we face challenges that affects our decision-making and helps us avoid despair. Next time you feel anxiety creeping up on you, remind yourself that Hashem is right there next to you leading the way. Allow this feeling to hug you as your distress slowly fades away. That is bitachon!

Mind Control

Our thoughts define us. They motivate us. They govern our *ratzon* (will) to enable us to get things done. As they are so powerful in nature, it becomes vital to know how to control or channel them.

Our thoughts give way to our emotions. Our emotions are then inspired by things that we are interested in. By way of example, if someone is starting to think negatively of their own marital relationship, they may notice and compare others' relationships. This in turn may inflame emotions such as jealousy and competitiveness and ingratitude.

In order to avoid this negative spiral, the person has a choice. One option would be to stop the thoughts from going down this road of jealousy and comparison ("Why do they have what I want?", "Why can't I get what they have?").

Instead, we should turn our thoughts to gratitude for what we do have. Just as two thoughts cannot occupy the mind at the same time, so we cannot have two desires inhabit our heart at the same time. We can replace every negative thought with a positive one — finding the good in our hardship. Eventually, this will strengthen ourselves and focus our thoughts on the love and care that is being showered onto us from the Borei Olam.

Alternatively, if we cannot control our drive to look at others, we can replace one drive for another. Since we are emotionally invested in the issue, we can use our drive to improve our personal dilemma, investing our energy in a place that will heed positive results. We can take our desire to look at others and let it serve as a motivator to beseech the Melech HaOlam for help on ways to remedy our own marital situation.

GETTING PRACTICAL

Challenges are intended to motivate us toward self-improvement. Let's use our mind and eyes to look at others for the sole purpose of learning to emulate their virtuous behavior; not to foster thoughts and feelings of jealousy and self-pity.

| **Shabbos Is Dedicated to the Soul**

Each Jew is imprisoned in their own personal exile. We are in *galus* and thus not living where we should be. Due to the darkness facing our current generation, we all require tremendous effort to see beyond the human eye and view life from a spiritual perspective.

Shabbos affords us a day to step out of time and provides us with a chance to view our lives from a global and more objective perspective. By taking a break from our worldly responsibilities, we are able to nurture the seed planted in our soul, igniting it anew. Shabbos frees us from bondage and takes us out of the darkness. It nourishes us and infuses us with holiness for the rest of the week.

Shabbos completes the universe because it is a day dedicated to the soul — the true purpose of our creation. On Friday night, our hearts should be full. Just as wine overflows the Kiddush cup, so our hearts should spill over with love for HaKadosh Baruch Hu. We are enveloped in the sweetness of Hashem's creation.

The light of the Shabbos candles themselves illuminates peace in our home. After lighting the candles, we wish each other "*Shabbat Shalom.*" Rooted in the Hebrew word *shalom* is the word *shleimus* (completeness). Peace is signified by unity; it is the joining of separate parts that leads to wholeness. Candle lighting also carries with it a message of peace in the home. When a Jewish woman lights two separate flames, the ultimate light created is unified into one. This reminds her that even though she and her husband are two separate beings, they are one soul. The *avodah* (work) of a couple uniting the two halves of their soul is the work of a lifetime.

A candle is also likened to the soul. Just as a candle always reaches upward and strives to reach aloft to its source, so do we, on Shabbos we await to be rejoined to the Ribbono Shel Olam. We are advised to use pure olive oil to light the Shabbos candles.[124] *Tehillim* teaches that Torah scholars are compared to olives and olive oil.[125] When women light with pure olive oil, they are said to be rewarded with sons who are Torah scholars.[126]

There are many possible reasons given to us. One is taught by the Ben Ish Chai, where he comments that olive oil burns a clean and steady light, which serves as a protection from negative moods and energy. Essentially we wish to illuminate our home in the brightest way which encourages marital peace and a joyful spirit. Light that illumines from olive oil is steady; a peaceful atmosphere free of flare-ups.

GETTING PRACTICAL

We need Shabbos as a sanctuary in time dedicated purely to holiness, and to remind us of our eternal bond to Hashem. Whereas our focus during the week is on physical pursuits, Shabbos provides us with an oasis in time for us to nourish our souls and recharge!

124　*Shulchan Aruch* 264:5.

125　*Jerusalem Talmud, Shabbos* 15:3.

126　*Machazik Berachah*, cited in Yalkut Yosef.

100% Precise

Those who have internalized *bitachon* to the extent that they apply it to everyday life situations experience far less anxiety than otherwise. *Bitachon* is the strongest indicator that he has cast his burdens onto HaKadosh Baruch Hu. If we can simply say "I accept the circumstances of my life for what they are," we remind ourselves that whatever Hashem desires is just and good and we accept it with love.

Ultimately, *bitachon* is **the** only true answer to all of life's queries. No falsehoods, just unassuming *emes* (truth). Our Creator wants us to serve Him in purity and simplicity. Accepting the conditions of life with humility implants the knowledge that we do not know what is best for us, only the Ribbono Shel Olam does. Humility works hand in hand with contentment.

The Vilna Gaon teaches us that innermost serenity is achieved when we are satisfied with the physical possessions that we have, without any desire for more. The opposite of contentment is desire, a major transgression. *Bitachon* should not stop us from following natural paths to achieve what we need in order to survive. That is our *hishtadlus*. However, yearning for more than this minimum requirement is acting with desire — a trait to be wary of.

For instance, let's consider a person searching for his *bashert* (soulmate). Many people invest extensive time and energy into finding their marriage partner. This search is often fraught with tension and glitches. Things may not seem to work out the way one predicts. When one finally thinks they have found the right one... it falls through.

Yet, brewing under the surface, from a place where you least expect it, a new prospect is proposed. *Baruch Hashem* he or she is The One! Only in hindsight can many people appreciate Hashem's handiwork in arranging that the previous possibility fell through. Though it was all for the best at the time it fell through, without *bitachon* we may only see the brilliance of Hashem's plan with hindsight.

GETTING PRACTICAL

Hindsight is an exact science. Emunah is trust in the perfect masterplan of the Borei Olam, also exact, albeit in a different way. Sometimes we are privy to see the precision and sometimes not. Let's practice being humble enough to say that although we cannot fully understand, it is 100% precise!

No Matter Who, What, Why, Where, When or How!

We cannot fathom Hashem's ways or be certain about the message or meaning behind anything that He does with us. As creatures of control and knowledge, this can be frustrating to us because we like to comprehend everything that happens in our lives.

We do not see the full dimension of reality. Hashem deliberately conceals His plan to bring the universe to its ultimate perfection. In due time, Hashem will proclaim before the entire world the reason for every reprimand and affliction. We simply cannot comprehend the awesomeness of Hashem and the intention behind every act. Whereas only the top layer of every act is apparent, there is a core of truth that remains hidden.

Our sins distance us even further from feeling HaKadosh Baruch Hu's control. They cause an even thicker veil to spread over us, consequently hiding more of Hashem's spiritual light which shines upon us. This leaves us with an even greater sense of feeling alone. In order to reconnect we need to do *teshuvah* for our sins in order to regain the feeling of connection to the Borei Olam.

Emunah translates as believing that all that Hashem does is for the good. In spite of the fact that we may feel distanced from Him, we do have *emunah* deep inside that Hashem is just in all of His ways, no matter who, what, why, where, when and how. It is vital to fill our heart's storehouse with this knowledge so that we have a place to draw strength from when life's challenges arise.

We are never alone. Hashem is with us, guards us and shares in our suffering. No matter how difficult it

In memory of
Malka Baila
bat HaRav Yona
Shmuel z'l, who
embodied the
meaning of true
emuna
Dedicated
lovingly by
Elisheva
Goldwater

may be to comprehend and accept difficulties, it is all for our eternal best. The Ramban brings down that all of Iyov's suffering does not add up to even one moment of Gehinnom.[127] It is comforting to remember that HaKadosh Baruch Hu is *Kel Maleh Rachamim* (full of compassion). Any difficulties that Klal Yisrael does experience are less exacting than we deserve. As it says in *Sefer Iyov*, "Hashem exacts less of you than your iniquity deserves."[128]

GETTING PRACTICAL

As challenges arise, saying words such as, "Somehow, someway this is serving my ultimate best" opens up the emunah channels. Every challenge originates from a point of compassion and endless love, which is important to keep in mind.

---

127   Commentary on the introduction of *Sefer Iyov*.
128   11:6.

| Life Is Compared to a Machine

What is the ultimate level of *bitachon*? It is a place of total trust in Hashem's care to the extent that we do not perceive anything in life as bad. As it says in *Megillas Eichah*, "*Mi-pi elyon lo teitzeh ha-raot v'hatov* — By the command of the most high, neither good nor evil come."[129] It is living with the feeling that all Hashem does is for my ultimate best, both in this world and the next. Hashem is the Judge of truth and exact in all of His decrees.

The foremost student of the Arizal, R. Chaim Vital teaches us that the creatures of the universe are like screws in the great machine called creation. HaKadosh Baruch Hu tightens the screws or loosens them, and adjusts their actions according to the workings of the machine. The events in this world occur in accordance with the precious Divine plan. Hashem brings *neshamos* down to the world and takes away those needed above in the next world.

Just as with a machine, there are no extra pieces. Each part has its own function in the makeup of the contraption, and so it is in this universe by G-dly design. This world and the World to Come both work toward the same end, yet we are not privy to the intrinsic function of every nut and bolt in the mechanism.

I came across a quote by someone anonymous that read, "Life is like a washing machine. It twists, turns and knocks us around, but in the end we come out cleaner, brighter and better than before." From our limited position in this world, we are often not able to grasp the unity of the two worlds. Hashem knows what is good for us better than we do. We are

---

129 *Eichah* 3:38.

never alone. He is always holding our hand and guiding us on our journey called life.

The manufacturer holds the blueprints which illustrates the particular purpose of each element. Let us take refuge in the fact that the Manufacturer of the world maintains full control and care over the productivity of His creation.

GETTING PRACTICAL ⎯⎯⎯⎯⎯⎯⎯⎯⎯⎯

Trusting in Hashem often requires us to defy intellect. Though we live in galus ha-da'as and often perceive painful events to be bad, we can remind ourselves that we are all screws in a unified machine which is created, managed and maintained by Hashem with love.

A Powerful Remedy to Dissatisfaction

The materialism of this life is a powerful but dangerous illusion. It plants within us a feeling of emptiness and harmful craving, leaving us with a feeling of dissatisfaction which may permeate every aspect of our lives.

Our generation has been described as the one where "darkness will cover the land" and concealment will rule. Rashi explains that in our era, it will appear as though all hope is lost.[130] There will seemingly be no leaders, prophets or kings to guide us.

Our generation's task is the perfection of *emunah*.[131] We are believers, children of believers and stand against all odds and defy all logic. Both Klal Yisrael and prayer itself are above nature. As Klal Yisrael, we have the power to change nature via prayer. *Hisbodedus* is a powerful antidote to unhappiness. It is necessary to combat our physical drives and channel our negative emotions.

The *tzaddikim* who have departed from this world rely on our *hisbodedus* as ammunition to arouse *rachamei Shamayim*. One of the challenges of a *hisbodedus* session may be finding the exact words to say. In *Sefer Tehillim*, Dovid HaMelech suggests in such a predicament the following, "My heart was hot within me. While I was musing the fire burned; then I spoke with my tongue."[132]

In other words, if we focus on and yearn to bond with Hashem, that ache can turn our heart aflame

---

130   *Zechariah* 14:6–7.

131   Our generation, the generation of the footsteps of Mashiach, carries this particular mission as our sages explain the *pasuk*, "A righteous man will live with his *emunah*," *Makos* 24.

132   39:3.

which in turn can fuel our words. Praying often requires deep contemplation. During this time of contemplation, we may not utter a word yet love may
still brew in our hearts. With such passionate and
positive intent, words will eventually begin to form
which will enable us to speak.

This process itself is a priceless gift to HaKadosh
Baruch Hu. The longer we immerse ourselves in deep
thought, attempting to bond with Hashem, the more
we will successfully connect with Him. Every word we
speak to Hashem advocates against the decrees hov-
ering over Klal Yisrael.

GETTING PRACTICAL

Hisbodedus is an irreplaceable tool for spiritual growth and the
main weapon for invoking Heavenly compassion onto our personal
and collective plights. Try today to strip away the layers and reach
deep within the soul by having an open heart talk with Hashem.

The War on Faith

In this generation, many Jews have lost their *emunah*. Most have lost their optimism for the future and have become numb to any hope of change. This is what the holy Baal Shem Tov calls *galus ha'da'as* (exile of spiritual knowledge). This is the most powerful war that we must fight — a war on our *emunah*; it is a fight to remain faithful to the idea of a better future.

This world as we know it is at the finish line. The *nisyonos* (trials and tribulations) are intended to rectify, purify and cleanse our souls. Rather than a sign of abandonment or punishment, our difficulties serve as wake-up calls to alert us at detour points in our lives. It is important to embrace them rather than running from them. It is necessary to step up to the plate and admit our weaknesses — the demons we hide in the closet and our wrongdoings. Rather than make us feel helpless, they should challenge us to grow. As any good athlete knows, going uphill, not hiking on plateaus, increases muscle tone. Difficulty brings greatness.

"Hashem, You love me, care for me and have put me into this world to do only good for me. It is all good." This should be our *emunah* mantra repeated over and over again. Accept Hashem's justice and completely believe that how harsh it may seem, His justice is infused with endless mercy and compassion. It could have — and should have — been worse. We are working for our eternity. Reflect on the word "eternity" and you will begin to see your struggles minimalize.

Beg Hashem to fortify your *emunah* to see you through your personal and our national troubles. It is a treasure that, once found, is priceless!

In memory of Yaakov ben Aaron z'l (27 Elul) Dedicated lovingly by the Picker Family

GETTING PRACTICAL _____

Emunah embraces everything in the Torah. It is the key to winning all wars and negating harsh decrees. Challenges are intended as opportunities to strengthen our resolve to spiritually grow and overcome our natural tendencies. This is an essential teaching to incorporate into our daily lives.

Suffer for Nothing or Struggle for Something

Our lack of *emunah* creates distance between us and Hashem. This kick-starts a vicious cycle, for the further we feel from Hashem, the more pain we endure. In other words, a weakened *emunah* is grounds for more suffering. In contrast, reinforced *emunah* brings about *yeshuos* (salvation). It is essential to maintain a close-knit relationship with Hashem to ensure that we not feel left alone in the midst of trouble.

When we do experience a *nisayon*, we should constantly remind ourselves that hardships build us, they have a purpose, and that they are tailor-made to complete our *tikkun* (soul rectification) in this world. R. Ashear, who writes the "Daily Chizuk" teaches a beautiful parable of a man who found a butterfly emerging from a cocoon. The man watched the butterfly struggling for hours, trying to wiggle itself out of a little hole in the cocoon wall. At one point, the butterfly stopped struggling. The man presumed the butterfly had given up. He felt sorry for it and snipped a bigger opening in the wall to allow the butterfly to escape. However, the emergent butterfly had a swollen body and small, shriveled wings. The man watched the butterfly, expecting its wings to expand and body to reshape itself. However, nothing changed. For the rest of its life, the butterfly remained stunted, never to recover or fly. In his kind ignorance — sometimes referred to as misplaced *chesed* — the man failed to understand that the restricted state of the cocoon was deliberately designed to allow for the fluid in the butterfly's body to spread

In memory of Rivka bat Miriam z'l (29 Elul) Dedicated lovingly by the Riter Family

to its wings in order for them to fly. The butterfly needed its period of struggle. Just as Hashem created this perfect cocoon system to maximize the butterfly's potential, so too He designs the struggles in life exactly in the manner we need in order to be able to soar. Struggles build us.

Still, we have a choice. We can stay as we are or we can choose to grow and extract the maximum potential that Hashem has planted within each of us. We continuously face forks in the road. No matter which path we choose, there will always be challenges. Do we want to suffer for nothing, or do we choose to view these bumps as a struggle for something?

GETTING PRACTICAL

We can choose to view hardships as a means for strengthening our emunah muscles. Instead of resenting Hashem for our struggles, we can focus on how we can grow and what we can learn from each challenge in life. This will enable us to remain focused on the long term advantages in spite of current pain.

| ## Shabbos: Hashem Is the Creator

We have been granted the ability to emulate HaKadosh Baruch Hu and partner with Him as a creator, so to speak. However, the danger with this power to create during the week is the fact that we may become so carried away with the powerful feeling of creating and control that we may attribute our actions to "our own might and wisdom (*kochi v'otzem yadi*)." Therefore, Hashem created Shabbos. The idea of Shabbos is the cessation of creative work. By abiding by Hashem's commandment to cease work for the day, our actions are proclaiming to the world — and also to ourselves — that Hashem is the Creator.

On Shabbos, we are required to stop and remember Who is in control. On Shabbos, all of creation is equal, for no one works, not the maidservant or the cattle. We all release ourselves from different activities so that we may enter a world of delight.

On Shabbos, our mind is also given a chance to rest. Our thoughts should not be focused on any act of creativity whose purpose is constructive. We should not exert effort on any deed that demonstrates our mastery of nature. Rather, Shabbos is a time to pause and reflect over the past week, to refresh our energy for the week to come, both mentally as well as physically.

On this precious day, we strengthen our awareness. During the work week, we are so busy taking care of our personal needs that we often miss the chance of seeing Hashem in the whole picture of life. In fact *Sefer HaChinuch* teaches that we drink wine on

Shabbos in order to create excitement.[133] Over what? Over the fact that Hashem is our Creator and is personally active in our lives.

During the working week, we seldom have the time to appreciate life's purpose. We may feel less joy because we are so consumed with physical activity and mental overload. Shabbos represents a time-out in order to gain perspective on the meaning of life. Shabbos should be the goal of our entire week, with the weekdays being a means to that end.

Chazal teach us that *emunah* is ingrained into the groundwork of Shabbos. Instead of watering the plants, on Shabbos, we should water the seeds of *emunah* that we have worked so hard to plant. These seeds grow keen awareness that Hashem is with us every step of the way.

GETTING PRACTICAL

Shabbos is a time to stop and think about our true purpose and who is in control. In spite of the darkness that may have covered over our spiritual senses during the week, on Shabbos let's immerse ourselves in spiritual delight.

---

133   Mitzvah 31.

How Long?

In *Tehillim*, Dovid HaMelech is renowned for his ability to sing songs of praise to Hashem when facing struggles. This is particularly remarkable because he praises Hashem before he even experiences the *yeshuah* (salvation); he praises in anticipation of Hashem's salvation. We can learn from this that when crises arise, we can emulate Dovid HaMelech's confidence in Hashem's salvation.

However, it is difficult to maintain this level of *emunah*, particularly during a long crisis. A fundamental human fear is that of abandonment. When we suffer an affliction, the worst part is feeling Hashem has forgotten us. Dovid HaMelech himself writes, "*Ad ana Hashem tishkacheni netzach, ad ana tasteer es Panecha mi-meni* —How long Hashem will You forget me forever? How long will You hide Your face from me?"[134] The eyes of Dovid HaMelech are so drenched in pain that he begs Hashem to "*Ha'ira einai pen ishan ha-maves* — Enlighten my eyes lest I sleep the sleep of death."[135]

Yet, in the face of our present suffering, it is also Dovid HaMelech who provides the template for our appropriate response. Like him, we can raise our pain-drenched eyes and look into a future bright with joy and hope. As he writes, "*Ve'ani b'chasdecha batachti yagel libi b'yeshuasecha* — But I trusted in Your loving-kindness, my heart will rejoice in Your salvation..."[136]

Jewish history is reassuring because we can learn that just as Hashem has brought about our

---

134 *Tehillim* 13:2.
135 13:4.
136 13:6.

redemption in the past, so He will redeem us in the future. This provides strength and *emunah* to face present challenges. Turning to Hashem in a situation of need helps us to internalize the *emes* that everything is under Hashem's control. This, in turn, can lead to tranquility. Prayer is the vessel through which we can achieve this tranquil state. Dovid HaMelech speaks to Hashem with the *emunah* that He is listening. It is a great *zechus* to live with *emunah* and to speak directly to Hashem, confident of being heard.

GETTING PRACTICAL

Despite the depth of pain Dovid HaMelech endured, he lifted his eyes and continued to sing, praise and trust Hashem. We can learn from him that even throughout lengthy challenges when we feel like Hashem has hidden His face, singing, praising and trusting that the Borei Olam hears us can lead to hope and tranquility.

The Eisav in All of Us

Hashem does not need to justify His actions. It is important to understand the ramifications of feeling angry *chas v'shalom* with HaKadosh Baruch Hu. Feeling resentment toward Hashem weakens us, yet it does not affect Hashem or our outcome. We are the ones who suffer if we attempt to humanize Hashem or understand His ways with our limited human minds.

Despite emulating Him, we are required to accept that we can never fully understand His workings. There is an eternal distance between us and our Creator. In fact, when we attempt to fathom the infinite nature and ways of the Borei Olam, we should be left feeling dumbfounded and awestruck.

For example, with regard to *parnasah,* earning a livelihood, many of us fail to recognize that our requirement to toil in order to sustain ourselves is a curse — the curse of Adam. Unfortunately, our society considers work a blessing, to the extent that we often work over and above what we need rather than spending time considering our true mission in life of connecting to Hashem. For instance, think about how much time many of us dedicate to work compared to the time we focus on spiritual matters.

This devotion to the physical world represents the Eisav in all of us — the ultimate workaholic who severed his ties to the spiritual realm, all for a bowl of lentils! This is the part of us willing to substitute spirituality with material fulfillment, after which we are still left feeling unsatisfied.

Overworking in order to earn a higher income is useless and often leads to physical and emotional exhaustion, which may consequently make such a person feel angry at his lot in life. As with everything in life, true *emunah* in the case of earning a living is seeing Hashem's hand in our livelihood and knowing that wealth is not built on our own efforts. It is all orchestrated from above for reasons that only He can truly fathom.

GETTING PRACTICAL _____

Anger at Hashem at our lot in life stems from a mistaken belief that we understand His ways. If we embark on the emunah path and adhere to the words of Chazal, we can avoid making mistakes such as working for its own sake. Rather, let us remember that spirituality and connection to Hashem is our true purpose in life.

Spiritual Elevation

Let's be prepared to fight for our spiritual elevation. In order to climb the spiritual ladder, we need to act contrary to our bodily desires. The Gemara teaches that we should take the *yetzer hara* with us every time we perform a mitzvah and engage in Torah study, in order to let it bow to the will of the *neshamah*.[137] Since the *yetzer hara* constantly battles with us and causes our *mitzvos* to be done without pure intent, we should drag it to accompany us when we are involved in good deeds. This will result in quite the opposite — *mitzvos* being done *l'shem Shamayim* (for the sake of Hashem's glory).

The process of *teshuvah* actually involves giving the upper hand to our G-dly side while weakening our bodily side. As human beings, we are naturally drawn toward self-indulgence. However, herein lies the challenge of this world because Hashem does not shine His infinite light in places where one is involved in self-gratification.

Despite the temptations of self-gratification, we can transform darkness into light and cause Hashem to dwell in our midst by increasing the spiritual intentions of our actions. Though this process may not change our deeds from an external perspective, internally the *kavanah* (intent and purpose) becomes *l'shem Shamayim* and the effect is vastly different as a result. The intentions behind our actions essentially serve to invite Hashem's Presence to enter previously dark spaces.

We may notice a transformation has taken place when we feel uplifted and experience immense joy

---

137   *Sukkah* 52b.

from the mere fact that we are bringing *nachas ruach* to Hashem. The spiritual nature of this transformation means that we will not feel a personal ego boost from this joy, but rather a pure connection to Hashem. In this way, we will have refined our thoughts and our *neshamah*, and will have given new life and meaning to each deed we perform.

This process of overcoming our nature and elevating our intentions is a laborious and lifelong task. It requires a continual assertion of *ratzon* (will) to move forward and grow. Hashem makes us aware of our weaknesses so that we act to improve them. Hashem gives us challenges and tests to compel us to seek ways to grow and thus uncover our best potential. Reaching a low point is meant to stir us to move forward and rise again. As a result, with Hashem's blessing we will reach a higher level than before.

GETTING PRACTICAL

Our spiritual intention and kavanah behind each mitzvah and action remain hidden from the outside world. Though it is unseen, it is an essential spiritual force that enables us to form a close, personal relationship with Hashem. Let's try to strengthen our minds, focus and attention on Hashem's constant Presence in our lives.

| <h1>Healer of the Brokenhearted</h1>

Residing in Meah Shearim, R. Ofer teaches a well-known *segulah* (spiritual practice that increases one's merit) to remove sadness. He recommends reading chapter 147:3 of *Tehillim* seven times consecutively without interruption upon feeling melancholy. This *pasuk* says, "*Ha-rofeh li'shvurei lev, u'michabesh l'atzvosam* — He Who is the Healer to the brokenhearted will also bind up their wounds."

In order to fully understand the meaning of this *pasuk*, we also need to analyze the previous and latter *pesukim*. The previous *pasuk* reads, "*Nidchei Yisrael yichanes*," which, when taking the first letter of each of these three words, spells the word *yayin* (wine). Some interpret this as suggesting that when we are downhearted, we should sip wine to lift our spirits. Elsewhere in *Tehillim* it is written, "*Yayin yisamach levav enosh* — Wine makes glad the heart of the man."[138] The Radak's commentary on this *pasuk* is that when wine is drunk — in moderation! — it leads man to be happy.

The latter *pasuk* (147:4) reads, "*Moneh mispar la'kochavim, l'chulam sheimos yikrah* — He who fixes the number of the stars calls all of them, too, by name." This *pasuk* teaches us that each and every one of us is important in Hashem's eyes because Hashem knows each of His dispersed sons by name. The Ibn Ezra writes that no one is lost in His count. Just as He is aware of every star and their particular task, He is aware of our pain, our *tikkun* (soul's path of rectification) and our hardships, and He is there for us through it all. Remembering this wisdom will prevent us from ever feeling alienated or alone.

---

138   104:15.

The Baal Shem Tov suggests that we turn to *tefillah* which eventually leads to an elevation of our spirits. *Tefillah* should be done from a place called *lev nishbar* (a broken heart) rather than a state of hopelessness or of complaint. It is ideal to pray to the Borei Olam through a voice of hope rather than of anguish — with a broken heart in need of mending and dependent only on the Borei Olam to send him his *yeshuah*. Consequently, through *tefillah* our broken heart will be mended and we will be uplifted to a state of joy.

Tefillah should always begin on an optimistic note. As is written in *Yirmiyahu*, "*Mikveh Yisrael moshiyo b'et tzarah* — O' Mikveh Yisrael, the redeemer thereof in time of difficulties."[139] We should not read the first word as *mikveh*, but rather as *m'kaveh* (From hope, Yisrael will be redeemed in their time of difficulties). We should call out to Hashem from a place of *emunah*, believing deep inside that He has, is and will make everything good.

GETTING PRACTICAL _____

Next time we find ourselves sad or downhearted, reciting chapter 147 of Tehillim can help elevate us. It reminds us that Hashem heals our wounds and that we are all special and individual in Hashem's eyes. Our davening can also elevate us as long as it comes from a place of hope. Hashem treats our wounds of sadness. He wants us to feel His loving care.

---

139   14:8.

Humility

Anavah (humility) is considered a very important character trait. Whoever believes that their own "strength and might" creates something or causes something to happen actually drives a wedge between himself and Hashem. The Torah itself warns us against the tendency: "You may (erroneously) say in your heart, 'My strength and the might of my hand made me this wealth.'"[140]

However, humility is not a denial of one's worth. It does not require us to feel self-effacement or to become an aesthetic. Rather, it means recognizing that the talent, skills, knowledge or wealth we possess comes only from Hashem. Rabbeinu Yonah teaches us that personal merits are only due to Hashem's *chesed* and *rachamim*. In essence, humility is both a healthy self-awareness and recognition that one's talents and fortunes are gifts from Hashem. This is the challenging balance to maintain.

Hashem assists the humble to draw closer to Him via enlightening them with Torah knowledge. This additional Torah enlightenment can enhance their original humility. However, there is the possibility that such additional Torah insights may lead to arrogance. *Gaavah* (arrogance) is the opposite of humility. In the presence of such *gaavah,* the Gemara suggests that the Torah insights can be forgotten because they are no longer granted Heavenly assistance.

The following points represent some additional teachings by our holy Rabbanim on the attribute of arrogance.

R. Raphael of Bershed said, "Some people pursue acclaim and thrive on being honored. Little do they

In memory of Yaakov Natan ben Mordechai Shalom Dedicated lovingly by the Ledder Family

---

140 *Devarim* 8:17.

realize that in order to receive honor, you must actually lower yourself. One can only pour into a container when it is held lower."

R. Pinchas of Koritz said, "Every sin requires some action or object. Vanity requires nothing. A person may be lying under blankets and think, 'How great I am.'"

R. Mendel of Kotzk said, "A person who seeks recognition is much like a goat that wears a bell around its neck to announce its whereabouts."

A vain person came to see R. Avraham the Malach. He found him standing by the window, looking out. "See that hill?" he said. "It is only a pile of earth, yet it stands high as if it were superior to others."

GETTING PRACTICAL

Torah flows to those with anavah (humility). Humility means recognizing that any talents, wealth or knowledge we attain are from Hashem. The next time you are granted success, saying the three words, "Thank You Hashem" will reinforce this idea.

Energize Your Soul

How does the soul become sick? We can learn the answer from the *pasuk* in *Sefer Devarim*, "*Shochad me'aver einei chachamim* — A bribe will blind the eyes of the wise ones."[141] Even those who are wise cannot withstand the effect of a bribe.

Arguably, one "bribe" of the current generation is materialism. Many feel the pull to "make it" and achieve financial independence or achieve retirement security. However, when we internalize *emunah*, we realize that this striving for independence is a mistake. Independence from whom — the Borei Olam?

Materialism may sway our ability to make wise, calculated decisions regarding our spiritual aspirations. Contrary to popular belief, the soul will not be satisfied by chocolate cake! It needs a connection to Hashem to survive and be healthy. It is negligent to nourish our physical bodies, while failing to provide proper sustenance for our spiritual *neshamos*.

Emunah can help us reach the point where we realize that we are not in control and therefore cannot secure anything without His will. Curbing our appetites for materialism is one way to restore and enhance our *emunah* and help cure our ailing *neshamos*. Showing Hashem that we value His Torah and valuing spiritual pursuits over material can help purify our hearts so that *emunah* can enter. Conversely, when *emunah* enters, the pull of materialism starts to fade.

How can we minimize materialism's esteem and seduction on a practical level in order let *emunah* flourish? We need to live, breathe and act with *emunah* as our life force. We need to immerse ourselves

---

141   *Parashas Shoftim*, 16:18–20.

in *emunah* for as much of the day as we can, while still leading a productive life. Examples may include davening with more intent, speaking words of *emunah* such as "*Baruch Hashem*," "*Im yirtzeh Hashem*," and "With G-d's help," contemplating Hashem's *hashgachah* and doing chesed.

By relinquishing our focus on our own issues, we are able to reach out in the spirit of *Ahavas Yisrael* and care for others. We are all part of Hashem's creation, so in helping others we are truly caring for His creations and for another part of ourselves. If we give without expecting anything in return, we gladden the heart of another and bring *nachas* (Divine pleasure) to *Abba She'baShamayim*.

GETTING PRACTICAL

Repeatedly talking, thinking, thanking and acting for Hashem's sake will revitalize our emunah and bring more energy into our souls' powerhouses. Try it!

Genuine Peacefulness - Shabbos Kodesh

When describing the creation of the first Friday, the Torah ends with the words, *"Va'yaar Elokim es kol asher asah ve'hineh tov me'od* — Hashem saw all that He had made, and behold, it was very good."[142] This suggests that Hashem defined the world on Friday as being beautiful and perfect. *Chazal* ask, "Why did Hashem need the seventh day of Shabbos if the world was considered perfect after six days?" They answer, "Shabbos came, *menuchah* (rest) came." To interpret this answer, let us explore the relationship between the number six and seven.

If we were to take six identical coins and lay them flat, forming a circle, we would find something extraordinary. The vacant center will have room precisely for one more identical coin. This phenomenon will not occur with any other number of coins. You should try it, I already did! This geometric trick may be used to demonstrate that whereas the number six (that is, six days) represents external perfection, the number seven (that is, the seventh day) achieves inner perfection.

The materialistic side of creation was complete on the sixth day. Yet, something was still missing — the internal core of life found only on Shabbos. This internal core is rest. Without rest, life is not complete. When we team up with Hashem to perform His will during the week, we can stop and rest on Shabbos, reveling in the peaceful feeling of having worked hard and created during the week.

In memory of Esther bat Minna z'l (9 Tevet)

---

142 *Bereishis* 1:31.

Shabbos encapsulates the inner essence of all the other six days. It completes the week. Shabbos brings out the beauty of the other six days. It reveals the inner kernel of all physical things. For instance, the common expression, "a taste of Shabbos," reflects the fact that more than the taste of the physical foods, we appreciate their additional, spiritual spice.

On *Shabbos Kodesh*, all of creation returns to its original form, their completed form. Shabbos is a time of contentment and inner serenity, delight and happiness for those who see themselves as partners in creation.

GETTING PRACTICAL

Whereas the six days of the week are together considered perfect from an external perspective, the seventh day of Shabbos is necessary to enjoy inner perfection. This day of rest is a day of completion and relaxation after having partnered in creation all week.

The Power of Our Thoughts

Shlomo HaMelech, the wisest of all men, teaches us to beware of our heart. In *Sefer Mishlei* he wrote, "*Mikol mishamer nitzor libecha, ki mimenu totzaos chaim* — More than any other guard, control your heart, because it has tangible results in your life."[143]

Many of us often confront the challenge of how to bring our mind's knowledge down into our heart. For instance, we know it is important to daven, say *berachos*, do *chesed*, etc. Yet, sometimes we are not able to bring feeling for these things down into our heart. Also, our minds may be filled with other thoughts and distractions. This can interfere with our *kavanah* for the holy task at hand.

Feelings are formed by images, sensations and experiences, which are then transformed into emotions. For instance, we may hear of someone else's great marriage and start thinking about the gaps in our own marriage. This may create a flood of emotion, leaving us drained and mentally exhausted and perhaps our *kavanah* for the *mitzvos* may suffer as a result.

If our minds are elsewhere, our emotions will be similarly caught up in other realms. This may be an indicator that it is time to regain control of what goes in to our minds. After all, our thoughts ultimately are the key directors over our hearts. We are where our minds are.

The key to controlling our emotional state is to understand that it is the work of the *yetzer hara*. One of its tasks is to switch off our rational minds. Our head might dictate that it is wasted energy to

In memory of Rivka Shaindel bas Label Halevi z'l (13 Tishrei) Dedicated lovingly by Sora

143   4:23.

want something that isn't ours or to feel bad because someone else has it. However, emotion can defy logic. When we understand this interplay between thoughts and negative feelings, we can begin to control our rational minds and thus govern our emotions. It is exciting to think that we can battle the *yetzer hara's* power over our emotions — just by changing our thoughts.

GETTING PRACTICAL

Negative emotions can wear us down and interfere with our kavanah for the mitzvos. When damaging thoughts come to mind, place a loving image in your mind's eye and stay focused on it until you feel in control.

Walk in His Footsteps

People are called *bnei adam*. The word *adam* is derived from the Hebrew word *adameh* (to resemble, emulate). The Gemara in Shabbos states one should be similar to Hashem. We are taught to walk in His ways, to walk in His footsteps. "*Mah Hu rachum, af atah rachum, mah Hu chanun, af atah chanun* — Just as He is compassionate and merciful, so should you be."[144] We have the ability to be G-dlike and control our natural animalistic tendencies.

In *Maseches Yoma* it is written, "*Haba'im l'taheir mesayim lo m'Shamayim.*"[145] A person who sanctifies himself to a small degree is then sanctified to a tremendous degree, as his efforts are from below yet he is helped from above to reach a greater level of holiness. A relationship with Hashem starts with our will. It begins with a fiery, intense desire to attach ourselves to our Creator. We make the first move to demonstrate that will.

Two ways of demonstrating to Hashem that we want to connect to Him are *limud haTorah* (the study of the Torah) and performing His *mitzvos*. Learning Torah is compared to reading a personal letter addressed to us from *Avinu she'baShamayim*. It is like receiving a warm embrace from Hashem, for this is the way that He communicates with us. Torah speaks individually to each of us; this is highlighted by the fact that many find that their learning seems geared to exactly where they are currently holding in their lives.

In order to demonstrate our will to connect to Hashem via Torah, we might for instance find a *shiur*

---

144   *Shabbos* 133b.
145   39a.

in the area that we can commit to and attend it on a regular basis. Excluding unforeseen circumstances, we should make every effort to go. This discipline creates a vessel in which Hashem can pour His blessings and will serve to draw us closer to Him.

In terms of *mitzvos*, we can also use these to connect to Hashem. The word "mitzvah" originates from the idea of creating a *tzavta* (companionship). When we merit doing a mitzvah with proper awareness of its worth, we gain perfect bonding with Hashem. Performing *mitzvos* with the proper intent is likened to creating a complete body and soul companionship with Hashem. By aligning our thoughts, speech and actions prior to doing a mitzvah, we concentrate on the eternal value and in this way connect to Him to an even greater extent.

GETTING PRACTICAL

Hashem has given us a great gift — to be co-creators in His magnificent universe. Learning Torah and performing mitzvos are the only tools given to us to fulfill such an awesome task. Keeping this thought in mind will heighten our awareness and change the way we approach Torah study and mitzvos.

The Concept of Trust

Elaborating on the concept of *emunah*, the Chazon Ish explains, "There is a common misconception regarding the concept of trust. The word 'trust' is often misunderstood to imply that in every uncertain situation in which the future may hold success or failure, one is obligated to believe that everything will be successful. And if one remains uncertain, one lacks *emunah*."[146] The central idea to internalize is that whatever happens is Hashem's will, and since Hashem only wants what is good for us, whatever happens is by definition good.

The Chazon Ish clarifies that true *emunah* is rather the belief that nothing happens by chance and that everything is ordained by HaKadosh Baruch Hu. This fundamental concept of *emunah* is represented by a certainty and an acceptance that difficult and painful circumstances are being orchestrated by HaKadosh Baruch Hu.

The *sefarim ha-kedoshim* explain that the danger of not placing our trust in Hashem is that we may by default place our trust in another person or in our own strength and wisdom. Placing our trust anywhere other than with Hashem distances us from Hashem because we may come to see life's events as being separate, *chas v'shalom*, from Hashem's order. As a natural consequence, HaKadosh Baruch Hu removes His care from us and allows nature to take its course. Unfortunately, being completely in the hands of natural order may lead to a feeling of vulnerability, helplessness and confusion.

There is a fine line between placing our trust in Hashem on the one hand, and undertaking the requisite effort to meet our needs for survival (*hishtadlus*). This

---

146   *Emunah uBitachon*, Chapter 3

balance can be managed by making a reasonable effort[147] and yet acknowledging that it is HaKadosh Baruch Hu who determines outcomes according to exact Heavenly calculations. It is important to remind ourselves that no matter what the effort, the result only occurs if and how Hashem ordains it.

This brings us to a central question: how much effort is required by us? Obviously, the answer varies with each situation, and again Hashem will decide whether that effort is fruitful. However, it is interesting to note that those on an elevated level of *emunah* may need to invest less effort than those in the process of acquiring *emunah* in order to achieve their desired results.

Building on this concept, we may extrapolate that as we advance in our levels of *emunah*, we may need to invest less effort with every challenge we face. Ironically, this phenomenon may be due not to the fact that the challenges we face become smaller, or even that the results change in essence, but rather because our attitude to what constitutes a good result changes as our *emunah* grows. Our *emunah* enables our perspective to change to the extent that we are satisfied with less, and feel that whatever happens truly is in our best interest and is for the best.

GETTING PRACTICAL

Trust does not imply that events will unfold precisely as we wish, though we must do our hishtadlus, remain hopeful and unremittingly pray for an outcome that we consider favorable. Let's practice having true emunah — the recognition that Hashem orchestrates the results and that all results are therefore truly for the best.

---

147 The subject of *hishtadlus* and *emunah* is beyond the scope of this lesson, however, a central teaching points out that the greater one's *emunah*, the less effort one needs to invest. Likewise, the weaker one's *emunah*, the greater one needs to extend *hishtadlus*.

► DAY 143 | A Tzaddik Lives by His Emunah

It is all a matter of *emunah*. An indication as to whether *emunah* is a stronghold in our life is the extent to which it guides our every move in life. Do we first think of Hashem and see Him as being The Boss? Or do we naturally think of ourselves and our choices? Who is at the center?

The *Chovos Halevavos* guides us as to how much effort we should invest when we approach anything in life. Once we employ effort, we are taught to leave the outcome and our worries to HaKadosh Baruch Hu. Actually, Hashem does not need us to exert any effort in order to achieve any result. He could arrange all results without any human intervention. Our actions will not affect any decree. Rather, our efforts are required because they represent the obligation that we must fulfill due to the curse of Adam HaRishon.

Hashem is testing us by concealing His hand in our lives and seeing whether we can still see it. All of life's events are camouflaged to allow for our free will — the basic system of creation — to exist. We are being placed in an illusory position where we think we are in control, and that all results are due to our own actions. In the face of such illusion, are we able to stand up to the challenge with steadfast *emunah*?

We choose how hard we work. Once we have done our share, we can convince ourselves that we need to work harder and that there is "no other choice." However, with greater *emunah* in Hashem we would realize that we are not ultimately in control. Often, in dire situations we fail to have patience but rather lose *emunah* very quickly. Rather than give up in such a case, we should trust that Hashem never has, does or will forsake us and that the *yeshuah* will surely and eventually come.

"*Tzaddik b'emunaso yichyeh* — A *tzaddik* lives by his *emunah*."[148] A real *tzaddik* believes this in his heart, not just in his mind, since his whole life and all the decisions he makes resonate with *emunah*. *Emunah* flows in his arteries and pumps life into his body, sustaining him every moment.

The word *tzaddik* means righteous one. The numerical value of the letter *tzaddik* is ninety. *Pirkei Avos* teaches that when one reaches the age of ninety, one is bent over. On a physical level he is bowed in weakness, however, on a spiritual level, it is indicative of being humbled before Hashem. A *tzaddik* no longer sees himself as independent, but rather as an extension of Hashem Himself.

GETTING PRACTICAL _____

We are a ray of G-dliness. Next time we undertake a task, let us tap into this holiness and see ourselves as being totally dependent on Him and His blessings. Whatever the outcome, it is the best one for us.

---

148   *Chavakuk* 2:4.

Levels of Trust

Hashem alone guides everything! Although we are required to do our share (due to the sin of Adam), we ought to be careful not to attribute the results achieved to our efforts. R. Dessler suggests principles governing the amount of concerted effort we must invest. Essentially, these principles are based on the notion that the sole purpose of our efforts is to reveal Hashem in this mundane world. Nature has no control over anything. It is all Hashem!

The more *hatzlachah* we receive when we invest time and effort into something, the more *emunah* is required to recognize Hashem as the source of the results. The Midrash on *parashas Pinchas* teaches that the *yetzer hara* will try to trick us into feeling that it is "our might and wisdom that has brought about the results." The Maggid of Mezritch expounds on this lesson. He teaches that once we put our trust in anything other than Hashem, we break our connection to Him and allow that thing or person to control the outcome.

Chazal teach that there are different levels of *emunah*.

- The highest level is where one does not distinguish between natural and miraculous interventions, viewing them as all equally emanating from Hashem. Such individuals may warrant open miracles.

- At the other end of the spectrum are those still striving to reach a minimum level of trust. They see a vast distinction between natural causes and Hashem's involvement, failing to attribute "natural causes" to Hashem at all.

- Finally, there are those of us somewhere in the middle of the spectrum (*beinonim*), who acknowledge that everything comes from Hashem, yet in practice distinguish between nature and a miracle. For instance, we might be in awe over Hashem's miraculous hand in the birth of a baby, yet fail to see His hand in the fact that we wake up each morning.

Whatever our current level of *emunah*, it is clear from the Midrash that, ironically, the more *emunah* we display, the more *hatzlachah* we will actually receive. Thus, the higher our level of *emunah*, the less we need to busy ourselves on the natural plane. Correspondingly, the lower our *emunah*, the less Hashem will smooth our way and the more we feel the need to intervene and partake in worldly activities.

GETTING PRACTICAL

Simply speaking, emunah is the belief that there is none other than HaKadosh Baruch Hu. Which level of emunah are we on? Can we experience Hashem's kindness when it rains — a relatively natural occurrence — acknowledging that it is coming from His nourishing hand in order to take care of the world's vegetation?

Ashrei - Happy Is He (Part I)

The well-known chapter of *Tehillim*, *perek* 145 — *Ashrei*, contains within it immense praises to Hashem, thus serving to reaffirm our *emunah* and declare that everything that occurs is for our ultimate best. The significance of this chapter is demonstrated by the fact that whoever reads it three times a day is considered a *ben olam haba*, a recipient of the World to Come.[149]

Why is this *perek* so lofty? This *perek* contains powerful messages on how to increase our awareness of all the good that Hashem imparts upon His creation. Specifically, it contains beautiful praises to Hashem, listed from *alef* to *taf*. The other special feature is its inclusion of the verse, "*Posei'ach es Yadecha...* — You open Your hand..." which reminds us that HaKadosh Baruch Hu provides for our every need.

The first *pasuk*, "*Ashrei yoshvei beisecha, od yehalelucha sela* — Happy is the one who sits in Your home, they will praise Your name," offers practical advice on how to approach our *tefillah*. It has been translated as "Happy is the one who sits (contemplates) *before* he enters Your home (the place where we daven) because it will enable him to praise Your name.

Taking a few moments before we approach our *tefillah* to contemplate Who we are davening to enables us to daven with more *kavanah* (intent). This is the simplest but most powerful way of davening effectively and it leaves us with a sense of genuine happiness.

The next *pasuk* states, "*Aromimcha Elokai haMelech* — I will lift You up, Hashem." Why does Dovid HaMel-

---

149 *Berachos* 4b.

ech find it necessary to "lift up (*aromimcha*)" Hashem? Isn't Hashem already above His creation?

Though Hashem is obviously above us all, this *pasuk* reminds us to expand our consciousness whereby we become more aware of His holiness and can serve Him in awe. It is working on our frame of mind. Lifting HaKadosh Baruch Hu up from the depths of our heart and bringing Him into our tangible reality enables us to sense His *hashgachah* in every aspect of our lives.

GETTING PRACTICAL

Chapter 145 of Tehillim is so special it has been included in our daily davening. It contains powerful praises to Hashem, reminders that we should pay attention to how He provides our every need, and lessons on how to pray most effectively and to serve Him in awe. Consider how He is involved in your life, and rejoice.

Taste the Presence of Hashem

We cannot fully appreciate the extent of Hashem's love for us. The only way to delve into His gift of love is to stand before His creation in awe and gratitude. On Shabbos we use all of our senses to see, taste, smell, hear and touch the Borei Olam. We celebrate Hashem's artistry, appreciating the intricacies and care that go into His landscape.

Shabbos is the best day of the week. During the working week, the goal of life is hidden. On Shabbos, Hashem reveals the purpose of creation — to bask in His goodness. It is a day of joy to taste the presence of HaKadosh Baruch Hu. It separates us from the mundane and allows us to enter into a realm of *kedushah* (holiness). It prevents us from getting too immersed in the sea of the working week. Shabbos stands alone, illuminated by its own light and glory.

Shabbos requires separation in order to permit us to enter into the realm of sanctity. It enables us to release all the worries and stresses which may clutter our mind and cause inner congestion during the week. When we are carried into Shabbos mode, we allow our burdens to drift away and we are loosened from our routine ties to this world.

Shabbos Menuchah can be defined as rest with a twist of happiness and stillness, peace and harmony. There is no place for strife or fear, only pleasure. Yet, despite being relaxing and pleasurable, we must remember to observe Shabbos precisely because it is a commandment. Thus, we honor Shabbos for the sake of sanctifying the Borei Olam and because He commanded us to, since He knows what is in our best interests.

In loving memory of Leo and Becky Schamroth

Rather than viewing Shabbos as a day off or a break from work to give us renewed strength to return to work, let's remind ourselves that Shabbos provides a weekly, intimate date with Hashem and is thus the central highlight and purpose of our week.

GETTING PRACTICAL

Shabbos is the purpose of the week and of creation. It is not simply a day to reinvigorate us for the working week, but rather the purpose for which we work. Use this Shabbos to delve into Hashem's Presence and embrace the Oneness of life.

Ashrei - Happy Is He (Part II)

The following *pesukim* focus extensively on the importance of announcing Hashem's greatness and proclaiming it to the world. In the *pasuk*, "*Bechol yom avarcheka*," we are reminded that "Every day I will bless You..." This is the world of *asiyah* (action) and this *pasuk* suggests that our daily actions should be to praise Hashem. Repeated phrases such as "I love you Hashem" or "Thank you Hashem for ..." are ways to do this. Once we train ourselves to constantly praise Hashem in this lifetime, then in the World to Come, "*Va'ahalela Shemecha l'olam va'ed* — I will praise Your Name forever."

"*Ugedol chossed... ve'rachamav al kol ma'asav* — And great in bestowing kindness... His compassion is on all His works." No matter if we sin and are undeserving, Hashem showers His creation with loving-kindness, always.

This *perek* also teaches that Hashem is "*Erech apayim* — Slow to anger." It is comforting to know this about Hashem and we should emulate His ways. Instead of being angry at our *nisyonos*, we can choose the route of *emunah* — viewing our difficulties as priceless opportunities to do *teshuvah* or strengthen our faith.

The above lessons are particularly crucial for us as parents. **We** have to work on our *emunah* and exemplify our solid trust in Hashem before imparting them to our children and family. Using phrases such as, "It is from Hashem and it is for the best," "I know it is difficult, but it must be good," "Hashem loves us, no matter what" will spread *emunah* to future generations.

When they face an inevitable *nisayon,* challenge of faith, each child will be less likely to despair and more likely to recognize challenges ultimately as being an act of benevolence from Hashem. When our children are taught *emunah*, they trust that everything Hashem does is for their ultimate best and grow to be optimistic adults with a healthy emotional outlook.

GETTING PRACTICAL

This part of perek 145 teaches us to praise Hashem and Hashem's characteristics and kindnesses that we can emulate. Only after internalizing the message of emunah can we teach these fundamental lessons to our children.

Ashrei - Happy Is He (Part III)

Many of the *pesukim* in this *perek* suggest how to show appreciation for Hashem.

Specifically, the phrase, *"Yoducha Hashem kol ma'asecha* — All Your works shall thank You, Hashem,"* is an expression of thanks which is written in future tense. This may suggest the idea of giving thanks before one has even experienced a kind act. Perhaps it refers to the fact that in this world we are limited and cannot see "all Your works." Whereas in the World to Come, when all the masks are removed, we are privileged to see the entire scope of Hashem's *chesed* and then we "shall thank You, Hashem."

The following *pasuk, "L'hodia li-vnei ha'adam gevurosav u'chvod hadar malchuso* — To inform the children of mankind of His strength and the glorious magnificence of His Kingdom,"* teaches that we should publicly praise Hashem, rather than keep our praise for Him to ourselves. This is because we are *am echad* — one people. It is *ahavas Yisrael,* a demonstration of loving others as we love ourselves, to allow them to enjoy appreciating Hashem's gifts just as we do.

It is comforting to remind ourselves that *"Somech Hashem l'chol ha-noflim v'zokef l'chol ha-kefufim* — Hashem supports all the fallen ones and straightens all the hunched ones." Those who have fallen and are in need of additional help are the recipients of HaKadosh Baruch Hu's aid. He is attentive to those who are powerless and proclaim their need before Him.

The *pasuk* stating, *"Tzaddik Hashem b'chol derachav* — Hashem is righteous in all of His ways,"* suggests that Hashem is honorable and true. We may not understand some of the things that happen to us, but *emunah* means accepting and believing things that we mortals cannot fully understand.

GETTING PRACTICAL _____

The pesukim of Ashrei continue to teach us about Hashem's kindness to us, to accept that His ways are always good even if we cannot see them, and how to proclaim this emunah to ourselves and to the world.

Ashrei - Happy is He (Conclusion)

The belief outlined in the *pasuk*, "*Karov Hashem l'chol korav l'chol asher yikrouhu ve'emes* — Hashem is near to all those who call upon Him, to all who call upon Him in truth*," is a precondition to living a true life of *emunah*. In spite of His awesomeness, it is reassuring that He comes down to His frail creatures and "is near." Hashem is as near as we let Him be.

However, just as we should not merely call upon others only when in need, we should not only connect to our Creator in hard times either. We should seek to be close to Him at all times. Our awareness of His *rachamim* should be continuous. For instance, if our bodies are working smoothly one day, we should not take this for granted or presume that this will always be the case. Rather, we should try to appreciate that Hashem is so near that He recreates every breath anew. We should value each new moment that we are alive to praise him.

Dovid HaMelech also reminds us that "*Shomer Hashem es kol ohavav* — Hashem preserves all those who love Him." Hashem loves us no matter what. He yearns for us to long for Him. He waits for our hearts to open up to His love. When we manage to fulfill His will with love and joy, we achieve a higher level of awareness of His constant Presence.

This mutual love between us and the Melech HaO-lam grants us different lenses by which to view life's difficulties. We can learn to see hardships as messages, flag posts and impending danger signs calling out for our attention. When we perceive the *nisayon* in this light, it brings us closer to Hashem because it can be viewed as a blessing in disguise.

Finally, in the last *pasuk* of this powerful *perek*, "*Tehillas Hashem yedaber pi* — My mouth will speak of praises to Hashem," Dovid HaMelech reminds us of the important *avodah* of singing songs of gratitude to Hashem for the free gifts He gives us. In the beginning, the process of noticing and appreciating the little things in life may be hard work but with time this appreciation process will become a regular habit until we can sing endlessly of His constant kindnesses.

GETTING PRACTICAL _____

A life of emunah cannot be compared to a life without. This perek teaches us to slow down the pace of life and pay attention to the story of our lives. It takes us on a journey on how to praise Hashem and spread this awareness to others. Hashem's love and care can be felt in every verse. May we hold such intent every time we recite this perek.

Hallelukah!

Dovid HaMelech composed the words of *Tehillim* to serve as a key to open our individual hearts through his words. In the last *perek* of *Tehillim*, chapter 150, Dovid HaMelech sings songs of praises to HaKadosh Baruch Hu. There is a clear sense of orchestration, a bonding of numerous instruments coming together for the sole purpose of glorifying Hashem's name.

We are a *Klal,* a whole unit. Yet a unit is made up of its individual parts. Every Jew must internalize the notion of individual responsibility for the sake of our brethren, and yet come together to sing to our Creator.

"*Hallelukah!* Praise Hashem in His holy place; praise Him in the sky that contains His might."

Hashem is so very good to us. Our words of praise in appreciation for His endless kindness bring Him *nachas ruach.* Contemplating the continuous goodness that Hashem bestows upon us should humble us.

"Praise Him for His acts of strength; praise Him as much as befits His greatness."

Just as each musical instrument is different but necessary for the orchestra, each one of us sees Hashem's greatness differently. We articulate our feelings according to our understanding and our role to play in this world.

"Praise Him accompanied with a *shofar* blast; praise Him using a lyre and harp."

In memory of Yehudit bat Aaron z'l (21 Shevat) Dedicated lovingly by the Picker Family

Hashem is the Conductor of the world. Every one of us plays a unique musical instrument of praise to the Ribbono Shel Olam. Whether we are a *shofar* or a harp, it makes no difference because an orchestra needs each instrument to make it sound complete. Each of us plays our own special, irreplaceable notes.

"Praise Him using a drum and flute; praise Him using various musical instruments."

We are all needed. If one musical note is played out of key or at the wrong time, the whole symphony is disrupted. No one can replace the personal task of another.

"With the entire soul, praise Hashem. *Hallelukah!*"

Though we each have our unique role to play and thus praise and express appreciation individually, ultimately we are all one soul, the soul of Hashem's children. What a gift. This is true praise, this is true love!

GETTING PRACTICAL _____

Chapter 150 in Tehillim demonstrates how we as individuals experience the beauty and love of Hashem in different ways, but also as Klal Yisrael we are part of a full orchestra of sound, being all one soul from the same Creator.

The Dawn

I found my way through jagged streams,
Through distant shores and broken dreams.
I climbed the rocks that pierced my skin,
Believing that I still could win.

With aching bones and broken heart,
And fear my world might fall apart,
I looked up high, as not to see
The loss and pain that called to me.

And with my head held up so high,
I felt as though my soul could fly.
I turned to You with all my might,
Until the darkness turned to light.

And now I moved beyond the pain
The sun's come out, there is no rain.
The storm is gone, I see the shore
And I shall smile forever more.

Poems by Leah Rubabshi, copyright 2015.
Used with permission.

In *Koheles,* the wisest of all men, Shlomo HaMelech, teaches, *"Hevel havalim, hakol havel* — Vanity upon vanity, all is vanity." Life is transient — we must search for the everlasting meaning of it all.

Let's focus on materialism. A shopping-center environment appeals to the human need to feel good, look good and thus increase happiness. What's wrong with that? One problem is the temporary nature of the happiness associated with this materialistic focus — a fleeting feeling that usually passes immediately. Like vapor (another meaning of the word *hevel*), which makes a big impression yet disappears into thin air almost as quickly as it appears, material satisfaction dissipates almost immediately.

By living and engaging in this world, we are often drawn under its spell. We may become so caught up in materialism, we forget that its magic is temporary. Our daily chase for materialistic wealth can be likened to cloud-chasing — frustrating and ultimately unrewarding. Or it can be likened to the process of painstakingly renovating and decorating a hotel room, only to be moving out in a few days' time.

Shlomo HaMelech teaches that in order to combat the transitory nature of this world, we should spend our time delving into the book of eternal value, our holy Torah. This enables us to connect to the only eternal source — HaKadosh Baruch Hu. Though difficult to grasp, the concept of the World to Come being eternal must nevertheless be internalized in order to live an *emunah*-filled, fulfilling and rewarding life.

One purpose of *emunah* is to substitute transitory pursuits with the eternal.

GETTING PRACTICAL

Living in a materialistic world serves a purpose and is valuable so long as we use the physical as a source of elevation. For example, next time we indulge in material pleasures, let us feel gratitude to the One Who has given this pleasure to us.

It is vital to serve Hashem to the best of our capability. It is also vital for us to retain the *middah* (attribute) of humility in all aspects of our lives, including *avodas Hashem*. Recognizing that all our successes, talents and attributes are a gift from Hashem combats arrogance (*gaavah*). Excessive pride distances us from the Borei Olam. It creates a balloon full of air (an arrogant person is described as someone who is full of himself) between the arrogant person and those wishing to come close to him.

Ultimately, true humility requires honesty. Honesty is necessary to defeat the deception caused by the *yetzer hara* — who may disguise pride as humility! How? A person can pretend that they are modest, and yet still take pride in the very fact that they are being humble. A cunning trick of which we must be aware!

Practically speaking, in order to enhance our humility, we should constantly remind ourselves that our *avodah* to Hashem is incomplete. There is always more we could be doing. In the *sefer Chovos Halevavos* it is suggested that a person look forward to those in front of him (learn from those more spiritual than him) yet look backwards (not place his attention) toward those less fortunate than him materially.

Another way of enhancing humility is to avoid broadcasting our *mitzvos* to others in order to claim honor for them. Rather, we should be doing the *mitzvos* solely in dedication to HaKadosh Baruch Hu, for Him to place them in His treasure box.

Ramban's famous letter enlightens us further about humbleness. He writes, "I shall explain how you should become accustomed to the practice of humility in your daily life. Let your voice be gentle and your head bowed. Let your eyes be turned earthwards and your heart heavenwards. When you speak to someone, do not look him in the face. Let every man seem superior to you in your own eyes. If he is wise or rich you have reason to respect him. If he is poor and you are richer or wiser than he, think to yourself that you are therefore all the more unworthy and he all the less, for if you sin you do so intentionally whereas he only sins unintentionally."

GETTING PRACTICAL

Humility is a fundamental trait necessary in order to serve Hashem. Let us treat each person we meet as someone superior to us, and be aware of becoming proud about our newfound humility!

Shabbos Wholeness

Just as in the days of Sarah Imeinu, when we wave our hands over the illuminating radiance of the Shabbos candles, we can imagine them enveloping our home with holiness which lasts beyond Shabbos until the next Shabbos.

Yet, are we in love with Shabbos? One way of finding out the answer to this question is to see whether we are capable of sitting with Hashem and doing nothing but show our love for Him. In other words, can we occupy our minds and thoughts only with spirituality and Hashem's Oneness for more than a few seconds? The longer we can do this, the more Shabbos has reached the deepest and highest place in our hearts.

We greet others with the expression, "*Shabbat Shalom* (from the Hebrew root word *shalem*, whole) because on Shabbos we should feel a sense of wholeness. In fact, the feeling of completeness serves to remind us of the time before the sin of Adam HaRishon. After Adam transgressed, part of his soul remained in Gan Eden, even though he was banished. As Klal Yisrael are all comprised of sparks from the soul of Adam HaRishon, this part of our soul which remained in Gan Eden is released back to us every Shabbos. This is the possible origin of our extra Shabbos soul.[150] Consequently, every Shabbos essentially provides us with free entry back into Gan Eden.

On Shabbos, inner healing flows into the world in the form of spiritual vitamins and minerals that

---

150   The Shabbos soul comes from the Tree of Life from which souls blossom. *Zohar HaKadosh*, 2:98a and 3:173a.

refresh our souls. Our task is to make the vessel of our body clean and pure in order to be able to absorb these essential nutrients. In contrast to the working week, our *neshamos* on Shabbos are not passive. Rather, they are on such a holy, high level that we must ensure that our thoughts match and are involved in the spiritual realm as well. Since Hashem provides easy access to this holiness on Shabbos, reaching this match is relatively achievable — we need only to tap into it.

GETTING PRACTICAL

Shabbos is a special, holy gift representing our time in Gan Eden. On Shabbos we can easily tap into this higher, spiritual feeling of serenity and completeness. Let's embrace our extra Shabbos soul.

All Hashem Does Is for the Best

We often waste time on emotions such as worry, fear or anxiety. Though logically we may understand that these emotions do not solve anything, we often become caught up in their web. A solution to this struggle is to realize that the *yeshuos* (salvation) to all issues comes about from Hashem instantaneously, often without intervention on our part. This emphasizes how little we control the outcome of life's occurrences.

We can never be completely impartial and objective in viewing our own circumstances. An analogy is that of a tailor who receives beautiful silk to sew a royal gown. An observer may lament that the tailor is ruining the expensive material. But those with wisdom may understand that the cutting of the silk is a necessary precondition for a useful, beautiful gown. The parable teaches that something which appears bad or senseless to the observer may actually be fundamental in order to complete something good or ultimately for the best, such as the rectification of this world.

As Rabbi Akiva often said, "*Kol ma d'avid Rachmana l'tav avid* — All that Hashem does is for the best." The Talmud reminds us to memorize these essential words and say them often.[151] Yet, internalizing this teaching may be difficult for many of us. We can beseech Hashem to assist us in this process. Contemplative prayer is the way to do this and thus to purify our hearts. Sharing with Him our innermost thoughts, fears and feelings every day will draw us closer to Him and ideally lead us

---

151 *Berachos* 60b.

In memory of Moshe ben Aaron and Chaya z'l (10 Adar II) Dedicated lovingly by the Farajun Family

to believe in our hearts, and not just intellectually, that everything truly is for the best.

GETTING PRACTICAL

Emotions such as fear or anxiety can be alleviated if we are able to internalize the understanding that everything Hashem does is for the best. Teach yourself to say "Kol ma d'avid Rachmana l'tav avid — All that Hashem does is for the best."

Surrender Your Ego! | DAY 155 ◀

Feeling Hashem in our lives requires dedication and work. We should be prepared to surrender our egos in order to delve into Hashem's Presence. Living "ego free" means being at peace with what we have and having *emunah* that whatever we have is exactly what we need.

Often we live under the false impression that life unfolds through a natural course of events; the more one invests the more one gains. In order to overcome this false notion, we need to constantly remind ourselves while undertaking our deeds that ultimately Hashem's decrees will prevail. Hashem does not need any help from us to help bring forth His judgments.

Simple acts can strengthen the awareness that results are not in our hands. For example, when visiting a doctor we should remind ourselves that the cure is completely in Hashem's hands. Though we are obligated to take prescribed medications and seek out the most skilled doctors, the end result may be the same regardless of which path we choose, because Hashem's decrees will always prevail.

The difficulty lies in the feeling that once we work hard to attain something, we naturally feel that we earn or deserve the results. Overcoming this struggle requires us to surrender our ego and remind ourselves that our effort is just a superficial show that Hashem requires of us as His servants. If we are able to achieve victory in this battle, we will have succeeded at strengthening our *emunah*.

GETTING PRACTICAL

We undergo a constant struggle in life to see that our efforts are not responsible for any results. Though it is necessary for us to do our hishtadlus (invest concerted efforts), ultimately Hashem is in charge of all the results. Internalizing this fact strengthens our emunah.

An Uphill Battle |

This is the world of *asiyah* (action) and we are here to work — work on building our and our families' perpetuity in the World to Come. To improve and ascend on the spiritual ladder we can do the following:

- reevaluate our goals in life

- clearly define the direction in which we are heading

- truthfully gauge what motivates us to act

- honestly and objectively identify our selfish ego and how it affects our behavior and decisions

The road to self-improvement can be an uphill battle. We naturally want to relax and enjoy life without exerting excessive effort. This road may seem even more difficult to traverse if there is no immediate reward in sight. Human beings are naturally wired for reward — happy chemicals in our brains such as dopamine are reinforced when we achieve a goal and merit a reward. Thus, investing our energies in acts that bear only eternal rewards in the World to Come may initially appear worthless because such spiritual pursuits do not provide instant gratification. We may feel discontent since we may not witness the product of our efforts in this world at all.

Despite this, we should continue in our quest for the truth and a meaningful relationship with HaKadosh Baruch Hu because this is the path to spiritual redemption. The opposing forces within us may constantly nag us and belittle the value of our spiritual development. We may hear an inner voice harping, "What are you going to gain from this?"

and may not have a logical answer. Yet, we do have an *emunah*-based answer: "I am working for my spiritual future."

Throughout our lifetime, we need to beg Hashem to shower us with *emunah shleimah v'peshutah* (complete and simple *emunah*) — the power of faith to guide us in working for this non-tangible reward of the World to Come. When Hashem illuminates our eyes everything will become clear and worthwhile.

GETTING PRACTICAL

Just as the material world embraces the idea of a pension fund for our physical retirement, Judaism teaches us to invest in our future in the World to Come. Let us try to view our work and life in this world as a profit-producing business for the World to Come, requiring regular review and investments.

Emunah Softens the Suffering

Emunah serves as an ointment for an aching soul. Rather than a band-aid, it is a genuine, deep inner healing that eradicates emptiness and confusion. Knowing that Hashem is with us always helps ease our pain. It is relatively straightforward to have *bitachon* in Hashem when everything is smooth sailing. However, the measuring rod for gauging our true *emunah* level is how we react when we are met with life's difficulties.

Klal Yisrael is bound to one another and considered one body. In the *Path of the Just* (*Mesillas Yesharim*), the Ramchal teaches that "Everything in this world is a test." A righteous person who is on an exalted level may be tested and suffer in order to carry the world's transgressions on his shoulder. It may be through the righteous person's affliction that Klal Yisrael is protected and saved from having to endure harsh decrees. This serves to protect the world. Although intellectually this may be difficult to understand, we should still accept that this is part of Hashem's master design of creation.

The subject of pain and suffering in this world is complex. However, there is a thread of knowledge attached to every hardship — the inner awakening of a lesson well-learned that serves to increase spirituality and our connection to Hashem. Deep down, our soul (if not our body) knows that it is the hard times, the tests and the challenges which help us to grow.

My diagnosis of MS has elevated my *emunah* in ways that cannot be explained. My husband regularly jokes, yet it rings a note of truth when he says, "Hashem gave you MS so you can write the

Daily Dose of Emuna." Our *emunah* and strength increases with suffering if we realize that we do not control reality. The comfort lies in acceptance of *Hashem's emes* (truthful and just ways), that is, that what we don't understand will be revealed to us in the World to Come. I know that my MS was intended to shift me to a higher spiritual task. Accepting this certainly contributes to my overall emotional and physical health.

Instead of remaining silent, our soul needs to petition HaKadosh Baruch Hu to reveal His Presence in the world. We should proclaim our longing to be united with the Borei Olam and live with clarity, a reality where the veil of confusion will be lifted and all will be revealed. However, until that awesome day arrives, *b'karov b'rachamim* there is no better way to live than with profound *emunah*.

GETTING PRACTICAL

Life's trials and tribulations present us with opportunities to increase our emunah and bitachon in Hashem and to grow spiritually as a result. Let us internalize the profound teaching that we become spiritually elevated through challenges. Our emotional and physical health will benefit as well.

In our generation, many of us are bankrupt in our thoughts. Our entire system of thinking has been stolen by the Western world. We are being spoon-fed what to think, how to act and what to desire, often following modern Greek culture without even noticing it!

Jewish thinking and Western (or Greek) thinking are as different as the heavens and the earth. Modern-day thinking primarily focuses on us taking care of our own needs. In contrast, Jewish teaching guides our thoughts to holy matters and getting to know Hashem, ultimately leading us to act for His Name's sake, not our own.

The holy Baal Shem Tov explains that Am Yisrael's thoughts initiate from above. R. Aryeh Kaplan explains that all thoughts stem from above and are planted in our minds with the purpose of leading to our soul rectification. Hashem is the Giver of thoughts. All is in line with His will. The profound message from this lesson is that our thoughts are G-dly-sourced, but that we must channel them to do good. We are granted the free will to respond (or not respond) to these thoughts in a way that we choose.

There is an idea taught to us by the Baal Shem Tov that you are where your thoughts are. With this in mind, it is interesting to note that the Hebrew word *machshavah* (thought) is closely related to the Hebrew word for *b'simchah*, happiness. The Chernobler Rebbe teaches that Jewish thought can be naturally saturated in joy despite our difficulties. This joy originates from the idea that living

In memory of Esther bas Aaron Dovid Singer z'l (1 Sivan) Dedicated lovingly by Chaya Edelson

serves a greater purpose and that we are greatly loved and cared for by Hashem.

When a thought randomly pops up in our minds we can choose whether to accept, fight or ignore it. We elect how we will respond to it and how it will motivate our actions.

GETTING PRACTICAL

The origin of free will lies in our response to life's happenings, including our thoughts. We choose what we wish our minds to dwell on thus giving us the opportunity to make the choices along our path in life. Strive to be mindful; the way we think is the way we live.

"I Am with Him in Sorrow" DAY **159** ◄

The word for suffering in the Hebrew language is *yissurim* which is rooted in the word *mussar* (rebuke). The Chafetz Chaim brings from this the idea that suffering is a form of reproof from *Shamayim*, rebuking us to change and improve our ways. The father of the *Shlah HaKadosh,* R. Avraham, instructs us to be humble and bless Hashem when we experience suffering. We should recognize the goodness in it and understand that it is all a result of the Borei Olam's benevolence. We should not kick the *yissurim* or reject them, but rather accustom ourselves to say, *"Kol ma d'avid Rachmana l'tav avid* — All that Hashem does is for the best."[152]

The *Be'er Mayim Chaim* comments on the verse, *"Imo Anochi b'tzarah* — I am with him in sorrow,"[153] that when we suffer, the *Shechinah* suffers along with us. As the Gemara teaches, when we suffer, the *Shechinah* says, *"Kalani me-roshi, kalani me-zro'i* — My head is hurting, My arms are hurting."[154] Hashem loves us so much that He is willing to metaphorically go through pain Himself — because this is what is best for us.

Knowing this helps us appreciate the depth of Hashem's kindness and goodness. We can adopt a viewpoint on life of wanting to be wherever Hashem wants us to be, and doing whatever Hashem wants us to do. Internalizing the following six concepts may be beneficial in helping us accept our difficulties:

- It is all from Hashem.

---

152 *Berachos* 60b.
153 *Tehillim* 91:15.
154 *Sanhedrin* 46:1.

In memory of Dr. Yosef Herbert ben Sholom z'l (12 Tevet) Dedicated lovingly by Orit Esther Riter

- There is no suffering without sin (*Ein yissurim l'lo ahvon*). We cannot complain because our sins are the cause of our suffering.

- We should accept the *din* (judgment) because Hashem knows best.

- This suffering is for our ultimate benefit. Note that when we rejoice in the suffering we bring *yeshuos* (salvation) to the entire world.

- Our troubles could and should have been worse.

- Hashem's salvation may come in the blink of an eye (*Yeshuas Hashem ke'heref ayin*).

If we keep the above points posted within eyesight, we can learn them by heart, internalize them and act as if we'll be tested on them — the test of our lives!

GETTING PRACTICAL

Am Yisrael is never alone, neither collectively nor individually. Repeatedly, we are taught in the Torah that Hashem is with us and will never forsake His beloved nation. We should always keep this in our minds and hearts as this will ease us through many of our challenges.

Preserving the Holiness of Shabbos

Hashem built Shabbos into the world from the very beginning of creation. No matter where we are, Shabbos inevitably arrives as soon as the sun sets on Friday evening. However, we can prepare for this holiness by dedicating our activities in its honor. One way to do so is to consciously redirect our thoughts, deeds and speech from mundane to holy. The inverse mental shift is necessary when Shabbos departs as well.

Havdalah is the ceremony distinguishing between the holiness of Shabbos and the rest of the week. One reason for lighting the *Havdalah* candle is to symbolize Hashem's gift to us of His holy Torah. Learning Torah is represented by fire, a form of powerful energy which is needed to ignite our activities all week long. We take hold of this "fire" on Shabbos and carry it through the entire week.

There are Kabbalistic reasons for the particular order involved in the *Havdalah* ceremony. Reciting the *berachos* over wine, *besamim* (spices), the fire and then the *berachah* to separate holy from mundane represent our senses in an ascending order. The wine uses the mouth and must be tasted to enjoy it. We use our noses to smell the fragrance of the spices even from a short distance, whereas the ability to see the fire can be identified even from far. Our minds, the highest level, can discern the significance of the *berachah* of distinguishing between Shabbos and our workweek in abstract without requiring proximity at all.

It can be difficult to let go of Shabbos. Those who have internalized the genuine difference be-

In memory of Chaya Etta bas Benyimin HaCohen z'l (11 Av) Dedicated lovingly by Sora

tween Shabbos and *motza'ei Shabbos*, light and darkness, may feel this stark change from sacred to mundane. After taking part in a sliver of time enveloped in tranquility, we then face the storms of everyday reality.

But there is no need to leave behind all the holiness acquired on Shabbos. We can tap into the remnants of holiness, allowing the aura of Shabbos to filter into our everyday lives and to permeate through our entire week. Rather than viewing *Havdalah* as an end to this week's Shabbos, we can see it as a call for the coming Shabbos instead. There is a *minhag* (custom) to allow some of the wine from the *Havdalah* service to spill over the cup, symbolizing this holiness of Shabbos spilling over into the workweek.

GETTING PRACTICAL

Shabbos is a beautiful gift and enables us to experience life on a different plane for twenty-five hours. If we relished in the Shabbos experience we may be able to infuse some of the holiness into the coming week. Havdalah is the ceremony which spills this holiness into the mundane. Let's infuse one reality into the other.

Life without Hashem Is Intolerable

The ideal level of *emunah* to strive for is the attainment of intense love and closeness to Hashem. This heightened reality should be our lifetime's goal and *avodah* (work). We should strive to reach a point where life without the Borei Olam is simply not tolerable.

In reality, we often spend the majority of our lives busy with temporal pursuits to meet our material needs. Unfortunately, spiritual goals often take second place. Many in this generation actually scoff at spirituality as being absurd. We can be drawn into this mode of thinking if we allow our common sense or intellect to overpower our inner spiritual yearning to connect to Hashem.

The main objective of the *yetzer hara* is to occupy us so that we cannot even spare a moment to think. Contemplating who we are, where we are and what we are doing with our lives are questions that the evil inclination does not want us to ask. Yet, it is precisely the process of searching for these answers that will lead us to cleave to Hashem.

The *yetzer hara*'s best-known tactic is to distract our need to perceive HaKadosh Baruch Hu by letting us soak in worldly pleasures, thereby dulling our spiritual sensations. Placing diversions to distract us is a good scam. We are rushed from place to place, task to task and led astray from our eternal ends.

In such cases, it is essential to listen to our spiritual voice within and continue on our spiritual path by pleading with HaKadosh Baruch Hu to reveal Himself to us. Generally, the more one devotes himself to acquire something, the stronger the desire grows to attain it. The degree of longing to connect to Hashem corresponds to the bond we create with Him. How much effort are we willing to exert in our relationship with HaKadosh Baruch Hu? Is our yearning so great that our severed relationship with Him anguishes us? Are our *tefillos* drenched with heartfelt cries over the sadness and distance we feel?

GETTING PRACTICAL

In the past, many people were more spiritually aware and connected to Hashem. In this generation, our yetzer hara often tricks us into thinking that we can find happiness elsewhere. Now it is time to find our way back home, to that place so secure and wonderful — back into Hashem's arms.

Thanking Is Acknowledging

Hisbodedus offers an ideal setting to thank Hashem for everything He has done for us and continues to do in our lives. When we give thanks, we are in essence acknowledging the gifts that Hashem has given us. This recognition serves to remind us that Hashem has fulfilled our previous requests, and engenders within us feelings of hope that He *does* listen to us and will listen to our future pleas.

In terms of what we can be thankful for, the list is never-ending!

Aside from the more obvious things such as our family, health, income, we can also be grateful for the *zechus* (opportunity) to perform *mitzvos*, every act of kindness that we are given an opportunity to do, every prayer we utter, the Divine assistance in overcoming our *yetzer hara*, etc. Instead of focusing on what we are lacking, we can train ourselves to see the big picture of all the good He bestows on us.

Gratitude strengthens our *emunah* as it positively affects the way we perceive Hashem's Presence in our lives, thus our thoughts and outlook on life. As we habituate ourselves to give thanks, we shift our mindset to focus on the good. In spite of how pretentious it may be for us at times to give thanks to Hashem, it will increase our spiritual awareness. Paying lip-service may not appear to be useful; however, it will eventually open up our eyes to actually see the good in everything.

Another valuable benefit to expressing words of gratitude is that we cease taking things for granted. This removes the detested trait of entitlement, bitterness and self-pity which eventually leads to

*In memory of
Rut bat Isaac
and Sadie z'l
(13 Elul)
Dedicated
lovingly by the
Farajun Family*

complaining and depression. This is the first fundamental step paramount to all prayer. Verbally expressing words of thanks to Hashem brings us to a great sense of appreciation and humility.

GETTING PRACTICAL

Hisbodedus is an ideal time to thank Hashem for everything in our lives. If we struggle to see the good in our life and are not able to appreciate how much good we really have, maybe we should take a walk to the local hospital, to an old age home or a cemetery. That will certainly help keep our perspective in line with gratitude.

In the book, *Trust Me*, Eliezer Parkoff writes, "Idolatry is seeing the hand of Hashem in front of your eyes, and still worrying about what tomorrow will bring." We should meditate upon this statement often because it is extremely significant and relevant to our generation.

These days, the most common idol worship is of *ourselves*. It is me who accomplished and it is me who is a failure. It is me who works and earns a living, gives *tzedakah*, has smart children or who knows how to save a buck for a rainy day. But is it really me? And do we also take credit for negative events such as children acting with *chutzpah* (defiance) or losing a home because we are financially strapped?

One of the greatest challenges to our *emunah* is our worshipping of the ego. To avoid this, we have to remove the "me" and replace it with *Melech Malchei HaMelachim, HaKadosh Baruch Hu*. We must internalize the idea that *Ein Od Milvado* — There is NOTHING else but Him.

We *schlep* our bag overflowing with the burdens of life, packed with all of our worries, trials and tribulations. Yet, there is a camel nearby onto whose back we can place our package, thus no longer feeling the weight of carrying it. As Dovid HaMelech writes, *"Hashlech al Hashem yehovecha v'Hu yechalkelecha* — Cast your burden onto Hashem and He will take care of your needs."[155]

Hashem is always with us, actively involved in every circumstance of life. He grants success and *chas*

---

155 *Tehillim* 55:23.

v'shalom failure. It is all from You, Hashem. I will not serve me, I will serve YOU, Hashem, and cast my burdens onto You.

GETTING PRACTICAL

This generation is considered the "Me" generation. We are so focused on ourselves and consider everything that happens to and around us as caused by us. Let's remember that Hashem causes everything — both successes and failures.

We Are Hashem's Children

The word *emunah* is closely related to the Hebrew word *l'hitamen* (to train). From here we learn that *emunah* requires training.

In light of this, let's learn some basic *emunah* strengthening tips:

- The first stage is the belief that everything that happens is ordained from *Shamayim*.

- The second stage is living with the reassurance that Hashem is compassionate and will stand with us in our time of need.

These two stages of *emunah* are a product of our own effort. We build our *emunah* by increasing our awareness of Hashem's tangible Presence and learning how Fatherly He is to us.

- The third and highest stage is absolute unwavering trust. This is gifted directly from Hashem.

One of the main obstacles standing in our way of attaining stage two of *emunah* (as outlined above) may stem from our feeling of unworthiness to merit Hashem's kindness. However, the Torah reminds us that "*Banim atem laHashem* — You are Hashem's children."[156] We are deserving of Hashem's unconditional embrace for the simple reason that we are His children.

We can learn how quickly Hashem forgives us when we come clean and do *teshuvah* by examining the way a parent forgives their child after they have asked for forgiveness. No matter where our actions take us, HaKadosh Baruch Hu awaits our return. He

---

156 *Parashas Re'eh* 14:1.

wants our return because He knows it is for our ultimate good.

One of Hashem's manifestations in this world is that He is *Chanun* — a derivative of the word *chinam* (for free). He was, is and will always be with us — *for free* — independent of our actions and even if we become angry or we rebel at times. We must strengthen the belief that Hashem loves us and will remain eternally kind to us as His children, regardless of our actions.

GETTING PRACTICAL

Let us train ourselves in exercising stage one and stage two of emunah. B'ezras Hashem, we will ultimately be gifted with stage three — the ability to have absolute, unwavering trust. If we feel unworthy, we can remind ourselves that we are worthy of receiving His unconditional love and intervention for the sole reason that we are His children.

All Roads Lead Us Back to Hashem

Chazal raise a philosophical question: How is it possible to hear Hashem's voice? We can properly hear Hashem's voice only when we shake off the falsehoods that cling to us and trick us into believing that Hashem *chas v'shalom* is not in charge of all life's circumstances. If we believe that a force other than Hashem, such as nature, is responsible for events, we will not hear Hashem's voice. If we assume there is another force that presides over the world, this creates a tear in the bond between the Jewish nation and Hashem Yisbarach.

What other force would a person possibly assume is having an impact on the outcome of her life? We ourselves — we are what come in the way between us and *emunah* in Hashem. When we believe our efforts affect the outcome, this is an indication that we believe in our might. The test of whether we have actually internalized *emunah* lies in our emotional state when we do invest less effort. How calm, cool and collected are we after we have extended *hishtadlus* onto any given action?

The Torah certainly teaches that we need to be involved in this world because Hashem recognizes that most people cannot rely on pure *emunah* without becoming anxious. In addition, making an effort to solve our own troubles enables us to draw closer to Hashem because by doing so we partake in creation and thereby emulate HaKadosh Baruch Hu. Yet, the challenge remains to be aware that any result coming forth from our effort is a result of Divine will only.

Attributing events to nature and not seeing them as Hashem's decrees in disguise, weakens our

In memory of Safta Shoshana bat Rivka z'l (13 Tevet) Dedicated lovingly by the Riter Family

emunah. In fact, Hashem is angered by the slightest implication that an event may have occurred as a result of chance. This is confirmed in the Torah, "If you behave as if you are punished by chance, then I will treat you in a chance manner."[157]

GETTING PRACTICAL

Despite appearing natural, all events are actually in sync with Hashem's rulings. All roads always lead us back to Hashem should we choose to follow them! When we do our hishtadlus let us continue to be mindful of Hashem's intervention which is at the forefront of every effort we make.

---

157 Based on *Vayikra* 26:21.

Rabbeinu Yonah teaches that Hashem's rebuke is solely for our benefit. Hashem reprimands us to encourage us to atone for our sins and remind us to do *teshuvah* for them. Our task is to improve our ways. This self-improvement serves to benefit us. Thus, Hashem chastises His people with love just as a father cares for his son and chastises him over his wrongdoings in order to make him the best person he can be.

In his book *Derech Hashem,* the Ramchal brings down an astounding teaching on the purpose of suffering. Hashem truly desires that we do not sin in the first place. Yet, in the event that we do sin, we should do *teshuvah* (repentance). Those who fail to take advantage of the gift of *teshuvah* may then endure suffering to rectify their transgressions this way. When hardships arise this should serve as a motivating factor to charge us to do *teshuvah.* Only after a person chooses not to heed that call does he have to be subject to a form of reprimand.

The Hebrew word for test is *nisayon.* This word contains within it the word *nes* which corresponds to the word banner. Perhaps this wording can be used to demonstrate that a person's tests are held up like a banner, denoting one who is raised up to his potential. The pain that one experiences in life is credited to him forever and therefore is looked upon as an act of kindness from Hashem.

All of Hashem's ways are just. We cannot always see this clearly because we are simply not shown the entire picture. The Chafetz Chaim describes the case of a soul being judged in the Heavenly court for its misdeeds. The soul begs to be born again and brought

In memory of Rinat bat Shoshana z'l (14 Tevet)

back into the world to live a life of suffering to allow the opportunity to correct past transgressions. However, during this second lifetime he bemoans its misfortune, forgetting that it was *he* who had pleaded to be given this suffering as a rectification. This illuminates the concept of what it means to see the entire picture and allows us to better understand *chesbonos Shamayim* (Heavenly calculations).

GETTING PRACTICAL

Though it is difficult to take a global view of our tests in this world, we should believe that Hashem sent them to us to rectify us. We can take advantage of the powerful gift of teshuvah in order to rectify our sins and reduce our suffering. Just a moment of secluded thought and regret, uttered from a place of honesty, can repair so much.

A Soul for the World

For the first six days of creation, the world was solely a body, a material body of nature. On the seventh day, Hashem gave the world a soul. Thus, the dimension of spirituality was added to the world with the celebration of *Shabbos Kodesh*. On Shabbos we celebrate togetherness with Hashem — the birth of a united world.

Three things are labeled with the word *chemdah* (longing): Shabbos, the Torah and Israel. We yearn to connect to our ultimate purpose in life. During the workweek, our finite and infinite selves are separate. On Shabbos, they are brought together to coexist in harmony. Shabbos is the purpose for creation. Shabbos belongs to eternity.

Unlike other days of the week, Shabbos is not divided into day and night. The phrase, "And there was evening and there was morning," is not mentioned after revealing Shabbos. Hashem ceased creating and took pleasure in His creation on the seventh day. Shabbos serves as a reminder that Hashem is the Creator and the world was deemed to be complete on the seventh day. There is no further need to mention a day and night, since this was the end for all of Hashem's intended purposes.[158]

R. Samson Raphael Hirsch teaches that Shabbos is an eternal covenant with *Bnei Yisrael*. Shabbos was given over to mankind to continue to fill this world with holiness. During the workweek, we are expected to mingle and interact with the mundane world to meet our physical needs. On Shabbos we return the world to Hashem, acknowledging that it was on loan.

---

158 This was prior to the sin of Adam HaRishon, which changed the course of history as we know it.

Refraining from working (and creating) on Shabbos proclaims that our use of the world to meet our own needs is a gift from Hashem. It also serves as a proclamation that we are not masters over the world, only the Borei Olam. When we relinquish mastery over the world on Shabbos, we also find ourselves humbled before Hashem because we realize that we need Him and do not control things ourselves. It is a reminder that nature is controlled solely and completely by Hashem!

GETTING PRACTICAL

This Shabbos, let us humble ourselves before the Borei Olam. The more we surrender ourselves to Him, the more strongly we will feel His embrace.

Each and every one of us in Klal Yisrael has been hand-picked and selected to be Hashem's child (*bnei melech* — children of the king) and should honor this status accordingly. However, in order to do so, we should act primarily from our G-dly soul by weakening our animal soul and its control over us. Our success in achieving this weakening depends on our *ratzon* to emulate Hashem's ways and devote our thoughts to perform His will.

An egocentric person often focuses on what pleasures they have and measures this relative to what others have. This way of thinking leads to comparisons and results in inevitable dissatisfaction. Though Jewish life is not ascetic and we are not meant to live a life devoid of pleasure, our aim is to avoid looking at what others have and rather to be happy with our lot. This attitude stems from the realization that we receive exactly what Hashem feels is best for us personally. Though equal, we are all different from each other and have different *tafkidim* (life tasks) and *tikkunim* (soul rectifications).

Without Hashem's help we are not capable of separating good from evil. Similarly, we cannot discern what is beneficial for us and what is harmful. It is only when we are tightly linked to HaKadosh Baruch Hu that we receive the necessary clarity to decide what is for our own eternal benefit.

The biggest obstacle to attaining this clarity is our physical side (also known as our ego or animal soul). Since the Borei Olam is concealed, and the voice of our animal soul is extremely loud, it requires enormous strength of will to ignore it and its demands. When cornered or feeling very distanced from our spirituality, we may be tempted to believe that our animal soul is the only true reality and that our Divine soul is imaginary. However, this reasoning stems from a place of darkness, a place void of Hashem's light and truth.

Ultimately, in order to overcome the pull of our animalistic soul and attain the necessary clarity, we must redirect selfish motives and instead carry out tasks and make decisions *l'shem Shamayim* (giving for the sake of Hashem only). This redirection will allow the *Shechinah* to shine upon us, bringing us *berachah* and spiritual elevation. The resulting state of happiness we will experience as a result of carrying out Hashem's will is incomparable to any joy this corporeal world can offer.

GETTING PRACTICAL

The most important and challenging task in life is to overcome our natural tendency to pursue our personal desires to the neglect of our spiritual needs. Let us summon a strong enough will to connect with the Borei Olam by acting purely l'shem Shamayim.

How Do We View Challenges?

It happens... maybe even often. We set a goal for ourselves but cannot keep up with it for long. Unfortunately, many times we give up in the middle of the journey because we do not see it as a process but rather only as a goal which seems impossible to reach. As a result, we may become depressed, angry or frustrated due to our weakness and inability to meet our objectives.

Rebbe Nachman teaches that these obstacles are destined from *Shamayim*. One purpose of hindering us from reaching our goals is to remind us that we are human beings — works in progress. Often our egos may mislead us into thinking that we have attained a level of perfection (or close to perfection) in certain areas of our lives. Confronting our weaknesses or obstacles clearly shows that there is still work to be done. Ideally, this crush to the ego will be paired with an outpouring of humility, enabling us to begin the process of *teshuvah* and continue on the path of self-improvement.

Alternatively, our disappointment may serve to draw us closer to Him. For instance, when working toward spiritual elevation, we may interpret lack of success as Hashem pushing us away, not wanting our closeness. However, in actual fact it is quite the opposite. By creating distance, HaKadosh Baruch Hu is actually bringing us nearer to Him since it strengthens our yearning and longing to want to bond with Him. The obstacles ensure we need to work harder which commits us to our spiritual path and makes our love for Him even stronger.

We can better understand this by example. When shooting a bow and arrow we must pull the arrow further away from its target in order for it to reach its destination. The same thing occurs when we want to read something. Our eyes cannot focus on written words unless we pull the page back from our eyes. The gap is intentionally created and ultimately assists us to come closer.

A famous quote by Harriet Beecher Stowe describes the importance of picking oneself up after a blow and advancing onward: "When you get into a tight place and everything goes against you, till it seems as though you could not hang on a minute longer, never give up for that is just the place and time that the tide will turn."

Life is an unraveling passage strewn with obstacles. Each stumbling block brings growth. This knowledge will change our perception on how we view life's challenges, so that we do not despair or stop continuing to move forward. Rather, we can choose to view every challenge as if it was the first time confronting it, from the perspective of a child undertaking an exciting obstacle course.

GETTING PRACTICAL

Life is about perception, not circumstances — all based on how we view them. This is the central point to free will — choosing to see life as challenges that empower us vs. conditions that debilitate us. Choose life!

Why does Dovid HaMelech describe HaKadosh Baruch Hu as "my shepherd" and therefore conclude that "I will not lack"?[159]

Upon close examination, we can learn what he means from observing the ways of sheep and their shepherds. Whereas sheep love to graze lazily, feel they know which pasture is best for them and want to remain there indefinitely, they do not see the wisdom of the shepherd's ways in moving them on to other greener pastures.

Similarly, we often feel we know the best place for us, and fail to understand Hashem's ways in moving us on or keeping us in particular situations. Though we may not see it, our shepherd Hashem is leading us to "lush pastures" — the best place for each of us.

Hashem is the source of all compassion. Dovid HaMelech teaches us that,[160] "*Olam chesed yibaneh* — The world is built on loving-kindness." In Eichah, it is written, "*Lo tizenah ha'raot me-haShamayim* — Nothing bad ever comes down from the Heavens and above it is always good."[161] However, whether we can see the good in all that He sends us is really up to us.

Just as the sun has the ability to soften butter, the same sun can have an adverse effect on salt — it causes it to harden. Similarly, we receive the same goodness from Hashem but it can affect each of us differently, depending on our ability to receive.

The person who is on the path of righteousness can take what Hashem sends, put it to good use

---

159   *Tehillim* 23:1.
160   89:3.
161   1:3.

In memory of Isaac ben Yaakov Tzvi and Chaya Rachel z'l (22 Nissan) Dedicated lovingly by the Farajun Family

and spiritually grow from it. In contrast, those with weakened *emunah* or those whose hearts are enclosed in *klipos* (husks of impurity, not immersed in Hashem's ways) may interpret the very same message as being bad.

Emunah helps us remember that nothing is intrinsically bad — everything is from Hashem and thus serves our ultimate benefit. Only the ignorant would want to remove healing ointment from his wound because it stings. A wise person endures the sting with patience, knowing the pain of this medicine will eventually heal him. Suffering for our sins is such a stinging ointment, yet it heals and is not considered bad.

Currently, when bitter events occur, we recite, "*Baruch Dayan haEmes* — Blessed is the True Judge." However, in the World to Come there will only be one blessing over all happenings, "*HaTov v'ha-Meitiv* — The One Who is good and does good". In the future, *b'karov* (soon) we will see everything in its true light — all good.

GETTING PRACTICAL

Hashem is leading us to greener pastures. He only sends us good since it is intended to be a healing balm; something to keep in mind next time an event stings.

Do Not Detest Hashem's Rebuke

Chazal teach us to accept hardships with love. Acceptance in the face of hardship certainly requires *mesirus nefesh* (self-sacrifice), yet it is vital in order to achieve a life of tranquility.

The purpose of life's challenges is to strengthen our *emunah*. *Mishlei* teaches, "*Mussar Hashem b'ni al tim'as* — My son, do not detest Hashem's rebuke." Rabbeinu Yonah comments that this *pasuk* teaches an essential lesson in *emunah*. In order for us to reach a heightened level of *emunah*, we should not detest or rebel against Hashem's rebuke. Rather, as Ramchal advises in *Mesillas Yesharim*, our main task is to hold strong when such *nisyonos* arise.

Often our *nisyonos* are accompanied by a list of questions and doubts in Hashem or in ourselves, for instance, whether we are worthy of Hashem's eternal goodness. By preparing ourselves in advance and expecting that these thoughts will arise together with the *nisayon,* we will be able to equip ourselves to overcome them.

When facing a challenge in life, a most powerful tool is to focus on praying. Our prayers should center mostly on asking Hashem to do what is right in His eyes, because it is only He Who knows what is truly best for us.

Additionally, we should ask that we be granted Heavenly assistance to implant in our hearts the knowledge that it is all for our very best. We should pray that the truth and trust in Hashem be woven into our hearts — to be granted the certainty that it all comes from our loving caring Father, *Avinu she'baShamayim.*

GETTING PRACTICAL ————————————

To prepare ourselves for difficulties, it can be expected that we may start to question ourselves or Hashem. Instead, let's actively choose to recognize that they come from Hashem, Who is our closest and caring Father.

Just Look Up and See Hashem

In the *sefer Emunah u'Bitachon*, the Chazon Ish writes, "The essential level of faith to which a person should strive is complete acceptance of Hashem's conduct of the world for good or for bad, without resorting to misdirected and uncalled-for forms of *hishtadlus*, but instead turning only to *tefillah* and *teshuvah*."

Hashem can do anything. He is able to take away the pain and suffering or prevent it from happening in the first place. If we do experience a challenge, we may be tempted to over-control our situation by entering into "misdirected and uncalled-for forms of *hishtadlus*." However, though we must take acceptable steps to solve the problem, anything beyond this is a waste of time and represents a lack of *emunah*. It will only hurt us spiritually and distance us further from reaching our goal of achieving *emunah*.

The *Nefesh Hachaim*, R. Chaim of Volozhin, teaches that we can earn salvation from our troubles to the degree that we strengthen our faith that everything is brought forth by Hashem. Just believing in this hastens the approaching *yeshuah*. We need to remind ourselves that Hashem is here with us. Rather than a distant entity, Hashem is a tangible reality in every Jewish life.

This point can be highlighted via a beautiful parable. A young child is being wheeled into an operating room. Afraid of the scary lights and strangers dressed in white, he feels alone and begins to cry. Suddenly, he notices a smile beaming in from a small window in the corner of the room. He sees his mother's face. She is watching and reassuring him. Now he feels more secure and stops crying, even managing a watery smile.

What happened? Essentially, nothing changed. The child remained in the same room with the cold lights. So why is he less frightened? Because he looks up and becomes aware that his loving, caring mother is with him.

Being aware of the Heavenly hug that accompanies us all the time makes all the difference for our journey in this world. If we just look up and see Hashem, we will feel Him right here with us, bearing our pain. Our job is to believe that He is there and to pray at the onset of troubles. The process of praying voluntarily changes who we are by humbling us. It also serves to comfort us that our situation is all from the Borei Olam.

GETTING PRACTICAL

The best way of tackling a problem is to remind ourselves that Hashem is right there with us in our pain. We are never alone. Let's daven to Hashem and await His yeshuah.

No Such Thing as Religious Retirement

We are all very busy. In between taking care of our precious family, Torah learning, *chesed* projects, preparing for Shabbos and *Yamim Tovim* and performing *mitzvos*, time management is crucial. *Pirkei Avos* teaches, "Rabbi Tarfon would say, 'The day is short, the work is much, the workers are lazy, the reward is much and the Master is pressing.'"[162] There is so much to do and so little time!

The halachah of *gezeilas z'man* (stealing another's time) demonstrates the value of time. Stealing time includes wasting other's time with idle chatter, keep others waiting or running late, and disturbing others sleep, to name a few. The Torah considers this a very serious transgression.

Pirkei Avos teaches that one hour used in this world for *teshuvah* and *mitzvos* is worth more than all of the pleasures of the World to Come.[163] Wow! This indicates just how precious our time in this world is and that our opportunities are priceless. Rabbi Tarfon's advice is to get busy! We ought to maximize our efforts to complete the *mitzvos* and *middos* at hand.

However, note that Hashem also values our unfinished deeds. Hashem cares about the process and our effort. He understands that each one of us has varying degrees of skills and that sometimes completions of tasks are outside of our control. As it says in *Pirkei Avos*, "*L'fum tzaara agra* — According to the effort is

---

162   2:15.
163   4:14.

the reward."[164] The reward is commensurate with the effort. We are offered eternal reward in accordance to the sincere effort.

Our religious responsibilities are never complete in this world. We are all a work in progress and can continue to strive for greater spiritual achievement. After spiritual growth and successes, we should use the momentum to continue developing more and pushing further. There is no such thing as religious retirement!

GETTING PRACTICAL

Life is a tale of ups and downs and we should accustom ourselves to constantly strive for betterment. Our lives are a work in progress. Gain self-empowerment from this lifelong journey as you see yourself reaching higher heights.

---

164 5:27.

Grasp the Kedushah of Shabbos

Preparing for Shabbos requires clearing our thoughts and stirring our hearts in order to receive the outpouring of holiness that spills forth from this *kedushah*-filled day. Detaching ourselves from the mundane working week ought to begin well before sundown. The internal work includes doing a self-accounting such as releasing negative emotions which may have accumulated and generally loosening our bonds to the material nature of this world. When we make the time to review the prior week, essentially we quiet our minds and release the worries, fears and other feelings which may overrun our Shabbos mindset.

There is a famous saying which says that what we prepare for Shabbos we will eat on Shabbos. This principle applies to spiritual things as well as physical. The *neshamah* deeply yearns to connect to HaKadosh Baruch Hu, waiting to capture the holiness that spills forth on *Shabbos Kodesh*. However, in order to do so we must spiritually sensitize our hearts.

As humans, we are naturally bound by time and space, and are attracted to all things material. These aspects may make it more difficult for many of us to pick up the spiritual vibes of *kedushah* that radiate on Shabbos. Therefore, we have to exert effort to break these forces that constrict us and thus transcend the nature of this world.

One practical solution is to offer *tzedakah* to those who are less fortunate or offer to host them at our Shabbos table. Another way to help us absorb the spirituality of Shabbos is to purchase the tastiest foods and drinks and dress in the finest attire that we can afford. This gesture essentially "spiritualizes" our money and our hearts, thus enabling us to experience *Shabbos Kodesh* in the most uplifting way.

We can also spiritually prepare our minds to enable them to grasp Shabbos *kedushah*. On Friday, there is a traditional custom to read the *parashah* twice in Hebrew in addition to once in Aramaic. This serves to filter the mundane thoughts from our consciousness and empty it to allow the holiness of Torah wisdom to permeate.

GETTING PRACTICAL

From midweek, we can already start preparing spiritually for Shabbos by reading the parashah or purchasing sumptuous food items and specialties. We can attempt to empty our mind of thoughts that weaken our emunah, instead looking forward to replenish our spiritual strength on Shabbos Kodesh.

"I" and Hashem | DAY 175 ◄

Each of us possesses free will to choose to see the Borei Olam as the sole director over the outcome of events in our lives. A major part of character refinement in this world involves correcting the erroneous belief that we are in control. The goal of all our thoughts and actions should be for the sake of building a close relationship with HaKadosh Baruch Hu.

However, in order to cleave to Hashem, it is crucial for us to free ourselves of our ego. Who is the "I" in each of us? The Kabbalah teaches that the "I" represents the sense of one's self which Hashem has removed from Himself and placed inside of us. The more we are in tune with G-dliness in terms of our *middos,* in other words the more G-dly we act, the closer we feel to Hashem. Therefore, any feeling of distance that we feel from Hashem is a direct result of our unrefined animalistic nature. The bigger our egos, the further away Hashem feels from us.

Our egos create a void between the "I" and Hashem. This void can manifest itself in a feeling of hopelessness. This comes as a result of sensing ourselves alone and defenseless. Oddly enough, though this hopeless feeling often forces us to give up our worldly ambitions. Ironically, this forced detour often serves to weaken our egos, in order that we connect to Him once again. To avoid such suffering, we can strive to nullify our egos and thus avoid having to experience a forced detour.

If we could reach a level whereby we had no selfish interests in the outcome of our daily affairs, we would experience less suffering. Directing ourselves away from fulfilling our own personal delight and physical pleasures gives us an opportunity to experience the more eternal and greatest pleasure of uniting with Hashem in eternal love.

GETTING PRACTICAL

The greatest power comes from knowing that we are connected to the source of all strength. Next time we feel a need to seize control, let's envision that we are on a bus and Hashem is the driver. He has a Divine GPS system, driving us through the journey called life and taking us to the best destination.

For the Sake of Heaven or Not

Imagine performing a mitzvah with the sole motivating factor being to bring *nachas ruach* to Hashem! Or, let's envision that every action we take originates from an intense desire to come close to Hashem and a subsequent intention to avoid upsetting Him.

This is the characterization of serving Hashem *l'shem Shamayim* (for the sake of Hashem alone). Every day we can try to direct our thoughts, speech and actions in order to bring pleasure to HaKadosh Baruch Hu. By doing so, we will be able to develop a mindset of *emunah* and strengthen our feelings of selfless, unconditional love toward Hashem.

For example, let us look at our approach toward *tefillah*. *Tefillah* is thus called *avodah she'ba-lev* (work of the heart). Let's ask our hearts: what are we praying for? Can we honestly say that our thoughts, desires and even our bodily organs are aware and in support of what we recite? This is undoubtedly a high *madreigah* (spiritual level), but represents an ideal level to which we can strive for.

Achieving such a lofty goal is compared to the redemption, enabling us to leave our spiritual exile and enter a space of unworldly freedom. In order to start this process, we can try to become aware of where we are holding right now, and have a desire to improve our communicative skills with our Creator.

What is the measuring rod by which we can determine whether we are acting *l'shem Shamayim* or not? One gauge is the amount of time we spend thinking about factors *lo leShamayim* (that are not for Heaven's sake). Shifting our thoughts in a conscious effort, with the power of guided imagery, envisioning the *simchah* of being close to Hashem — all of these are powerful tools to activate change.

Another gauge would be the extent to which we think of Hashem when involved in a mitzvah. The mitzvah is valued based on whether we are performing it with pure intent, which should be the motive dominating every aspect of our lives.

GETTING PRACTICAL

Unconditional love in this world is often considered unattainable. However, we can give unconditionally if we are emotionally healthy and fulfilled. When we focus on acting only to bring pleasure to Hashem, this is the loftiest level of all.

The Source of Happiness

Sefer HaMiddos teaches, "When you perform a mitzvah with joy, it is a sign that your heart is completely with Hashem."[165]

Hashem wants us to be happy. Happiness comes as a result of inner satisfaction and knowledge that our actions are meaningful and truthful. Then, the heart feels content from within. Our heart then releases positive feelings that affect our actions, infusing them with a powerful life force.

Simchah comes from the joy and appreciation we feel in being chosen as His special people and in recognizing His goodness and love. Imagine sitting in a giant stadium of 20,000 people. We would feel extremely fortunate to be one of only ten that were picked to go up on the stage and meet the most important personality in the world. This is the status of the Jewish nation — out of the billions of inhabitants on Earth, we Jews were selected by the King of kings to assist Him to make this world more G-dly. This is a remarkable reason to be happy!

Sadness generally comes as a result of believing Hashem is not just, *chas v'shalom*, and that things are not the best that can be. Our minds are finite and therefore we cannot understand Hashem's infinite intentions; however, the Torah is the source of splendid light and strength. Even if we recognize this truth intellectually but it has not yet penetrated our hearts — smile! The outer appearance of a smile is contagious. Even if we fake it, it has a positive effect on us and those around us.

165　In the chapter on *simchah*.

*In memory of
Shemaya ben
Avraham Hirsch
Halevi z'l
(21 Adar II)
Dedicated
lovingly by the
Margolis Family*

When we realize we are blessed with the *zechus* (merit) of co-partnering with Hashem and revealing G-dly light into this world, each mitzvah we perform will be infused with joy, inside and out.

GETTING PRACTICAL

Let's celebrate the fact that we are part of a select, special and holy nation. We are chosen to reveal G-dliness to the world. Next time we feel downtrodden or sad, let's remember that we are a vital piece in the puzzle of this world. Without each of us, the puzzle is incomplete. This realization can create a lasting, internal happiness.

We Are Living in a Time of Dawn

We often fail to see Hashem's hand in life. The degree to which we think we are in control is inversely proportional to the *emunah* we have internalized. The calmest way to get through a time of difficulty is to stop wondering why we are going through it. Logic has no place due to the simple reason that as human beings our complete understanding of this world is limited. The *emes* is that we are being led to the exact place that Hashem sees fit for us to be. Even the suffering that we must undergo is precisely measured.

We are living in a time of dawn. The sun is yet to rise, thus things are still unclear. Hashem has hidden His beautiful countenance from us, preventing us from seeing His master plan with complete clarity. But despite His hand being concealed, Hashem has not forsaken His beloved children. Hiddenness does not mean abandonment, but rather that Hashem is merely in disguise.

One cunning way of the *yetzer hara* is to encourage the false belief that Hashem takes no part in our daily lives. A weakened *emunah* may falsely presume HaKadosh Baruch Hu does not rule over the entire universe. However, Hashem is our shepherd and pastures us. He places us in the right place, at the right time. We may not even realize or understand what is happening.

Sometimes, we may think Hashem is just causing us pain *chas v'shalom*. This train of thought is born only from a state of despair. It is a failure to truly internalize the belief that Hashem is looking out for our eternal good. We may not see the good in whatever is occurring and this false belief may lead us to complain as a result. However, we can avoid this state by relating to Hashem through *emunah*. *Emunah* is the firm belief in Hashem's eternal power and ability to control all happenings in the universe for the good. It is the recognition that not only does He control the world but that Hashem operates only from a place of goodness and compassion.

GETTING PRACTICAL

We may meet many pitfalls along the road of life. Foggy clouds will envelop us in the form of challenges that darken our clarity. Yet, during these times, let's implant emunah which helps us know that Hashem is embracing us all the way through, and that He is good.

Injecting Emunah into Our Relationships

Hashem links Jewish souls together in order for them to learn and grow from one another. Being infallible and omnipotent, Hashem does not err. He does not make mistakes when He orchestrates the people in our lives, whether it is in the marriage, friend, parental or any other relationship. His intention is to enable us to rectify and improve ourselves. Eventually, we realize that rather than changing the other person, we need to change certain aspects of ourselves. This realization requires honesty and deep contemplation, sometimes over a long period of time.

Peace between people, including husband and wife, evolves from resolving differences. We must learn to treasure our differences of opinion. When Hashem created Chava, she was referred to as Adam's *ezer kenegdo* (a helpmate opposite) partly to inspire an objective and different perspective. Although our differences may weigh heavily on our patience, resolving such differences and overlooking our irritations promotes *gadlus* (spiritual greatness).

Relationships also enable us to work on being objective and empathetic, and to consider the other perspective. This requires humility; that is, admitting that what we think and feel are not always objective but rather that there are different angles to everything we experience. There is no such thing as objective circumstances in life, rather it is about perspective. It is essential to internalize that although we are not personally experiencing the other person's view, their perspective is real and true for them.

In Memory of Frayda Malka Bat Baruch z'l - Lovingly your daughter Chana Levick

Relationships also thrive when both parties can compromise; that is, reach a consensus based on both viewpoints. Recognizing Hashem's hand in our lives enables us to reach a point of calm acceptance through which compromise is attainable. Hashem wants us to live in peace and harmony, but He also wants us to struggle in order to obtain this peace, rectifying our weaknesses along the way.

When we see each other as bodies, clashes often arise. However, seeing each other as souls, each possessing a *tzelem Elokim* (a G-dly spark), enables us to exercise compromise, humility and tolerance. Our conflicts will consequently wither and fade.

GETTING PRACTICAL

Peace results from seeing the hand of Hashem behind the people in our lives. When we view each other as souls rather than bodies, then we can practice humility, compromise and tolerance. Building healthy loving relationships enables us to thrive and reach our full potential.

"Hashem, I want to engrave the *pasuk*, "*Shivisi Hashem l'negdi tamid* — I have set Hashem before me always,"[166] on my mind and heart. Even when I realize this truth in theory, You know how difficult it is for me to incorporate this into practice every moment of every day. My mind constantly wanders from place to place and the road from my mind to my heart is long. Only You, Hashem, can help me internalize this great lesson.

Hashem, help me completely and authentically serve You. I need Your help to bolster my inner strength and follow all the laws of the *Shulchan Aruch*. Sometimes, I become so overwhelmed that I act foolishly.

Hashem, please help me to never forget from where I came and before Whom I stand, bowed in gratitude and humility. Hashem, help me avoid *gaavah* (pride) and jealousy. Help me be humble enough to admit my many errors and avoid making excuses for the events that surround me. Let me not leave this world without repenting for my sins. Please help me follow the advice of *Chazal* and make an accounting of my actions every evening.

Help me realize that there is nothing more important than serving You with love and fear. Let me realize Your hand in everything around me and not attribute it to luck or the regular course of nature. Help me to recognize Your hand in my life, protecting me from evil and mishap.

Ribbono Shel Olam, You have given me so many reasons to be thankful. Please enable me to be

---

166   *Tehillim* 16:8.

*In memory of
Hinda Miriam
bat Yehoshua
Dedicated
lovingly by the
Ledder Family*

completely and sincerely grateful for all of them all the time."

GETTING PRACTICAL _____

You can recite this prayer as is, or use it to jumpstart your own personal prayer. Let the words and ideas penetrate your heart. Daven with full conviction and feel the profound and beneficial effects on deepening our gratitude to our Father in Heaven.

Conclusion

This world is really an *emunah*-exercise room, providing all of us with the opportunity to stretch and strengthen our *emunah* muscles. It presents us with numerous opportunities to strive to internalize the ultimate truth that Hashem loves us and does everything for our ultimate best.

In order to remove the shadow that obstructs Hashem's light from shining on us; we need to nullify both our intellect and our egos. *Emunah* kicks in when logic ends. We are intellectual and logical beings. Darkness may make us feel confused and abandoned. Yet, it is precisely at these challenging moments that *emunah* becomes real and relevant. When our lives are smoothly coasting along, there is no reason for *emunah* and no opportunity to connect to Hashem through our faith in Him. When we fail to logically comprehend the reasons why things happen, *emunah* means the ability to nevertheless accept that the event is all good.

Emunah provides us with the *da'as* (wisdom) to accept and trust in what lies beyond our physical reality. Enhancing our spiritual sensitivity leads to greater awareness that there is movement behind those Heavenly curtains. It enables us to more calmly accept that everything that happens in our lives is for our best.

I hope that this 180-day program leaves you with a drive to want to learn and do more *emunah* learning and training. Adopting an *emunah*-based attitude to life requires constant practice, immersion and repetition, day after day, week after week, month after month. Yet, through contemplation, revision and repetition, we can all alter the way we see life. Eventually, we will begin to notice, accept and even dance in the face of a reality with which we may previously have felt downtrodden, defeated or frustrated. Reaching such levels is truly a cause for celebration!

However, we must also remember to be gentle on ourselves. Embedding *emunah* in our hearts is a lifelong process. Any changes to our levels may be obscure at first, or may be so subtle as to be unnoticeable to others. We must also celebrate even the subtleties! We all begin from a different point on the *emunah* ladder. Being able to increasingly delay our frustration by even one second, or to minimize it by even one degree, represents real progress.

I invite you to continue traveling on this *emunah* journey of spiritual self-discovery. Please feel free to visit our website **www.dailydoseofEmuna.com** to find out more information, view *emunah shiurim* and sign up to receive continuous *emunah* booster shots in the form of the *Daily Dose of Emuna* on-line emails. You are also welcome to contact me any time at **OritRiter@gmail.com** and share your *emunah* challenges and successes. I would love to share part of your *emunah* journey together with you!

With a warm *emunah* embrace and wishes,

Orit

About the Author

Orit Esther Riter was born in Brooklyn, New York. She is a caterer by profession, holding a culinary arts degree from the Culinary Arts Institute in New Jersey.

However, after being diagnosed with multiple sclerosis (MS) in 2006, Orit's life direction took a different course. She was forced to close her off-premise catering company which served the Tri-State area for over fifteen years. Despite her incurable illness, she found healing through spiritual empowerment.

In 2009, Orit made *aliyah* with her family from Monsey, New York. She began teaching *emunah* to others. Essentially she went from feeding the body at *simchahs* to feeding the soul *b'simchah*. She nurtures herself and others by emphasizing the importance of establishing a close-knit relationship with HaKadosh Baruch Hu. She focuses on learning and teaching the essential value of living a meaningful life with *simchah*.

Reflecting a common theme of the *teshuvah* path, Orit's path is infused with endless love to HaKadosh Baruch Hu. Growing up in Brooklyn, New York, she attended Yeshiva of Kings Bay until fifth grade. Family reasons led her to move to New Jersey and there she continued her schooling in a public school environment. This led her to stray from Yiddishkeit. She remained at this school for three years and then made *aliyah* with her mother and stepfather. After receiving her high school diploma, Orit served for six months in the Israeli Defense Forces, being discharged in order to get married.

Three years later, she traveled back to the States, earning her dream college degree in the culinary arts. After working for a caterer in New York City, she boldly opened her own catering business, Kosher Designers. In order to expand marketability, she decided to run her catering business under glatt-kosher supervision. This required a full time *mashgiach*. In her daily interactions with Torah observant Jews, she realized the *emes*, beauty, meaning and purpose of a Torah life and her Jewish heritage. Her family gradually transformed from being secular and unaffiliated to becoming *ba'alei teshuvah*. Her Torah learning took precedence and focus over her success as a caterer. Orit's path had detoured in order for her to seek out her true mission in life.

Orit currently authors daily online articles and emails about *emunah* to a growing list of over 1,300 daily subscribers. These emails inspire others to get through challenging times by drawing from the wisdom of our Torah sages, in particular the *derech* of *chassidus*.

Having recently created an innovative "caring and listening gemach," Orit spreads her *emunah* knowledge to other women via personal email, Skype or phone by lending a compassionate ear and open heart to others in need. She provides practical coping skills for self-healing and emotional strengthening. In addition, she gives *emunah shiurim* every Tuesday in the Beit Shemesh area. These *shiurim* are available for viewing on TorahAnytime.com, the *Daily Dose of Emuna* YouTube channel and as MP3 downloads.

Orit's daily efforts are based on her firm belief that it is only natural to share one's innate gifts bestowed by HaKadosh Baruch Hu with others. She passionately believes that her ability to guide and empower others by strengthening their reliance on Hashem will fortify them with essential tools needed to live a purposeful life.

Currently, Orit Esther has five children and two grandchildren living in Israel. She lives with her husband and four younger children in Ramat Beit Shemesh.

About Mosaica Press

Mosaica Press is an independent publisher of Jewish books. Our authors include some of the most profound, interesting, and entertaining thinkers and writers in the Jewish community today. There is a great demand for high-quality Jewish works dealing with issues of the day — and Mosaica Press is helping fill that need. Our books are available around the world. Please visit us at www.mosaicapress.com or contact us at info@mosaicapress.com. We will be glad to hear from you.

MOSAICA PRESS